EUROPE: A PHILOSOPHICAL HISTORY

PART 2

Europe is inseparable from its history. That history has been extensively studied in terms of its political history, its economic history, its religious history, its literary and cultural history, and so on. Could there be a distinctively philosophical history of Europe? Not a history of philosophy in Europe, but a history of Europe that focuses on what, in its history and identity, ties it to philosophy.

In the two volumes of *Europe: A Philosophical History – The Promise of Modernity* and *Beyond Modernity* – Simon Glendinning takes up this question, telling the story of Europe's history as a philosophical history.

In the wake of two world wars of European origin, Europe's modern promise of universal peace, freedom and well-being for all humanity lay in ruins. In Part 2, *Beyond Modernity*, Glendinning picks up the story of this promise after the Second World War. Taking in Isaiah Berlin's defence of a pluralist ideal, Francis Fukuyama's vision of a new 'end of history' in liberal democracy, and Jacques Derrida's critique of the very idea of an end of history, Glendinning invites us to affirm a new philosophical-historical self-understanding: not the history of the rational animal on the way to its final end, with Europe at the head, but a history of the unpredictably self-transforming animal without a final end. In this context, Glendinning argues, Europe remains promising, its cosmopolitan heritage opening a future beyond its exhausted modernity.

Simon Glendinning is Professor of European Philosophy and Head of the European Institute at the London School of Economics and Political Science.

'In these timely volumes, the idea of Europe – the site of so much contemporary political strife – receives a philosophical interrogation commensurate with its nature. Glendinning's rigorous and compelling delineation of modern Europe's conception of itself, as at once philosophy's historical cradle and its cultural offspring, deftly draws upon the very self-understanding he analyses to confirm its current exhaustion, and to affirm its capacity for radical self-renewal.'

Stephen Mulhall, University of Oxford, UK

'In this remarkable two-volume book, Simon Glendinning inhabits and works through a "philosophical history of the philosophical history" of Europe. This is exemplary work, its readings developed with erudition, patience, and rigor. By the end of the second volume we come to see how the traditional concept of Europe is "exhausted", but not thereby left entirely hopeless or without promise. This is a sustained, often brilliant, exercise of reading the unfolding deconstruction of the dominant European understanding of Europe, one that can indeed stand as perhaps its own best example of what the old name "Europe" can still call forth in philosophy today. A magnificent achievement.'

Geoffrey Bennington, Emory University, USA

EUROPE: A PHILOSOPHICAL HISTORY, PART 2

Beyond Modernity

Simon Glendinning

LONDON AND NEW YORK

First published 2021
by Routledge
2 Park Square, Milton Park, Abingdon, Oxon OX14 4RN

and by Routledge
605 Third Avenue, New York, NY 10158

Routledge is an imprint of the Taylor & Francis Group, an informa business

British Library Cataloguing-in-Publication Data
A catalogue record for this book is available from the British Library

Library of Congress Cataloging-in-Publication Data
A catalog record has been requested for this book

ISBN: 978-1-138-58035-0 (hbk)
ISBN: 978-1-032-01582-8 (pbk)
ISBN: 978-0-429-50742-7 (ebk)

Typeset in Bembo
by KnowledgeWorks Global Ltd.

To Alan Montefiore

CONTENTS

LIST OF ABBREVIATIONS

The list here is specific to this book, which is the second of two parts. The bibliography provides a complete list of works referred to across both Part One and Part Two, many of which were germane to both.

AC	Friedrich Nietzsche, "The Anti-Christ"
AE	Denis Guénoun, *About Europe*
APMR	Paulin J. Hountondji, *African Philosophy, Myth and Reality*
AT	Emmanuel Levinas, *Alterity and Transcendence*
BB	Iris Murdoch, *The Book and the Brotherhood*
BFM	Jonathan Hopkin and Caterina Paolucci, "The business firm model of party organisation: Cases from Spain and Italy"
BGE	Friedrich Nietzsche, *Beyond Good and Evil*
BNR	Jürgen Habermas, *Between Naturalism and Religion*
BS	Jacques Derrida, *The Beast and the Sovereign*
BT	Martin Heidegger, *Being and Time*
CES	Edmund Husserl, *The Crisis of European Sciences and Transcendental Phenomenology*
CF	Jacques Derrida, *On Cosmopolitanism and Forgiveness*
CHPR	Karl Marx, *Critique of Hegel's Philosophy of Right*
CHU	Stanley Cavell, *Conditions Handsome and Unhandsome*
CIS	Richard Rorty, *Contingency, Irony, and Solidarity*
CM	Karl Marx, *The Communist Manifesto*
CPR	Immanuel Kant, *Critique of Pure Reason*
CR	Samuel Beckett, "The Capital of the Ruins"
CV	Ludwig Wittgenstein, *Culture and Value*
DLFF	Rowan Williams, *Dostoevsky: Language, Faith and Fiction*
DN	Jacques Derrida, *Deconstruction in a Nutshell*

DP	Peter Frick, *Divine Providence in Philo of Alexandria*
DPC	Simon Glendinning, "Derrida and the Problem of Consciousness"
EC	Jacques Derrida, "Economies of the Crisis"
EDC	Kalypso Nicolaïdis, "European Demoicracy and Its Crisis"
EH	Francis Fukuyama, *The End of History and the Last Man*
EHO	Francis Fukuyama, "The End of History?"
EIT	Rodolphe Gasché, *Europe, or the Infinite Task*
EM	Jacques Derrida, "The Ends of Man"
FK	Jacques Derrida, "Faith and Knowledge"
GS	Friedrich Nietzsche, *The Gay Science*
GL	Jacques Derrida, *Glas*
GM	Friedrich Nietzsche, *The Genealogy of Morals*
GNH	Hagen Schulze, *Germany: A New History*
GPC	Jacques Derrida, "Globalization, Peace, and Cosmopolitanism"
HAP	Phillipe Lacoue-Labarthe, *Heidegger, Art, and Politics*
HG	Jacques Derrida, "The Aforementioned So-Called Human Genome"
HH	Friedrich Nietzsche, *Human All Too Human, Part II*
HP	Paul Valéry, *History and Politics*
HPP	Phillipe Lacoue-Labarthe, *Heidegger and the Politics of Poetry*
HPR	G.W.F. Hegel, *Philosophy of Right*
HS	Martin Heidegger, "Heidegger Speaks"
IB	John Gray, *Isaiah Berlin*
IBWD	Bernard Williams, *In the Beginning was the Deed*
IC	Benedict Anderson, *Imagined Communities*
IM	Martin Heidegger, *Introduction to Metaphysics*
INP	Simon Glendinning, *In the Name of Phenomenology*
IOG	Jacques Derrida, *Edmund Husserl's 'Origin of Geometry': An Introduction*
IPH	G.W.F. Hegel, *Introduction to the Philosophy of History*, trans Rauch.
IRH	Alexandre Kojève, *Introduction to the Reading of Hegel: Lectures on the "Phenomenology of Spirit"*
Kant	Immanuel Kant, *Kant's Political Writings*
LC	Ludwig Wittgenstein, *Lectures and Conversations on Aesthetics, Psychology and Religious Belief*
LF	Judith Shklar, "The Liberalism of Fear"
LH	Martin Heidegger, "Letter on Humanism"
LLF	Jacques Derrida, *Learning to Live Finally*
LT	Jürgen Habermas, *The Lure of Technocracy*
MA	Martin Heidegger, "Memorial Address"
MC	Isaiah Berlin, "Message to the 21st Century" (unpaginated online text)

MJ	Simone Maria Emms, *The Modern Journeyman*
MK	Adolf Hitler, *Mein Kampf*
MPP	Robert Pippin, *Modernism as a Philosophical Problem*
MU	Louisa Passerini, *Memory and Utopia*
NW	Martin Heidegger, "Nietzsche's Word: God is Dead"
OH	Jacques Derrida, *The Other Heading*
OG	Jacques Derrida, *Of Grammatology*
OL	J.S. Mill, *On Liberty*
OP	Immanuel Kant, *Opus Postumum*
OS	Jacques Derrida, *Of Spirit*
PAF	Jacques Derrida, "Politics and Friendship"
PDAT	Stanley Cavell, *Philosophy the Day After Tomorrow*
PF	Jacques Derrida, *Politics of Friendship*
PG	Robert Blanch and Julian Wasserman, *From Pearl to Gawain*
PH	G.W.F. Hegel, *Philosophy of History*
PI	Ludwig Wittgenstein, *Philosophical Investigations*
PL	Simon Critchley, "The Problem with Levinas" (unpaginated online interview)
PMC	Jean-François Lyotard, *The Postmodern Condition*
PMF	Stephen Mulhall, *Philosophical Myths of the Fall*
PTT	Jacques Derrida, *Philosophy in a Time of Terror*
R	Jacques Derrida, *Rogues*
RB	Emmanuel Levinas, *Is it Righteous to Be?*
RC	Mitchell Cohen, "Rooted Cosmopolitanism"
Rhees	Rush Rhees, *Ludwig Wittgenstein, personal recollections*
RL	Rowan Williams, "Rome Lecture: 'Secularism, Faith and Freedom'"
S1	Geoffrey Bennington, *Scatter 1*
SA	Myrto Dragona-Monachou, *Stoic Arguments for the Existence and Providence of the Gods*
SAS	Stephen Mulhall, *The Self and its Shadows*
SFV	John Adams Wettergreen, Jr., "Is Snobbery a Formal Value? Considering Life at the End of Modernity"
SM	Jacques Derrida, *Specters of Marx*
SMSW	Daniel Johnson, "Seven Minutes that Shook the World"
SN	Bernard Williams, *Shame and Necessity*
SR	V.I. Lenin, *State and Revolution*
TC	Isaiah Berlin, "Two Concepts of Liberty"
TDC	T.S. Eliot, *Notes Towards the Definition of Culture*
TFI	Jean-Paul Sartre, *The Family Idiot* (Vol. 4)
TI	Friedrich Nietzsche, "Twilight of the Idols"
TIML	David Wiggins, "Truth, Invention, and The Meaning of Life"
TLP	Ludwig Wittgenstein, *Tractatus Logico-Philosophicus*
UM	Friedrich Nietzsche, *Untimely Meditations*

UNESCO	Jacques Derrida, "Of the Humanities and the Philosophical Discipline"
UWC	Jacques Derrida, "The University Without Condition"
WP	Martin Heidegger, *What is Philosophy?*
WPC	Gabriel Citron (ed.), "Wittgenstein's Philosophical Conversations with Rush Rhees (1939–50)"
WS	Jacques Derrida, "What I would have said..."
WTP	Friedrich Nietzsche, *The Will to Power*

ACKNOWLEDGEMENTS

I would like to thank the following people for their support, encouragement, inspiration, and suggestions, large or small: Catherine Audard, Sonja Avilijaš, Matthew Bell, Robert Bernasconi, Chiara Bottici, Richard Bronk, Kevin Cahill, Amit Chaudhuri, Rebecca Comay, Robert Eaglestone, Kevin Featherstone, Katrin Flickschuh, Cristóbal Garibay-Petersen, Rodolphe Gasché, Victoria Glendinning, Denis Guénoun, Robert Hancké, Bjarke Morkore Stigel Hansen, Stephen Houlgate, Christine Irizarry, Peggy Kamuf, Anna Ksiazczakova, Oisín Keohane, Mareike Kleine, Ingrid Kylstad, Elissa Marder, Michael Morgan, Alan Montefiore, Michael Naas, Kalypso Nicolaides, Paula Zoido Oses, Alois Pichler, Tahir Rashid, Alison Stone, and Jonathan White.

This volume is dedicated to my friend and teacher Alan Montefiore. Alan took me under his wing when my future in philosophy looked – for internal and external reasons – bleak, and I have remained indebted to him ever since. Alan's contribution to philosophy and the culture of philosophy in Britain has been quietly transformative, and I know I am not alone in feeling profoundly grateful to him.

Material from this book has been presented at academic conferences, seminars and lectures at universities in Amsterdam, L'Aquila, Baltimore, Cambridge, Edinburgh, Groningen, Haifa, Little Rock, London, Luxembourg, Memphis, Moscow, New York, Nottingham, Oxford, Rochester, St Petersburg, Utrecht, Warwick, and Wolverhampton; at public events in Edinburgh, Hay-on-Wye, and London; and at various schools, primary and secondary, in England. I would like to thank the participants at all of these occasions for their thoughtful comments and contributions.

Most of the thinking that belongs to the development of this book was first presented in lectures to my students in the European Institute at the London

School of Economics and Political Science. I would like to thank them for their patience, enthusiasm, and ideas.

The first draft of this book was completed while I was Visiting Professor at the University of Bergen, Norway in 2015–16. I am extremely grateful to Alois Pichler for facilitating that. My sincere thanks go to Geoffrey Bennington and Stephen Mulhall who read through the penultimate draft of both volumes, and offered generous and helpful suggestions for their improvement. I would also like to express my thanks to Tony Bruce for taking on this project and, with Adam Johnson, overseeing its development. Above all, with endless gratitude, I would like to thank my wife, Anjali Joseph, who read everything, provided numerous detailed comments and objections, and saw before I had got there the other heading.

Oxford, 2021

INTRODUCTION

#Philosophy #Europe

We are backing into the future

– Paul Valéry

I

This book is the sequel to a partner volume, *The Promise of Modernity*. In that volume, I explored the historical self-understanding of those who have called themselves "Europeans", and tried to show how Europe's distinctively "modern" cultural formation was rooted in a general sense of human history. It doesn't matter if you haven't read that book because I will summarily introduce its basic claim now.

The basic claim of the first volume is quite simple: namely, that European cultural identity since the Enlightenment has been most powerfully configured by a very distinctive conception of Man: of Man as a fundamentally historical and rational being created in the image of God. Human history is understood as the history of the self-realisation of this uniquely theomorphic and rational animal. As it has come down to us, the most familiar expression of this conception presents a picture of human history as a process of the progressive civilisation of Man; it is the idea that (as the OED puts it, citing Matthew Arnold) "civilization is the humanization of Man in society". Central to my account were two related thoughts. First, that this European discourse on human civilisation is a *philosophical* history of Man; and, second, that it is a history which positioned Europe at the head of the pack in that civilisational development: it is a *Eurocentric* history of Man.

This picture of human history and Europe's centrality took systematic form when philosophy itself turned to the history of Man as a theme. And it is there that Europe and its modern condition became a theme for philosophy too. Immanuel Kant's late essays on human moral and political progress are perhaps the greatest and most influential examples of this kind of history. The understanding of human history and Europe's modernity that Kant presented in the 1780s and 90s was the first in a line of related philosophical treatments which were the focus of the first volume; I especially looked at those found in Hegel (1820s), Marx (1840s), Valéry (after the First World War), and Husserl (on the eve of the Second World War).

However much Kant's thought prefigured later efforts (and it prefigured them a lot), the history of philosophical history after Kant was not one of simple continuity. At issue, in the first volume, was the fate of the European philosophical discourse of Europe's modernity from Kant to Husserl; which means, very roughly, an account of the historical development of philosophical history from late eighteenth century *optimism* to mid-twentieth century *despair,* covering the history of philosophical history from the Enlightenment to the outbreak of the Second World War.

The very idea of writing a philosophical history was itself a theme in the first volume. It is impossible today not to be deeply suspicious of the idea that philosophers might make an *a priori* contribution to understanding historical events and developments. Indeed, the idea of philosophical history is not just ambitious, it is deeply paradoxical. One might think, as Kant himself anxiously put it, that "only a *novel* could result" (Kant, pp. 51–2). This anxiety has only grown over time, and did so within the history of philosophical history. Nevertheless, the basic shape of this hoping-to-be-non-novel-like philosophical history in Kant had two striking features that I tried to show were invariable throughout the many variations that followed from Hegel to Husserl. First, all of the later efforts I looked at retained Kant's thought that there is a discernible narrative intelligibility of human history: namely, a *teleological* (end-directed) movement from a condition of primitive human animality to one of increasingly rational and civilised humanity, a movement which is pre-eminently a history of *reason* unfolding in time. And, second, all the philosophers explored in the first volume retained the idea that the empirical history of Europe, and especially the "golden thread" of its Greek-Roman-Christian-Modern development, leads the way in the heading of humanity towards its proper end or *telos.*

Europe, so it seemed to these thinkers, promised a future condition of, as Emmanuel Levinas puts it, "peace, freedom and well-being" for all humanity "on the basis of a light that a universal knowledge projected onto the world" (TI, p. 132). This promise, for philosophy, has been the fundamental historical sense and significance of Europe, and became central to its distinctive cultural or civilisational identity. The promise of peace, freedom and well-being for all humanity is Europe's modern promise; and philosophical history, the history of "world history", or "the history of the world", or "universal history" was the discourse through which it found its most systematic expression.

As I have just indicated, however, the history of philosophical history is not a story of ever-greater confidence concerning this promise. On the contrary, by the middle of the twentieth century, the discourse of Europe's modernity had become a discourse of modern Europe's crisis. In the wake of the first world war of European origin, and in a phase in which the imminent threat of "portentous upheavals" pervaded European life (CES, p. 6), Europe could no longer be so assured of its place in world history. Edmund Husserl saw the apotheosis of this crisis lying in the fact that Europeans conceived "history" as having "nothing more to teach us than that all the shapes of the spiritual world...form and dissolve themselves like fleeting waves" (CES, p. 6). European humanity had lost faith in the idea that history has a teleological sense, and had lost faith in itself as central to such a development.

And today? What can we say today about this Europe, its history, its promise? Today, in the temporal phase that is our today, it perhaps faces something more or other than even a crisis. Writing in the mid-1980s, Levinas specified it, first, as a matter of conscience: "the conscience of Europe [today] is a bad conscience" (AT, p. 132). With the undeniable shame and guilt that runs through its culture in the wake of two world wars, totalitarianism, Nazism, fascism, genocides, the Shoah, colonisation and decolonisation, this is a condition in which the sense of its centrality to world history – the idea of its exemplary modernity – is not just currently in bad shape (a sense of a life/death "crisis" for Europe), but in which the very idea of such centrality has become increasingly and rightly impossible to believe in good faith. As Levinas puts it, Europe, its modern promise, has become "worn-out" (AT, p. 132).

This volume picks up this problem, our problem today – philosophical through and through and yet not merely philosophical – with Europe's modern promise. I will refer to this contemporary phase as the emergence of a condition "beyond modernity". I will explain how I want to understand this later, but one thing I want to stress is that a "worn-out" condition is not the same as a shift to a new one. The modern idea of human history as a process of civilisation – an idea that European philosophy more than any other mode of thought has promoted – may be facing exhaustion, but a new way of thinking about the "humanity of Man" and human history has not come along to displace or replace it. A significant feature of our time is the *hanging on* of the old modern self-understanding, despite its considerable weakening. At the end of this volume, I will suggest that a new conception of Man and history, a new conception of being human, is in fact beginning to coalesce in European thought in our time, though still fairly obscurely and tentatively. I believe it has a future.

In order to get going again in this philosophical history of Europe, the first part of this volume will cover the ground between the time when the European world was dominated by Christianity and Christian ecclesiastical power, and Europe in our time, when it is not. I will do so twice. First, in a somewhat mythological (but still philosophical) mode, via Friedrich Nietzsche's story of

"The Madman". And then, for a second time, in a more routinely historical (but still philosophical) recapitulation. At that point, we will have made our way back into the second half of the twentieth century where the first volume stopped. I will then stake out a path that tracks philosophical history through, first, the Cold War (Isaiah Berlin) to its apparent ending (Francis Fukuyama), then into our time with its considerable disruptions, dissatisfactions, and dangers, where a number of more or less contemporary philosophers (Jean-François Lyotard, David Wiggins, Stanley Cavell, Bernard Williams, and Judith Shklar among others) will be discussed together, although Jacques Derrida's work will increasingly be to the fore. Historically speaking, we can say that this volume covers the history of European philosophical history from the end of the Second World War to Brexit and Covid-19.

It is not an altogether encouraging story. A basic characteristic of our time as I will present it is its historical opacity. We do not know how we got here, and no longer know where we are heading. On the other hand, as Iris Murdoch writes, perhaps every age thinks it is "on the edge of an abyss", and then the task, once more, is to "think onward, outward, into the dark" (BB, p. 244), and I want to make a contribution to that too, from and for our time.

Achieving some kind of orientation towards that opening to the future depends on the light granted us beforehand, by our approach. The approach taken in this book, over both volumes, is long-run historical, and mostly chronological. But it is not a work of empirical history or the history of ideas. While I want to take in events in the world which, like cat's eyes in the road, mark the way as we go along, my interest is in the cultural world within which such events unfold. That world is now, more than ever, not merely regionally European but global and planetary. We (all) live in a time, as the poet and essayist Paul Valéry says, which is the end of a time in which history and politics could be "localized" (HP, p. 15). However, this new "globalized" condition, this globalisation, is not, I think, best understood in an exclusively geopolitical way, but must also be grasped, as it were, geophilosophically; that is, in the terms of a philosophical history. It is also not best understood in English, but in French: not globalisation but *mondialisation*: world-wide-isation. And at issue is not, I will argue, just any world-wide-isation but the world-wide-isation of the Greco-Biblical European world – a world becoming increasingly both global in its hegemonic reach and, perhaps paradoxically, exhausted in its condition.

II

Thinking that the world of European humanity is increasingly marked by a sense of its wearing-out in the very movement of its growing world-wide may not be entirely new. No more than is thinking, with Murdoch, that we are on the edge of an abyss, or, with Hamlet, that "the time is out of joint". Indeed, another Shakespeare play, *The Tragedy of Timon of Athens*, seems to have it in its sights too. Set during the onset of a financial crisis for a wealthy Athenian merchant whose creditors call in their debts, it presents a way of configuring its time which seems, oddly, to belong to more or less any time. I don't know if Shakespeare heard the expression or invented it but the words of a grumpy house painter to a cheerful poet certainly voices it:

Act 1, Scene 1
Athens. A hall in Timon's House
[Enter Poet, Painter, Jeweller, Merchant, and others, at several doors]

POET: Good day, sir.
PAINTER: I am glad you're well.
POET: I have not seen you long: how goes the world?
PAINTER: It wears, sir, as it grows.
POET: Ay, that's well known: But what particular rarity? what strange, which manifold record not matches?

The house painter's gloomy assessment of a world that wears as it grows is assessed in turn by the cheerful poet as how things always are: wearing and growing is what the world always does. It is always becoming more worn out than it once was, and it seems always to be getting bigger too. But that's not enough for the poet. He wants to know whether there is something genuinely unprecedented taking place in his "today". I want to do the same. How should we conceive the "particular rarity" of the contemporary European world? What is distinctive about it which "manifold record not matches"? We might begin by noting two key developments.

First development: in a planetary way, the world has stopped growing. We live in the era of completed world-wide-isation. As Valéry put it, "there is no rock that does not bear a flag; there are no more blanks on the map; no region out of the reach of customs officials and the law...*The age of the finite world has begun*" (HP, pp. 14–5).

Second development: not only do we live in a time of a kind of geopolitical extensiveness without limit, but what marks our world-wide-world is the loss of any way of speaking of the unity of our world; we lack the kind of gathered and joined-up discourse that would be a discourse of the world as a world. Our worn-out world is, to use a formulation of Martin Heidegger's, "a world that is no world" (MA, p. 48).

What is most singular about our time? We lack a discourse through which to understand our time; we lack a conceptual horizon in which an understanding of the world and the significance of our lives might be framed. The old understanding – that is to say the "modern" understanding of world history and its crises – is no longer one we can entirely inhabit, but we do not have a new one. We try again and again to find a new way to speak the old language, "one more try to save the discourse of a 'world' that we no longer speak", one more try to "save a world that we no longer inhabit", as Derrida put it (EC, p. 70). Without inhabiting a new language, and with the old language not simply in crisis but worn-out, there is a shimmering perplexity over the sense of our lives and history. "*We are backing into the future*", says Valéry, and "*headed I know not where*" (HP, p. 113). "How goes the world?" It has stopped growing and it has worn out. The world of the old modern European self-understanding – it is both globally dominant and all but exhausted.

In calling this a movement beyond modernity, I am steering close to the thought of the French philosopher Jean-François Lyotard, who famously proposed in 1979 that we should understand the contemporary situation of the advanced Western economies as having entered a "postmodern" condition. As we shall see, he also defines this in terms of our no longer having a certain kind of discourse at our disposal: he defines the postmodern condition in terms of what he calls "incredulity toward metanarratives" (PC, p. xxiv). The overarching, sense-making discourses through which and in terms of which we had understood the more concrete twists and turns of our lives – discourses which were, he also insists, above all, philosophies of the history of Man – have become incredible, unbelievable, but not because we have converted to a new "postmodern" metanarrative, a new grand narrative through which we might make sense of the world as a whole and the overall significance of our lives. We have no such sense-making discourse, we inhabit only the ruins of the old one.

This volume does not begin with an affirmation of Lyotard's conception but it does join him in the attempt to come to terms with our time, and the sense that a language for doing so, as Derrida puts it, "seems to us to be withheld" (EC, p. 70). We need to understand this. The opacity of our time in a European world gone world-wide is its greatest singularity. Lyotard and Derrida were writing in the wake of earlier thinkers who were also trying to understand our time. And they were not alone in this ambition. Indeed, today, almost everyone is at it. It's not that we have nothing to say. We probably say too much. Within the very limited reach of my own competence, the focus of this volume is a series of philosophical texts – including texts by Derrida and Lyotard – that I have come to regard as most helpfully contributing to this task of understanding our time. I will not be exploring "postmodern philosophy" but – if we want to retain this word at all – philosophy of Europe's postmodernity, or (as I prefer to say) the philosophy of Europe beyond modernity.

In this volume, I will suggest that the old modern discourse of the history of the world reaches a kind of limit in our time: a time of the radical weakening of the modern European self-understanding, a time of its exhaustion and unravelling, leaving "we, the Europeans" (and I will count myself among them in this book) adrift with respect to the meaning of our lives and history. However, this unravelling of the modern sense of world history and of Europe's centrality retains a somewhat paradoxically modern form: it takes place within the still-dominant discourse of Europe's social and scientific progress, and especially of the process of democratisation that Europe's modernity itself freed up. Democracy is a political concept, but I do not intend to limit its significance only to a form of government or a given governmental regime. Following Nietzsche, I will speak of the "whole democratic movement" as "a pervasive cultural tendency" (NCD, p. 21), characterising what used to be called the "spirit" of a time. In "modern times" – the times of science, the times of secular and democratic Enlightenment – what we see is the ongoing retreat of an older default understanding of the world and the significance of our lives. The *profound trust* in God (the father, the judge) and the correlative sense of the world as made with Man in mind no longer holds sway. Instead, there is an increasingly *profound mistrust* of prevailing authorities; a cultural and not merely (institutionally) political conviction about the general rightness – in every domain of our lives – of our freedom to resist tyranny, and freedom to question authorities of all kinds.

This taste or preference for democracy – self-direction, self-determination, self-government and self-legislation broadly conceived – pervades our overall cultural identity and self-understanding. In that sense, it is not simply one "modern idea" among others. It is the fundamental "spirit" of a properly shaped modern life – autonomous, rational, scientific, progressive – in a society granting (promising) free speech, free inquiry, and equal rights. The process of civilisation was always understood as fundamentally a movement towards rational freedom: the de-alienation or emancipation or progress of rational subjectivity in its self-liberation from conditions of subjection, servitude and dogmatism. Philosophical history led the way in elaborating this understanding conceptually, representing the movement of world history as the unfolding of the universal reason in Man from a dormant potential to a realised actuality, a realisation that is inseparably a movement towards universal freedom – with Europe at the head. Hegel's summary of world history stands as an extraordinary paradigm of a (notably German-centred) Eurocentric discourse of the promise of Europe's modernity:

> The History of the World travels from East to West, for Europe is absolutely the end of History, Asia the beginning...The East knew and to the present day knows only that *One* is Free; the Greek and Roman world, that *Some* are free; the German World knows that *All* are free. (PH, pp. 109–110)

Hegel was no friend of democracy as the proper form of government for a free people. However, the history of philosophical history, the geophilosophical history of Europe's modernity, is invariably understood as a history of the progress of freedom, and today increasingly of democratic freedom and democratic legitimacy. How the unravelling of the modern self-understanding takes place within the movement of its own celebration of human freedom is something I will try to track as we go along. Equally important, however, will be to see how the ongoing appeal to and the appeal of democracy opens a future for democracy beyond the still-modern and the increasingly hollowed-out democratic spirit of our contemporary condition. While I will want to avoid what Judith Shklar calls "the politics of hope" – a utopianism of some kind of ideal arrangement to come – there is something not unhopeful in this for our discouraging times. In what Derrida called the "European, and *uniquely* European, heritage of an idea of democracy" (OH, p. 78, emphasis in original), we can still see a future for Europe's promise beyond modernity.

Indeed, it is in this dimension of Europe's heritage that the geopolitical and the geophilosophical come together. A key theme for this volume is that politics, all politics, presupposes a conception of Man. And the political implications of the argument of this book belong with the claim to see in our time the exhaustion of the understanding of Man which had held sway in Europe's modernity – an understanding which had promised a final "end of history" in human self-realisation.

In the course of the book, and especially in its final part, I will explore the possibility of an alternative conception: one which conceives Man (in Isaiah Berlin's suggestive phrase) as an "unpredictably self-transforming" being, and I will discuss the politics of this conception most directly in terms of Derrida's ideas around democracy as "democracy to come" (where we do not know what is coming in that name, nor what it will be like to be alive then). This approach to democratic politics will be seen to entail a distinctively "empty" but still universal promise. It is an empty promise because it has no specific future-projecting content as democracy's final or ideal end. Instead, it affirms a conception of democracy which pledges the possibility, beyond anticipation, of ongoing and strictly interminable deliberations and discussions concerning the future of democratic politics itself. The claim will be, however, that this empty promise is anything but an empty promise. It lacks the affective force of classically "progressive" political projects (it does not stir our souls or provide a flag to march behind by promising progress towards a final end) but it is not toothless, since it gets its strength from wanting there to be, for everyone, no end of democratic politics. Yes, it is free of what T.S. Eliot called "the specious glitter of unmeaning promises" that have wreaked havoc and continue to wreak havoc in our time. But in that, it is not at all unhopeful.

As will become clear, my thinking about this ongoing promise, and Europe's responsibility for it, owes a great debt, its greatest debt, to Jacques Derrida and to his readings of philosophical history and Europe's modernity. However, to launch this discussion concerning our contemporary condition, I want first to orient its considerations through a reading of what still stands as an astonishingly disorienting orientation into our time from one of the most extraordinary and "untimely" texts of nineteenth-century philosophy, a text that I will read as a fable or fairy story that stages a magical juxtaposition between what it is like to be alive now (when Europe's promise is barely hanging on) and what it was like to be alive then (in the world in which Europe's promise first emerged), a contrast between times that I will try to pursue more concretely in the chapter that follows it. First stop: a step back to Nietzsche's Madman.

PART I

Europe then and now

1

THE DEATH OF GOD

Towards no one is mankind so ungrateful as it is towards God, just because people have the sluggish notion that one can always have Him – why, He cannot even die some day, to let people feel what they have lost

– Søren Kierkegaard (1848)

THE MADMAN

Have you not heard of that madman who lit a lantern in the bright morning hours, ran to the market place, and cried incessantly: "I seek God! I seek God!" – As many of those who did not believe in God were standing around just then, he provoked much laughter. Has he got lost? asked one. Did he lose his way like a child? asked another. Or is he hiding? Is he afraid of us? Has he gone on a voyage? emigrated? – Thus they yelled and laughed.

The madman jumped into their midst and pierced them with his eyes. "Whither is God?" he cried; "I will tell you. *We have killed him* – you and I. All of us are his murderers. But how did we do this? How could we drink up the sea? Who gave us the sponge to wipe away the entire horizon? What were we doing when we unchained this earth from its sun? Whither is it moving now? Whither are we moving? Away from all suns? Are we not plunging continually? Backward, sideward, forward, in all directions? Is there still any up or down? Are we not straying, as through an infinite nothing? Do we not feel the breath of empty space? Has it not become colder? Is not night continually closing in on us? Do we not need to light lanterns in the morning? Do we hear nothing as yet of the noise of the gravediggers who are burying God? Do we smell nothing as yet of the divine decomposition? Gods, too, decompose. God is dead. God remains dead. And we have killed him."

> "How shall we comfort ourselves, the murderers of all murderers? What was holiest and mightiest of all that the world has yet owned has bled to death under our knives: who will wipe this blood off us? What water is there for us to clean ourselves? What festivals of atonement, what sacred games shall we have to invent? Is not the greatness of this deed too great for us? Must we ourselves not become gods simply to appear worthy of it? There has never been a greater deed; and whoever is born after us – for the sake of this deed he will belong to a higher history than all history hitherto."
>
> Here the madman fell silent and looked again at his listeners; and they, too, were silent and stared at him in astonishment. At last he threw his lantern on the ground, and it broke into pieces and went out. "I have come too early," he said then; "my time is not yet. This tremendous event is still on its way, still wandering; it has not yet reached the ears of men. Lightning and thunder require time; the light of the stars requires time; deeds, though done, still require time to be seen and heard. This deed is still more distant from them than most distant stars – *and yet they have done it themselves.*"
>
> It has been related further that on the same day the madman forced his way into several churches and there struck up his *requiem aeternam deo.* Led out and called to account, he is said always to have replied nothing but: "What after all are these churches now if they are not the tombs and sepulchers of God?"
>
> Friedrich Nietzsche, *The Gay Science* (1882, 1887) para. 125; Walter Kaufmann ed. (New York: Vintage, 1974), pp.181–82.

I

This chapter and the next will present a narrative description of the development of Europe's culture into our time. It will not, however, describe that development in the way philosophical histories of Europe did in the past. It will not narrate the kind of epic adventure that memorialises Europe's "modernity", describing its world-historical break into "a new human epoch" (CES, p. 274), or its unrivalled advance to global "pre-eminence in all fields" (HP, p. 31). It is not because such a thing has become forbidden. It is simply no longer possible. As Ludwig Wittgenstein put it in the 1930s, "the development of this culture… just is no longer an epic" (CV, p. 11). At the end of this book, and in company with Jacques Derrida, I will look for something like a new "epic gesture" to help give strength to a more subterranean European memory which perhaps still has a future, or a fighting chance of having one. It is there, it is "*taking place now*", but it is not "*presently* given" (OH, p. 30, italics in original). Faithful to that barely accessible memory, this new epic gesture will take us beyond – and no doubt in some respects betray – the epic narratives that have dominated Europe's self-understanding hitherto (OH, p. 31). At this point, however, as we begin, I will be giving a narrative description only of the becoming-unbelievable of those old epic narratives, the classic narratives of Europe's modernity. "Only a *novel* could result from such premises", we would likely now say – as, in fact, Kant had already anxiously worried in the 1780s when he wrote one, a worry he felt confident that he could dismiss (Kant, p. 52).

The classic epic narratives of European philosophical history – those presented by Kant, and after Kant by Hegel, Marx, and Husserl, for example – recount the deeds, misdeeds, adventures and misadventures of Europe's history in a way that conceives them as belonging to an extraordinary drama of human self-realization: describing the antagonisms, impulses and revolutions that will one day bring about a life proper to Man as Man. These will have been philosophical (hi)stories of the movement towards a universal cosmopolitan existence, or the progress of spirit, or the emancipation of the working subject as universal subject, or the *entelechy* of rational animality. One and all concerned with the history of Man, and with Europe's centrality to that history. None of this seems remotely plausible today. As Lyotard put it in the 1970s, philosophical history is "losing its functors, its great heroes, its great dangers, its great voyages, its great goals" (PC, p. xxiv).

Wittgenstein thought the time had likely passed in which a philosopher might elaborate an epic narrative of Europe's cultural development. His judgement hesitated, however: in Nietzsche he saw a philosopher who perhaps "passed close" to what he called the "problems of the intellectual world of the West [*Probleme der abendländischen Gedankenwelt*]" (CV, p. 11). I don't know what Wittgenstein had in mind, but it is probably uncontroversial to say that Nietzsche addressed problems inherent in Europe's modern self-understanding in a still recognisably "epic" way. Nietzsche's European story does not relate an ongoing process of the emancipation or progress of Man, it is not a story of the "heroism of reason" in a titanic struggle with its own deformations (as Husserl put it), but he wrote, as we shall see, with a certain hope for the future of Europe, and he has what he calls a "tremendous event" in view that prepares for it: "the greatest recent event", which is, he says, "already beginning to cast its first shadows over Europe" (GS, §343). Nietzsche will tell a long-run European story in its terms, and it is one that opens onto what he saw as a still-promising future for Europe, for a Europe beyond its modern ideas and modern politics.

I will not follow Nietzsche all the way on his voyage towards a new European horizon. Wanting to stick with an attainable but still-unattained promise of democracy that he also attests to, I will stop short of the hopes for Europe's future that were his. Nevertheless, in this chapter and the next, I will attempt to relate the tremendous event that Nietzsche invites us to see underway, and to affirm his effort as a great first attempt to do so.

What I want to bring into view with the description of this event is less a change in the world (a geopolitical development, for example) as much as a world-change: a radical changeover in our understanding of the world and the significance of our lives. It is a change that will be marked most profoundly by what the British philosopher David Wiggins calls a "formidable" difference between times (TIML, p.89): a difference between *what it was like to be alive* in Europe's not so distant past (when an epic description of Europe's cultural development was still possible in classic terms), and *what it is like to be alive* in Europe's more recent present (when, "unless we are Marxists", it is not). It is in terms of that difference between then and now, indeed as an effort to come to terms with that difference, that I will narrate the cultural development of Europe into our time. It is also, I will suggest in this chapter, the central concern of Nietzsche's little story "The Madman", the extraordinary text in which the "tremendous event" is first announced.

Nietzsche's madman will say that the event he is concerned with is "still on its way, still wandering": it is not only ongoing and not over, but it has barely even arrived: "it has not yet reached the ears of men". As we set out to read Nietzsche's text, we should note first of all that the words Nietzsche finds to announce the event were themselves already making their way, wandering already, in the European world. For example, while they were not, first, Hegel's words, they were already among Hegel's first words. In revolt against Kant's finding it "necessary" to deny *knowledge* of God "to make room for *faith*" (CPR, Bxxx), the young Hegel (taking words already to hand) famously-but-not-as-famously-as-Nietzsche expressed the feeling that, with the rising domination of Kant's philosophy in Europe, "God himself is dead" (HFK, p. 67). Kant's ruling out the possibility of genuine knowledge of God was not experienced by Hegel as a mere theoretical shortcoming of Kant's philosophy but as a profoundly irreligious contamination of European life. Seeking God, one should strive not only for faith but – as scripture insists, says Hegel – knowledge of God, or all is lost. Hegel's own life-long effort to displace Kant's hold on our time, to usher in a new time in which this threat not just to philosophy but to European culture in general, is overcome, may well have been felt by him to have fallen on deaf ears.

I am not saying that Nietzsche's madman is Hegel. Indeed, I do not want to suggest that we need to work out any (or every) particular historical person that Nietzsche might have had in mind with his astonishing announcer of the death of God. But the fact that Nietzsche effectively quotes Hegel in staging the madman's presence in our midst should not be entirely overlooked. It is fair to say that the ears of men today are pretty sure about what they have heard in Nietzsche's telling of the announcement: it is most often heard as *a critique of Christianity*. And perhaps it is also that or can belong to that. But what reaches the ear so loudly today seems to me to obscure the more intriguing thought – one that we can begin to think via Hegel's response to Kant, and one affirmed, as we shall see, by Heidegger in his reading of Nietzsche – that the one who is called "the madman" is himself *a defender of Christianity*. That's the reading that I will develop here, as we begin to make our journey between then and now.

II

Look again at the very first words of Nietzsche's text: "Have you not heard of that madman…". Well, by now many of us have. But when the story-teller tells us that what is recounted are the exploits of a madman, are we supposed simply to take that as read? Most readers seem content to take the narrator at his word, and don't raise the question of the madman's presumed madness at all. Stephen Mulhall – who is untypical of most commentators in being himself a defender of Christianity – takes the madman's madness seriously, wondering whether Nietzsche gives the announcement to a madman because it is not obvious that anyone could mean what he says (PMF, p. 20). Mad people can't be held entirely responsible for what issues from their mouth, and whatever issues from it might not make much sense either. And the point is compelling once it is pointed out: an atheist just as much as a theist would know enough about what we mean by God to accept that the one thing one cannot say is that He can die some day. So we might well wonder with Mulhall "how far Nietzsche himself thinks that one might succeed in meaning what the claim appears to say and still remain recognizable as a potential interlocutor?" (PMF, p. 20).

I will continue to follow Mulhall's pointers throughout this chapter, and I think he is right to question the status of the madman as "a potential interlocutor" with those he addresses. But how would things look if the madman were not supposed mad at all? The anonymous narrator has no doubts about it, and those he meets in the story seem to receive him as such too. But what if the one called (out as) "the madman" is attesting to a reality that the people he addresses are not yet prepared to recognise? Perhaps they can "understand him" as an interlocutor only in a transposed form that renders him merely mad.

In what follows, I will argue that what makes the relation between the one called the madman and those he addresses so disjointed, is that the whole set-up of the fable is staged in a "time out of joint": what is conjured up by Nietzsche is the juxtaposition of two times (then and now) in one time (now), creating an impossible happening "once upon a time". The times of these two times might be specified by the gloss that Nietzsche later gives to the situation of our time when he himself quotes the words of the madman: "The greatest recent event – that 'God is dead', that the belief in the Christian god has become unbelievable – is already beginning to cast its first shadows over Europe" (GS, §343). Our time is the time of the first shadows of the becoming unbelievable of belief in the Christian God – someone might want to bring a lantern to such a darkening world – and the other time is the time before that time, the time in which being-able-to-believe in the Christian God was still possible for Europeans. In other words, what Nietzsche compresses in his Once Upon a Time fable is a scene that enacts the difference between then and now through events taking place during a single day in one place and in one time, which is our place and our time. The one who speaks these now famous and familiar words has (as one should normally never say) literally "jumped into their midst" from that earlier time.

However, this midst that we in our time are amidst is also a time in which that other time is *still there* in the very language of our language – and is so even as the world of those words has, according to the madman, been sundered, the whole horizon of our lives wiped away. This is a world-change event rendered in the fable as a murder-event so extraordinary to the one who has jumped time and jumped right into our midst that he can only wonder what "atonement" those who have committed it might be able to conjure up to be "worthy" of it, and hence to have recognised its magnitude. It is not beyond exaggeration, and Nietzsche's fable certainly exaggerates it, but a changeover is afoot whose significance is immense.

Here, in summary, is how I want to read the fable. The *visitation*, for that is what it is, is from a faithfully Christian religious figure of our past. And while he is not or no longer, for that reason, simply "one of us" he remains in our time as a figure still haunting us in our here and now. In a visitation from the past, our past, the one who comes back speaks to our time – but cannot be heard, and so belongs as a non-mad interlocutor for us (since we can't go back) only to our future – when, presumably, it will not be a visitation anyway. His home-time has already gone – or is yet to come. For us, he is the madman, and yet we still, in some sense, inhabit the world of his words, but a world in ruins.

III

Nietzsche appends a little title for his fable: "*Der tolle Mensch*", translated in English as "The Madman". Reading this text, and writing in the language of Nietzsche's language, Heidegger asks the question of the madman's madness: "*Inwiefern ist diseser Mensch 'toll'*?" In what ways or in which respects is this man "*toll*"? – whatever "*toll*" means here, which is exactly what Heidegger is asking. And he answers, translating within German, "*Er ist* 'ver-rückt'", which the English translator nicely renders as "He is 'de-ranged'" (WN, p. 111). *Verrückt*, unhyphenated, means mad, crazy, or insane. Heidegger's hyphen does not altogether dismiss that sense but holds off the psychological reduction to mere madness that belongs to those who hear him in the fable. Heidegger wants to stress rather that *der tolle Mensch* is the one who is thrown out of place, he is "dis-lodged" (NW, p. 111). He is not out of his mind but, I want to say, out of his time.

And what did *der tolle Mensch* say? Note his first words: "*I seek God! I seek God!*" ["*Ich suche Gott! Ich suche Gott*!"] Who says things like this? In the translation of this text that Mulhall uses for his commentary on the madman the speaker of these words says "*I'm looking for God! I'm looking for God!*" Perhaps nearly everything that transpires in the rather too well-known scene that is anonymously related in this fable is visible in this re-arrangement of de-ranged words: "*I seek God!*", on the one hand, and "*I'm looking for God!*", on the other. Are these words different? On the face of it not so very different, and the latter can pass for the former. But there is a difference nonetheless. For the first is the typical expression of those who believe in God; the second, by contrast, is a typical expression of rearrangement of that religious expression by those who do not believe in God, concerning what they hear when they hear that typical expression of faith. As Mulhall notes (and we'll come back to this), the atheist's tendency to rearrange Christian words typically belongs with "an underlying assumption that God is an entity of some kind (even if a supernatural one)"; something on the list of what potentially "there is", something that one might, at a pinch, look for, and find, or not find, like a sock (PMF, p. 21). The translation of "*Ich suche Gott! Ich suche Gott*!" as the expression of looking for something or someone is just such a transposition. A re-arranged format, and a transposing into a more acceptable domesticity of the words of the one who is de-ranged into the language of an atheist interlocutor. It is perhaps "well-known", but even so you should remind yourself that when the de-ranged one jumped into the marketplace those he found "standing around just then" were precisely "those who do not believe in God" – the English-language translator transposing the words of the one who seeks God into the familiar pitch of the ungodly marketplace atheists, already, along with them, rearranging his speech.

The "news" of the death of God will be brought, first, to atheists. Isn't that a very striking fact? Moreover, they are marketplace atheists, merchants and traders, people confident in the monetisable equivalence of differences. Doubtless, they can trade beliefs in the same way: "You believe *p*, and I contradict you, I believe the exact opposite, I recommend the exact opposite, I believe not-*p*". (I will come back to this particular construal in Chapter 8). We are altogether in a scene of translation, of supposed equivalences of difference, whether between languages or within one language.

And we are all ourselves somewhere in this scene. Mulhall adverts to this when he notes that "critical commentary has tended to concentrate" on the first part of the story, the part that takes place in the marketplace (PMF, p. 20). The text is well-known but haven't you heard, Mulhall asks, that it finishes with *der tolle Menche* visiting "several churches"? When considering this concentration of commentary on the marketplace, Mulhall suggests that it may be due to the fact that "most such commentators would regard themselves as members of that first [marketplace] audience" (PMF, p. 20). Yet they often will have done so without even noticing that *der tolle Mensch* announces the death of God to atheists, to those who do not seek God, which is to say, *to them*.

We might say that "we" (mostly) more or less pass by the last words of the fable. Only we tend also to pass over the madman's first words too. Not coming to terms with what he says seems utterly pre-programmed in the thing; it is the very story of the story. Perhaps we can concentrate on that. We? All of us.

Thinking of that inclusive "we", Mulhall takes Nietzsche's text to divide over two different unhearing audiences: the atheists (in the marketplace) and the theists (in the various churches), and he conceives Nietzsche's aim as being to "reinterpret the self-understanding of both of them" (PMF, p. 21). There certainly are two events on the same day: in the marketplace and in several churches. But they are not only on the same day. They are also in the same place – a place both secular and religious. A characteristically European place, we might say. So let's not separate too quickly the self-understanding of those who are addressed more than we need to. Mulhall is right about Nietzsche's aim, but we should remember that it means that he aims to re-interpret all those who are implicated in the death of God, and that is all of us – "we, the Europeans", atheist or theist, who stand around in the "first shadows" of the tremendous event that is on its way.

Who is *der tolle Mensch*? Into the heart of modern European everydayness, he arrives as a fool ("he caused great laughter") and a noisy intruder ("led out and quieted"). But I think Heidegger is right to ask in what respects is *der tolle Mensch* "*toll*", and I think his answer is compelling: in our time "he is '*ver-rückt*'".

IV

Heidegger puts the word "*ver-rückt*" in quotation marks, and for that reason, one might wonder if it was one of Nietzsche's words. But it is not. It is, however, one of Heidegger's, and in an online video, you can hear him say it (see, HS). In the clip, Heidegger suggests that many atheists today, "for example communists", can be said to "have a religion" too; namely, their unconditional belief in modern science. This is not an individual affair, something had by each singly, but is something that exceeds any individual and binds them together, and "therefore", Heidegger rapidly concludes, is a "religion". ("*Religio*", we should recall, probably derives, in part, from "*ligare*" – to tie, to bind). And then rushing on faster still he adds that no man is without a religion, and every man is transcending himself, concluding: "and that means: *ver-rückt*".

We are all a bit *ver-rückt*. The English language translator of Heidegger's essay on Nietzsche's fable notes other related words in the two sentences following Heidegger's specification of *der tolle Mensche* as "*ver-rückt*" that bears on this understanding: "he is dislodged" [*ausgerückt*], and he is "carried out beyond" [*hinausgerückt*]. Heidegger had always contrasted Man (as such) from all mere (pure) animal life, with the thought that the latter "are lodged in their environment" (LH, p. 230), while Man "ek-sists", meaning that Man *is* at all only as "standing outside" or "dis-lodged" from animal immersion, as "Being-in-the-world" (LH, pp. 230–1). In this respect, there is, that is to say, an uncanny likeness of *der tolle Mensch* with every other. But, Heidegger will lodge a formidable difference between the visitor and the visited in Nietzsche's story, and first of all with respect to the marketplace atheists: the one who is *ver-rückt* as *der tolle Mensch*, because he seeks God, has "nothing in common with the kind of men standing about in the market place" who, Heidegger says, "are no longer able to seek God" – not because "*God* has become unworthy of belief" but because "*they* have given up the possibility of belief" (WN, p. 112). It is, first of all, from that presently attained "level of Man" that *der tolle Mensch* is dis-lodged (WN, p. 112).

Since he is not happily lodged in our time the one who has arrived in this visitation is, Heidegger says, "carried out beyond" the condition of Man attained in our time (WN, pp. 111–2). However, *der tolle Mensch* can be in that relation to us, he stresses, only because he is "drawn utterly" into the essential possibilities of being belonging to Man as that has been understood throughout the epoch in which Europe has made its way (WN, p. 112). This is the epoch of a self-understanding in which Man has been interpreted, first, from the Greeks, as the *zōon logon echon* (the living thing with the capacity for grasping the *logos*) and subsequently (as that was fatefully translated into Latin) as the *animal rationale*, coming down to us as the idea of Man as the rational animal. *Der tolle Mensch* represents possibilities of being for Man thus understood which Heidegger thinks that the innermost direction of European history (as attested by the very translation of the Greek into Latin just noted) has increasingly tended to occlude, and from which it leads us "off the track" (BT, p. 74). As we shall see in the next chapter, the Greeks lived with an unshakeable conviction that whatever happened in the world was the work of the gods, and Christians too saw Divine direction and control everywhere. But this is a conception of God that we, "we, the Europeans", are increasingly lost to. Our sense of ourselves has increasingly "glorified reason" (WN, p. 112) in terms of science and techno-scientific progress – about nature and about ourselves as natural creatures – and this has profoundly limited if not altogether erased any sense of our inhabiting a world made with Man in mind or with God or gods at its centre. In this visitation, we are haunted by something from our own past, something which, as we shall see more directly in the next chapter, opened the very path that leads us off the track.

Who is *der tolle Mensch*? Heidegger concludes, correctly I think, that he "is clearly, according to the first, and more clearly still according to the last sentences of the passage, for him who can hear, *the one who seeks God*" (WN, p. 112). And in the fable we find that he does not belong comfortably in our time: he is just a madman. But: he *is* our past, he *remains* somehow in our present, and his words still lie before us, ahead of us, carried out beyond us, yet to be heard.

V

Does the fact that *der tolle Mensch* is the one who seeks God make him closer, then, to the "level of Man" that belongs to the ones who "led him out and took him to task" [*hinausgeführt und zur Rede gesetzt*] when he went to "several churches" later that same day? Not really. The people in the churches clearly didn't want to hear the words intoned in his *Requiem aeternam deo* either. A requiem is a mass intoned for the souls of the dead, in this case intoned for the Christian "God eternal". This is not such an unfamiliar idea to Christians. After all, it is the Christian God who, as incarnate, was indeed murdered, and whose crucified body hangs heavily in every church, making of each one already something of a tomb or sepulchre of the dead God.

This is the incarnate God, as Mulhall notes, "whose time is both already gone and yet to come" (PMF, p. 28). In other words, Christians *already* live in the time of the death of God. "God is dead" – this is not just an Hegelian expression of grief and grievance but already a strictly Christian proposition, a fundamental part of the Christian creed, right from the start. Mulhall wonders whether the Christians in the various churches (mis)heard the intoned version of those same words as an insult; that they would be understood to "blaspheme against Christianity" rather than "recall believers to an aspect of their faith that is absolutely essential" (PMF, p. 31). At the end of the fable, we are told that the visitation to the churches was felt as a penetration [*eingedrungen*] of their places of worship, an invasive entry, and that he was escorted out and given a bit of a talking to. It was, perhaps, not so much felt as an attack on their faith as an intrusion on the good order of their good orders.

And perhaps for good reason. While the words of *der tolle Mensch* are Christian words they do not do normal Christian service, they do not follow the normal Christian order. In terms of that order, the once upon a time of this fable can be thought of as taking place, eternally, on Holy Saturday. In the order of normal Christian orders, that day is a day of pause, of waiting, a day between days, a day when (various) Christian churches have no services at all, and people might well want to "quieten" someone who is not suitably quiet on that day. In the fable, however, that day is unslung from being the day between Good Friday and Easter Sunday, hence unslung too from the incessant cycle of Christian memorialization: murder-death-resurrection. Indeed, also unslung from the staging of that cycle that takes place in the waves of Christian revivalism. Revival of the life of the church, restoration of vitality – this belongs to the life of the Church: its own death and renewal central to the staging of Christian life. But the madman sees in our time a decisive interruption of that cycle: "God is dead, God remains dead". And "now" – Nietzsche here marks the time as a new time, insisting *from now on* that we register a formidable difference between then and now – the life of the Church seems to him beyond revival, the churches now becoming tombs and sepulchres of the faith that had hitherto belonged to those who sought God.

The madman, coming from the time before our time, feels what we have lost, without our feeling it. Our churches may still be places of assembly (*ecclesia*), prayer and worship, but are they still, as institutions, houses of God (*kuriakos*)? Can you not see the churches emptying, hear the death-rattle? Smell the decomposition?

Of course, since the news of this tremendous event has barely arrived, Nietzsche's rupture-marking does not exclude ongoing calls for revival, even now. Indeed, if the event is nevertheless (in some sense) happening one might even expect growing calls for renewal, more intense recollection of fundamentals, and new fundamentalisms. But the world of the words of those who seek God, and the submission to that world which held it in its sway, has, the madman feels, been wiped away: we live increasingly without the profound trust that whatever happens, indeed everything that happens, is God's handiwork, and this leaves all of us only with the more "stodgy notion" that, whatever else, God "cannot die some day" – and that anyone who would think otherwise is…a madman.

Mulhall's conclusion to his discussion of the last sentences of the fable is that the song of *der tolle Mensch* can be understood to "confront Christendom in the name of Christianity" (PMF, p. 31). This seems to me exactly right. But in the end it should not be restricted to the last sentences. The visitation of *der tolle Mensch* in our midst, his invasive penetration into one of our places, to its marketplace and its various churches, simply shows up such places – our places, European places, the *remains* of Christendom – as peopled by Christians (theists or not) in a time of the first shadows of becoming no longer able to seek God. When Nietzsche later summarises the situation in Europe as he finds it as one in which increasingly "the belief in the Christian god has become unbelievable" – this is about everyone, whether they are theistic or atheistic Christians.

VI

Atheistic Christians? What? Don't they already find belief in the Christian God unbelievable? And why call them Christians, if they are atheists? In what ways or in what respects are they atheists? I will come back to this in greater detail in Chapter 8. But the basic thought here is fairly straightforward: in a European world in which Christianity has not been a mere walk-on part but for nearly two thousand years the playwright, set designer, lead actor and critic, it is not obvious how Europe's atheists could be other than Christian in their formation. Jean-Paul Sartre understood his existentialism as an atheist philosophy, but he had no illusions about the Christian historicity to which it belonged. In his biography of Gustave Flaubert, published in 1971–72, Sartre sketched the historical situation in the West as follows (TFI, p. 346):

> Flaubert writes for a Western world which is Christian. And we are all still Christians, even today; the most radical disbelief is still Christian atheism. In other words it retains, in spite of its destructive power, schemata which are controlling – very slightly for our thinking, more for our imagination, above all for our sensibility. And the origins of these schemata are to be sought in the centuries of Christianity of which we are the heirs, whether we like it or not.

Sartre's existentialism does not try to present any kind of refutation of religious beliefs. Rather it calls the religious theist back to his or her own responsibility for freely cleaving, with profound trust, to religious creeds. However, as we shall see in Chapter 8, Modern atheists do not see things existentially but epistemologically. For the modern atheist, religious theist beliefs are like, say, beliefs in an unobservable planet, or some other unobservable entity – but involve believing in their existence on ridiculously poor grounds. For modern atheists – and we have indicated that this is staged in Nietzsche's fable too – God is conceived as a being of some (weird) kind, an item in the entity-count of what one might take to be or to exist, and an item which, if we reason rightly, we would do better to cross off any rationally respectable list. Indeed, the modern atheist will suppose that, if we reason rightly, we are all likely, eventually, to come to agree that believing in God – which they hear only in the transposed form of "belief in the existence of God" as a being – is a childish superstition, something that has no place whatever in a mature life shaped by modern advances in our rational understanding of nature and ourselves as natural creatures. Seeking God – which they hear only in the transposed form of "looking for God" as a being – is, on this view, deeply irrational, simply mad. This is exactly how Nietzsche represents the thinking of those "who do not believe in God" in his fable.

VII

The marketplace atheists hear the one who seeks God as someone who is looking for someone or something, and they thus betray an understanding of belief in God as belief in an existent being. But when the madman responds to the marketplace atheists by speaking of God as having died, having been finally lost to us, he does not invoke the decline in belief in the existence of a thing, however significant or sacred a thing that might have been, but speaks to a loss that is the loss of significance itself: "the whole horizon" of our life has been "wiped away". How should we understand this?

Attempting to articulate a radical sense of our "thrownness" into the whereabouts of an historically specific time and place, Heidegger speaks of every Dasein as having "factically submitted to a definite 'world' – its 'world'" (BT, p. 344). Heidegger conceives this "world" as a whereabouts of sense, the home-land of a life, a meaning-world. But perhaps this "submission" to such a world is not entirely independent of, or at least has not always been entirely independent of, submission to God. Nietzsche puts it as follows (BGE, p. 84):

> Around the hero everything becomes a tragedy, around the demi-god a satyr-play; and around God everything becomes – what? Perhaps a "world"? –

As it is reproduced here, this remark is a self-standing aphorism in Nietzsche's text, belonging to a collection of short aphoristic remarks in a chapter of *Beyond Good and Evil* entitled "Maxims and Interludes". The remark may be self-standing but it only just stands up, and the long dash at the end, beyond the questioning "perhaps" (which may be all we have left to work with in our time) stands even more defiantly as a moment of incompleteness, perhaps pressing us on to wonder what is "around" when God… is dead; whether, for example, we are, as Heidegger also put it, increasingly surrounded by "a world that is no world" (MA, p. 48). ("God" and "the world" are "correlates", says Kant in the *Opus Postumum* (OP, p. 211).)

The "tremendous event" of the death of God, cannot be understood simply like the death of something or someone within the world, or an event within the domain of everything that is. Rather, it relates to something befalling the world within which all worldly events have their significant taking place, including the worldly crucifixion event which, we can now say, took place within the very world it came to open up. This world too has a history, a world-history – and, Nietzsche claims, it is altogether unravelling in our time. This greatest recent event – the death of God – is a deed done by "we, the Europeans" to our world – all of us are caught up in its happening. And yet today we (still) do not know what we have done. We live in our time in the becoming-shadow of the light of the Greco-Biblical world of Man. The theists are upstanding figures of European Christendom, and the atheists of the marketplace are through and through Christian atheists, not its radical overcomers. Indeed, if there is a "critique of Christianity" in Nietzsche's fable it is aimed just as squarely, perhaps more continuously, and certainly at greater length, with those Europeans "standing about just then" who do not believe in God. But: we are all in the shadow of this event. Nietzsche too can only conceive of a development of European culture beyond this shadow from under it. All available concepts are caught up in the closure he is trying to think beyond, and we have no others.

And yet, for Nietzsche, this condition of world-darkening, this old-world-exhaustion, this ruined world, is still promising. Indeed, while it might last for ages, for centuries to come, it is not, for Nietzsche, Europe's final fate. Speaking now in his own name, and quoting the words of *der tolle Mensch,* Nietzsche gives his reasons to be cheerful, and outlines the opening of a new European epic. In our floundering condition, he sees the chance for something new for Europe ("the sea, *our* sea, lies open again")?

> **The meaning of our cheerfulness.** – The greatest recent event – that "God is dead," that the belief in the Christian god has become unbelievable – is already beginning to cast its first shadows over Europe. For the few at least whose eyes – the *suspicion* in whose eyes is strong and subtle enough for this spectacle, some sun seems to have set and some ancient and profound trust has been turned into doubt; to them our old world must appear daily more like evening, more mistrustful, stranger, "older." But in the main one may say: The event itself is far too great, too distant, too remote from the multitude's capacity for comprehension even for the tidings of it to be thought of as having *arrived* as yet. Much less may one suppose that many people know as yet *what* this event really means – and how much must collapse now that this faith has been undermined because it was built upon this faith, propped up by it, grown into it; for example, the whole of our European morality. This long plenitude and sequence of breakdown, destruction, ruin, and cataclysm that is now impending – who could guess enough of it today to be compelled to play the teacher and advance proclaimer of this monstrous logic of terror, the prophet of a gloom and an eclipse of the sun whose like has probably never yet occurred on earth?
>
> Even we born guessers of riddles who are, as it were, waiting on the mountains, posted between today and tomorrow, stretched in the contradiction between today and tomorrow, we firstlings and premature births of the coming century, to whom the shadows that must soon envelop Europe really *should* have appeared by now –why is it that even we look forward to the approaching gloom without any real sense of involvement and above

> all without any worry and fear for *ourselves*? Are we perhaps still too much under the impression of the *initial* consequences of this event – and these initial consequences, the consequences for *ourselves*, are quite the opposite of what one might perhaps expect: they are not at all sad and gloomy but rather like a new and scarcely describable kind of light, happiness, relief, exhilaration, encouragement, dawn.
>
> Indeed, we philosophers and "free spirits" feel, when we hear the news that "the old god is dead," as if a new dawn shone on us; our heart overflows with gratitude, amazement, premonitions, expectation. At long last the horizon appears free to us again, even if it should not be bright; at long last our ships may venture out again, venture out to face any danger; all the daring of the lover of knowledge is permitted again; the sea, *our* sea, lies open again; perhaps there has never yet been such an "open sea." (GS, §343)

We will return to Nietzsche later in this book when we consider his anticipation, his *teleo-auto-poetic* projection or conjuration, of a newly epic movement for Europe beyond its present condition. As we shall see, Nietzsche conceived this as a movement that is likely to be mediated by a process of European political integration already nascent within the current processes of democratization. And while we will not follow Nietzsche to the end of his vision of what might become of the culture of this new supranational European culture, stopping short of that, we will draw on his radically decentered understanding of Man – a conception of humanity cut to the cloth of the death of God – when we draw our own conclusions.

VIII

"God is dead". The madman's words may not do normal Christian service but the whole visitation is still framed within a Christian conceptuality. The whole telling of the fable shines in and only in a Christian light, the light of a world – but a world which, we are given to understand, is darkening, a world in ruins.

And yet: we don't see it, hear it, smell it. As Robert Pippin nicely puts it, the culture of the places Nietzsche has in mind as undergoing the event described by *der tolle Mensch* is "the modern civilization [Nietzsche] describes in *Thus Spoke Zarathustra* as the 'city of the many coloured cow' [and it] is as stolidly contented as that bovine characterisation implies" (MPP, p. 86). Nietzsche had a thing about cows, and lines up women, the English, "and other democrats" with them – indeed, the "many coloured" character of this place recalls precisely Plato's image of a democracy as a distinctively female and many coloured kind of thing, a thing which is now, in the Europe of our time, dominated, Nietzsche says, by an "English" spirit, with its "profound averageness" (BGE, p. 156). This "democratic taste" and its "'modern ideas'" are at large right across Europe (BGE, p. 54). Moreover, as we shall see as this book develops, the primary vehicle for the unravelling of the times between then and now is precisely this general culture – rational, scientific, progressive – that belongs to "the whole democratic movement" in Europe.

Of course, as Pippin's description highlights, the most astonishing characteristic of the "tremendous event" that Nietzsche wagers to have happened is that it is simply *not happening* for those who are in it. Nietzsche, what a madman! He's not even describing how things are. The horizon of the world has, we are told, been wiped away – and apparently, we ourselves have wiped it. But, really? However "convinced" Nietzsche had become about it, Pippin finds it implausible to suppose that it can be straightforwardly described as an event that "we" are going through or responsible for. Indeed, in Nietzsche's own lifetime "among almost all of his contemporaries", there really is nothing to suggest it: "there is very little sense of any great moral crisis, or even any disaffection with modern ideals" (MPP, p. 87). One might well wonder, with Pippin, whether a condition of our existence that we do not attest to can be a condition of ours at all.

Pippin regards this as an objection to Nietzsche's interpretation of our time. But, for Nietzsche, this non-awareness of our situation is clearly part of the event and belongs to its description. This greatest recent event in Europe has (apparently) both already happened and is yet to arrive. How are we to understand this? Pippin finds it far-fetched. Nietzsche, however, invites us to find our condition of bovine solidity as structurally uncanny: complete disorientation is, he is suggesting, both our closest condition, the most near, and yet remains also the most distant, the most far.

Who and what to believe? Nietzsche himself says that he is guessing. On the other hand, one cannot give the casting vote to those who live without any great "disaffection with modern ideals" just because they feel stolidly contented. Isaiah Berlin will not be alone in wanting to "acknowledge the insight of Rousseau" that "to know one's chains for what they are is better than to deck them with flowers" (FEL, p. xxxix). And the same goes for life in a Christian world in ruins. The "strong and subtle" suspicion in the eyes of one exceptional thinker can make the scales fall from the eyes of others: suddenly the aspect of things that had been familiar can altogether change. And perhaps *since Nietzsche* the world-change he marks in our time is something becoming available for us to apprehend. Are we not in Nietzsche's wake? Hasn't he made a compelling thought about our condition available to us? Do we not live in a time marked by an ongoing loss of a sense or meaning or truth of human history, a loss which leaves us "straying, as though through an infinite nothing"? Are we not more alive in our today, as Wittgenstein seems already to have been in the 1930s, to the fact that Europe's old modern epic narratives for making sense of the world and the significance of our lives are weakening? Isn't it becoming plainer by the day that we no longer know where we are heading, or whether we are heading anywhere at all? Wasn't Jean-François Lyotard right to see a rising "incredulity towards metanarratives" (PC, p. xxiv)? Wasn't Bernard Williams right to see a widespread "scepticism" about "*les grands récits*" through which, in an earlier time, we had made sense of our modern lives, our lives as "modern" (IBWD, p. 47)? No?

If someone is determined to remain stolidly contented, no fabulous argument will convince them that Nietzsche's word on our time is its best first word. On the other hand, I do think the picture he gives us of the difference between then and now that I have followed in this chapter can be filled out in a more or less straight historical way too. I say "more or less" in part out of a strong sympathy with Bernard Williams, who, when accepting that he wanted to recognize "the significant role of Christianity in understanding modern moral consciousness", admitted that his "historical commitments" gave rise to a certain nervousness about whether he was writing "irresponsible history" (IBWD, p. 54). Nevertheless, and nervousness apart, in the next chapter I want to attempt an approach to the difference between then and now in a less fabulous and more historical way. Not as a historian might, in relation to the fate of peoples and fatherlands, but as a philosopher, and in relation to the fate of the narratives where, above all, the distinctively "modern" European self-understanding is most explicitly encountered: the epic philosophical narratives of Man and his history.

2

A WORN-OUT EUROPE

God lightly lets loose with his littlest finger

– St Erkenwald

I

This book speaks from and to what I want to call the perplexing opacity of our time: the fact that its sense, if any, seems withheld. My aim is not to clear it all up or to be a latter-day Mr Fixit who will explain "what is needed" or "what is to be done" to sort it all out and put things straight. But I do want to come to terms with our time.

When I say this I do not mean that I am trying to find a way to acquiesce to it. "Coming to terms with our time" means for me a project of making sense, finding the words that will clarify the opacity of our time, our "nowadays": to make sense of it as a time that does not make much sense. We will, then, I hope, be able better to see the movements in our time, already underway, that contribute most to thinking "onward, outward, into the dark".

There was a time, another "nowadays", not recently but not so long ago, say two hundred years ago, when most Europeans would not have been so perplexed about the sense of their world or time. Just by growing up then, most Europeans would have lived with a very distinctive way of understanding the world and the significance of their lives. There was a default world-understanding, a cultural default, which only a few resisted or found incredible (unbelievable), and through which and in terms of which the lives of most made sense to them. Speaking of our condition, in our time, that is to say, "during relatively recent times", as one in which we are "very perplexed" in the face of the obscurity of even the question of the sense or meaning of our own lives, David Wiggins contrasts our time with that time two hundred years ago, and summarises what he sees as a remarkable "shift" in perceptions on this matter: "History has not yet carried us to the point where it is impossible for a description of such differences to count as exaggerated. But they are formidable" (TIML, p. 89). Those Europeans of the day before yesterday, they are not (yet) everywhere foreign to us, but whereas we seem all at sea, they seem to have a very clear, specific and certain grasp on the question of the meaning of their lives. And their condition is one that we today might, for just that reason, quite understandably envy:

> It is impossible to reach out to the perplexity for which the question of meaning is felt to stand [today] without first recording the sense that, during relatively recent times, there has been some shift in the way the question of life's meaning is seen, and in the kind of answer it is felt to require... Two hundred years ago...the specificity and the certainty of purpose [is enviable]...The foundation of what we envy was the now (I think) almost unattainable conviction that there exists a God whose purpose ordains certain specific duties for all men.
>
> If we envy the certainty of the [old] answer, then most likely this is only one of several differences that we see between our own situation and the situation of those who lived before the point at which Darwin's theory of evolution so confined the scope of the religious imagination... [S]uch differences...are formidable. Accessibility to both the eighteenth and twentieth centuries of a core notion of God...cannot bridge [the gap between these times]. For recourse to [the idea of a common notion of God] exemplifies a tendency [on our part] towards an *a priori* conception of God, which, even if the eighteenth century had it, most of the men of that age would have hastened to amplify with a more hazardous or *a posteriori* conception. Faith in God conceived *a posteriori* was precisely the cost of the particularity and definiteness of the certainty that we envy... For us there is less specificity and much less focus. (TIML, pp. 89–90)

I will come back to the continuation of this text shortly, where Wiggins will try to bring our own time – with its distinctive lack of "focus" – into clearer focus. But I want first to draw attention to what Wiggins thought was available and accessible to Europeans of the eighteenth century that we in our time have lost, or, as he will later put it, increasingly "resist": namely, ways of thinking about our lives involving "faith in God conceived *a posteriori*".

When students explore *a posteriori* conceptions of God today they will likely be exploring traditional "arguments for the existence of God"; and the particular argument they will examine under the *a posteriori* head will typically involve an appeal to certain features or facts about the world (for example, the complexity of life physiologically understood) that might seem impossible to conceive without invoking a Divine Designer. The arguments are based on the idea that an adequate account of many natural things being what they are (for example, the human eye) has to make reference to what they are for. So a developing eye in a human embryo will only be developing as it should if it develops in a way that affords the developing human being the possibility of sight. The explanation of what it is, thus, draws in a developmental or teleological story concerning its purpose or end. But now consider there being any such thing as a human eye at all. How could such a complex structure required for sight come to be from absolute sightlessness? At this point one might feel the need to admit a teleology in nature quite generally: the coming into being of many natural things is not, as Kant puts it, "an aimless, random process" but exhibits an unfolding development which, when it goes as it should, develops "*towards*" and "in conformity with" "their *end*" (Kant, p. 42). And just as a human maker of things (a watchmaker, for example) puts things together in a planned and not aimless way, and does so in virtue of having a quite specific end in view (a reliable time-keeping-and-telling device), so natural objectivities which fulfil a purpose would, as Kant goes on to affirm, "seem to indicate the design of a wise creator" who has a benevolent "hand" in their development (Kant, p. 45).

Today, students looking at *a posteriori* conceptions of God are also very likely to have teleological claims of this kind called into question by an entirely natural science: we can claim today to have robustly natural explanations, in the wake of Darwin, of the evolution of organs, and indeed of life itself, that means we no longer need to invoke a supernatural Divine Designer at all.

I have invoked an experience of opacity, a perplexity and a lack of focus about the question of life's meaning for us in our time. But the text-book changeover just reviewed, from a time before and after Darwin, would seem to run in the opposite direction: it seems to have given us greater clarity, not less. Indeed, it would seem to provide for an understanding of the world and ourselves as natural creatures which is not only empirically well-established, but which perfectly fits our still ongoing sense of our own condition as "modern": it is an understanding which frees us from traditional prejudices, frees us from a worldview founded on myth, superstition and (at least in this area) religion. Why on earth should it go along with the "perplexity" Wiggins attests to?

We – we more recent moderns – are inclined to look at the *a posteriori* conception of God as a (not very serious if still sadly present) rival explanation for natural complexity and evolution. Indeed, this is one way (perhaps the standard way) of trying to comprehend what Wiggins regards as the differences between us and them that he thinks as so formidable. They still had that (supernatural) type explanation; we now have this far superior (natural) one. Not much to envy there.

How might we come to see this as a thin, weak, and shallow, assessment of the difference between times that I am trying to get into view here? One way would be to see it is akin to (indeed basically the same as) interpreting Nietzsche's madman's word "God is dead" as an oddly phrased but basically atheistic affirmation that "God does not exist". I do not want to deny the adequacy or legitimate authority of natural scientific explanations. Nor will I try to minimise the wider secular-cultural significance of the Darwinian upheaval in the sciences of nature.

Marx would not have been alone when he said in a letter to a friend in 1861 that *The Origin of Species* (1859) dealt "the death-blow...for the first time to teleology in the natural sciences" (RC, p. 345). For sure it mostly did. But this was not just a scientific achievement, replacing a non-empirical and unverifiable theory with an empirically testable and refutable alternative. Darwinian science struck a blow to the European self-understanding that made his scientific achievement into something like a world-historical event. I will come back to that "death-blow" in the final chapter. But what I want to emphasise here is that the *a posteriori* conception of God was not only a theological doctrine of nature and ourselves as natural creatures, in particular, it was not merely a doctrine about life in a physiological sense, a doctrine that Darwinian science provides such a fertile alternative to. On the contrary, it is also (and, as we shall see, this is why Marx's relation to the Darwinian blow will be so ambiguous) a doctrine about life, and especially human life, in a historical sense. As Paul Valéry put it in a letter to a friend in 1906, "no history can pass [Darwin] over. Just think: if he is right, the whole of history is changed. I mean all thinking about history" (HP, p. 516).

The idea that human life has a natural history predates Darwin, but the conceptual horizon for understanding what we are talking about when what we are talking about "human life" raises a more fundamental question of who we think we are *simpliciter.* In the tradition and heritage that belongs to European humanity, we call ourselves "Man". And even if Man is, physiologically speaking, an animal among other animals, Man was also understood as distinguished from or as having radically distinguished itself from all merely animal existence. Man is the being that he is precisely by virtue of living something other and more than a merely animal existence, indeed as having exited the state of nature (nature exiting itself); creating civilisations, cultural ways and works of the most astonishing variety, irreducible to instinctual animal life. An apparently completely unique characteristic of this being, then, is that it does not only develop or evolve physiologically, but even in a time when it hasn't developed or evolved in a physiological sense at all or barely at all (in the epoch of "modern Man" since Neolithic times, as we say), it has evidently (and on a more or less global scale) come a long way culturally. This is what we call "history", human history, the history of the (human) world, the history of humanity from a pre-historical and merely natural condition to the civilisations of ancient times, up to our own times, and, we hope, beyond.

This is where an *a posteriori* conception of God really entered into the lives of Europeans. And here, it seems to me, there is a powerful and fundamental connection to philosophy: for the significance to Europeans of the *a posteriori* conception of God emerges in the space of a self-understanding – a conception of ourselves as "Man" – that is rooted in Greek philosophy as it is drawn into Christian theology. Heidegger summarises:

> The originally Greek nature of philosophy, in the era of its modern-European sway, has been guided and ruled by Christian conceptions. The

> dominance of these conceptions was mediated by the Middle Ages. At the same time, one cannot say that philosophy thereby became Christian, that is, became a matter of belief in revelation and the authority of the Church. The statement that philosophy is in its nature Greek says nothing more than that the West and Europe [*das Abendland und Europa*], and only these, are, in the innermost course of their history, originally "philosophical". This is attested by the rise and dominance of the sciences. Because they stem from the innermost Western-European course of history, that is, the philosophical. Consequently they are able, today, to put a specific imprint of the history of mankind upon the whole earth. (WP, pp. 31–2)

It is not that, with the appropriation of Greek conceptual resources into a distinctively Christian understanding of the world (and within an increasingly wide-spreading Christian ecclesiastical power domain) philosophy is no longer "Greek" in its "nature". It is not that Christianity made philosophy religious or confessional. On the contrary, Heidegger's claim is that it meant that the Christian world *remained* within the sway of the Greek opening, the Greek *archē* of Europe. In other words, the major scansions of the history of Europe itself – Greek, Roman, Christian, Modern – all take place within a space opened up, first of all, by Greek philosophy as that moved into a world that was becoming Christian. "Europe", as Emmanuel Levinas said, "is the Bible and the Greeks" (RB, p. 182). The becoming-European of a world and its world-wide-isation – Europe's *geopolitics* – belongs to what one might call this Greco-Biblical *geophilosophical* history; a history which, as Heidegger says, has come to "put a specific imprint of the history of mankind upon the whole earth". And yet, today, even as it becomes world-wide that world is in a condition of exhaustion. We'll come back to that.

When the ontology of Greek philosophy was drawn into the theology of Christian creationism, when the "great epoch covered by the history of metaphysics" that began in Greek antiquity makes its way into "the narrower epoch of Christian creationism" (OG, p. 13), when, that is to say, (following Levinas's formula) a distinctively *European* world began to emerge as the place of a Greco-Biblical tradition of more than one tradition, when the passage of history of what the Greeks called the *zōon logon echon* becomes inseparable from a history of the *ens creatum* made in God's image, the elements were in place for a decisive interpretation of the history of this creature that the Europeans called "Man", a creature understood, via Roman Latinity, as the theomorphic rational animal: the created creature that is the rational animal. On that interpretation, human history is not without God. On the contrary, it is the time of the working out of God's plan for Man, a Divine Designer's "work" unfolding from an original departure from the state of nature to the attainment of Man's proper end as a rational-spiritual being. All human cultural (indeed, they would have said "spiritual") history, "the history of mankind", just as much as human organic physiology, belongs to God's plan. And for the animal that we, "we, the Europeans", believe ourselves to be, the end (*telos*) of Man is then grasped as the full actualisation or perfection of the reason in Man. History, the history of the world, is the emancipation and de-alienation of rational subjectivity in time. Marrying the "end" and "end time" conceptions of Greek teleology and Christian eschatology, human history is thus conceived in the self-understanding of an emerging European humanity as fundamentally providential; a divine providence controls it and guides it from its origin to its proper end, the proper end, that is, of theomorphic rational animality. The significance of the *a posteriori* conception of God belongs to an *a priori* anthropology and history, the *archeo-teleo-eschatological* "universal history" of Man.

One way of articulating the specificity and the focus of the old European understanding of life's meaning would be to say that they inhabited a world in which what Wiggins calls "submission to God's purpose" was at the centre of their lived-out-lives, central "to what it was like to be alive then" in a non-physiological sense (TIML, p. 90). Faith in God conceived *a posteriori*, having God and God's plan for Man at the centre of their lives, this, I would suggest, was the crux of "what it was like to be alive then". They inhabited a world, and its history was providential: it was a world made with Man in mind.

The invocation of an *a posteriori* conception of God thus belongs to an originally Greek conception of Man, as that conception makes its way into a world that is increasingly Christian. That world is the world that calls itself (to be) European.

II

The idea of divine providence that was so alive for European humanity not so long ago can be introduced with reference to one of its earliest known written occurrences in English during the Middle Ages. The OED cites its appearance in two texts from around the 1380s:

> "Þou…fader, gouernyst bi prouydence" [L. *providentia*, Gk. *πρόνοια*; *L.V.* puruyaunce]
> "Þe prouidens of þe prince þat paradis weldes"

The first quotation is from Wycliffe's Bible: "Thou…father, governest by providence". The line is from the Old Testament book of Wisdom and is a (Middle English) translation of the (Latin) Vulgate translation of the pre-Christian (Greek) Septuagint translation of the original Hebrew. Providence is (visibly in Middle English) connected with, prudence, meaning care, but it is sometimes translated as prescience, meaning foresight. Fundamentally, it is the protective and foreknowing care of God, which gives Divine direction, control, and guidance to His creation. It is worth noting that the Greek of the Septuagint, *πρόνοια* (*pronoia*), is thought on the basis of an original imminence of *reason* (Greek *νοῦς* (*nous*)) in "*everything that is*" or "*being*" (Greek *ὤν* (on) or *οὐσία* (ousia)) – a conception of the rational ordering of the universe that Hegel will later emphasise as the first of "two phases" which come together in his own thought that "Reason has ruled, and is still ruling in the world, and consequently in the world's history" (PH, p. 12); the second phase of which is "the *religious truth*, that the world is not abandoned to chance and external contingent causes, but that a *Providence* controls it" (PH, p. 13). So tightly are these two phases tied together in European history that classical scholars will affirm that the notion of providence "was upheld by more or less all Stoics" (SA, p. 131), and that even if it was a providence "of the gods" and not of the monotheistic framework of the Biblical God "absolute confidence in divine providence was one of the basic tents of Stoicism" (DP, p. 6).

The second quotation is from the Middle English alliterative poem "St Erkenwald" (author unknown, but believed to be the same as the author of "Sir Gawain and the Green Knight"): "the providence of the prince that rules paradise". I will leave buried for the reader to uncover for themselves the sublime substance of this astonishing poem and want to recall from it only Erkenwald's reference to the finger of God (p. 35), and to what Robert Blanch and Julian Wasserman call the "contrast between the finger of God" and the "all-but-useless" hand of humanity (PG, p. 67):

> But what is miracle to man amounts to little
> If put by the providence [*prouidens*] of the prince that rules paradise
> When it delights him to unloose the least of his powers.
> When man's might is mastered, his mind overcome,
> His senses destroyed, and he stands confounded,
> God lightly lets loose with his littlest finger
> What all the hands under heaven could never hold.
> When mankind with his craft and counsel goes astray,
> The creature must recover in the Creator's strength.

As Kant will put it, where Man is "powerless to fulfil [his hopes] himself" he "looks to providence" to "create the circumstances" in which they can be fulfilled (Kant, p. 91). God rules in paradise but can, with just a movement of even his littlest finger, move the world as a whole, and hence in a sense from outside it, at least outside the conditions and powers that belong to the "hands under heaven" that it will transform. And once you look at human history as the history of Man, as the history, that is, of theomorphic rational animality, the animal that has broken from a merely natural condition, *that* history seems of necessity to begin with a step both in nature (in the world) and yet fundamentally beyond it. What force could possibly interrupt the instinctual life of animal-Man in the state of nature? Doesn't there have to be something of the hand or finger of God…even in the Fall?

Before Kant, Rousseau had already attempted to provide a universal historical genealogy of human development. Rousseau advanced an anthropology of pre-historic humanity passing naturally through two stages: from an originally "savage condition", thence into a "barbarian" stage of "natural indolence" where humanity will have lived in "golden centuries", centuries in which Man simply lived according to his nature. But what, in such a fully natural golden life, could lead it out of itself? Rousseau refers then to "the touch of a finger", "such a slight movement" which would nevertheless set off a world-changing teleological development "deciding the vocation of mankind" (cited OG, p. 256). As Derrida comments on this "slight movement", it seems to produce "a revolution out of nothing": it is essentially "exterior" to the world whose axis it shifts (OG, p. 257). Although Rousseau does not name the one "who willed man to be social", Derrida concludes that while "it is *perhaps not God*", since it is an originary evil and opening onto alienation, nevertheless, "*it is probably God*", since "a movement of the finger is enough for God to move the world" (OG, p. 257, emphasis in original); a conclusion more emphatically affirmed in another text by Rousseau where it is explicitly affirmed that God could "tip the axis of the world with a finger" – which would be the same thing as for God to say to Man "cover the world and be sociable" (cited, OG, p. 257).

> It *certainly concerns God,* for the genealogy of evil is also a theodicy. The catastrophic origin of societies and languages at the same time permitted the actualization of the potential faculties that slept inside man. Only a [chance] cause could actualize natural powers which did not carry within themselves a sufficient motivation for awakening to their own end. (OG, p. 257, emphasis in original)

Rousseau's story of the development of humanity from prehistory, thus, "naturalizes the Biblical incident: he makes a natural accident of the Fall" (OG, p. 260). And while Rousseau sees society as it develops in the history of Europe, with its attendant ethnocentrism, as a sort of sickness and alienation of primitive Man, he also presents "the history and progress of tongues" as a natural progress of "*reason*" (OG, p. 271); a history of increasing alienation from golden harmony which is thus at once a progressive de-alienation of rational Man, so that the finger of God that "interrupted the state of nature" opens a movement of a return of Man to himself, a return to original harmony but in a higher form. This very classical European self-understanding of the history of Man as a passage from a primitive origin towards the final emancipation of reason is set into a real history, and yet, as Derrida notes, "a teleological and eschatological anticipation superintends Rousseau's entire discourse" (OG, p. 295).

Kant too in his "Conjectures on the Beginning of Human History" relates the Genesis narrative of the Fall in naturalistic terms – admitting all the while that it is a story "which human reason cannot deduce from prior natural causes". Like Rousseau, Kant does not start with people "in their wholly primitive natural state" (Kant, p. 222), but in a second stage of development in which they have attained a condition of radical harmony with instinctual life, a life that was "happy" (Kant, p. 233). The incentive to abandon this happy condition could not belong to this condition; there is no incentive to follow a desire where there was no natural impulse to do so, and so no incentive not to be "guided by instinct, that *voice of God* that all animals obey" (Kant, p. 223). And yet, some chance event, some event which in itself "may have been" Kant supposes "quite trivial" has the most world-transforming consequences: "it may have been only a fruit" that tempts "reason" to "quibble with the voice of nature" (Kant, p. 224).

Once again the fateful event was *probably not God*, for in this "quibble" Man takes the first steps away from nature, away that is to say from natural obedience to God, along a path that concludes with "man's release from the womb of nature" (Kant, p. 226): an expulsion from the "harmless and secure condition" of innocent obedience to God, in a movement that nevertheless takes Man on his first steps in a history of the development of his rational capacities. This is a development from a condition in which rational capacities are merely inherent potentials towards a condition of their actualisation in a form of sociality "within which all the original capacities of the human race may develop" (Kant, p. 51).

This is, Kant says, a development which is nevertheless also "intended by nature" (Kant, p. 41), and hence the agent of its inaugural event *probably is God*. Indeed, without this (in worldly terms "quite trivial") event "man would live an Arcadian, pastoral existence of perfect concord, self-sufficiency and mutual love", and "all human talents would remain hidden forever in a dormant state" (Kant, 45). Hence it *certainly concerns* God and "nature should thus be thanked": the step out of "perfect concord" into a life that "causes so many evils" is not "the hand of a malicious spirit" but "the design of a wise creator"; encouraging Man "towards new exertions" that develop his rational powers (Kant, p.45). Once again, therefore, philosophy has "its *chiliastic* expectations" (Kant, p. 50), a horizon of "teleological and eschatological anticipation" of a second Golden Age in which the alienation of Man in the Fall is overcome in a movement of the progress of reason – a movement that is unfolding in its most advanced condition, Kant insists, in the history "of our continent" (Kant, p. 52).

Hegel too, in section §24 of *The Encyclopaedia Logic*, interprets "the Mosaic myth of the Fall of Man" as the beginning of world history (EL, p. 61). Starting with human life "in its instinctive and natural stage" (which may or may not be the first stage, properly speaking), Hegel insists that the movement into a "spiritual life" – a life, that is to say, which "essentially involves the tendency to reasoning and meditation" – does not "continue a mere stream of tendency" in human-animal life but "sunders itself to self-realisation" (El, p. 62). This "severed life" is a condition in which Man falls away from "concord", but does so in order to "win its way to concord again", a "final concord" that it attains "in something higher" (EL, p. 62). The "occasion which led man to leave his natural unity" is once again represented as a "solicitation from without", although Hegel will insist that this exteriority also belongs internally to "the nature of man"; namely, in his "likeness to God" (EL, p. 62). Man then "participates" in his "original vocation"; namely, "to be the image of God" (EL, p. 63). Nevertheless, the "hand" that Saves "Man" is the same as the one that initiates his Fall: "the hand that inflicts the wound is also the hand which heals it" (EL, p. 61). In his interpretation Hegel takes a swipe, as he always does, at Kant's attempt to set limits to knowledge "to make room for *faith*" (CPR, Bxxx), insisting that the Mosaic myth does not end with the expulsion, but with God saying that "Adam is become one of us" (EL, p. 62), opening a reading of the history of the world that is essentially the self-realisation and passage to self-consciousness of "the Divine that is in him, which we designate as Reason" (PH, p. 36). The movement of this history is one which, for Hegel, "travels", like the Sun, "from East to West"; "for Europe is absolutely the end of History, Asia the beginning" (PH, p. 109). As a movement in society it is, Hegel stresses, "still incomplete" (PH, p. 27), but it would result in a form of self-knowledge that is inseparably a reunion with and knowledge of God. Hegel's philosophical history of the world thus wants to leave no room for conjecture; it does not "make a demand on your faith" regarding "the guiding hand of God" (PH, p. 13–14) but aims "to furnish the proof...that a Providence (that of God) presides over the events of the world" (PH, p. 13); Man finally attaining not just faith but "knowledge of God" (PH, p. 15). The agent of the inaugural event is *beyond question God*.

The history of Man is thus understood as *archeo-teleo-eschatological*: the meaning of "Man" understood as theomorphic rational animality implies an historical horizon of an *origin* and *end* of Man. This is invariably conceived as a movement from the Fall from natural innocence to redemption in self-conscious self-realisation. The history of the world thus conforms to a covenant theology – the theology of God's promise – that the history after the Fall will finally be drawn together for all humanity under the provisions of the covenant of redemption.

For all humanity – and yet as Derrida noted in a public lecture he gave at UNESCO in Paris in 1997, these philosophical histories of Man are configured quite as if God "had assigned Europe" a special place in this history, with a "special mission" (UNESCO, p. 6). What would call itself (to be) European humanity belongs to a culture with this special mission of being the advance guard of humanity on the way to its proper end. Europe assigned the task of putting "a specific imprint of the history of mankind upon the whole earth" (WP, p. 33). And hence, Derrida concluded, this discourse of world history "has become the tradition of European modernity" (UNESCO, p. 7), God's promise to Man inseparable from the promise of Europe. And here we reach a first conclusion for this history of philosophical history: the classic philosophical discourse of world history is a discourse of Europe's exemplary modernity. It is a Eurocentric history of Man.

A first thought dawns for the one who calls himself (to be) European. Paul Valéry expresses this dawning modern Eurocentrism as classically and as problematically as anyone has:

> A first thought dawns. The idea of culture, of intelligence, of great works, has for us a very ancient connection with the idea of Europe – so ancient that we rarely go back so far.

> Other parts of the world have had admirable civilizations, poets of the first order, builders and even scientists. But no part of the world has possessed this singular...property: the most intense power of radiation combined with an equally intense power of assimilation.
>
> Everything came to Europe, and everything came from it. Or almost everything. (HP, p. 31)

This history of the history of the world: it nearly all happened, says the European, first in Europe. The discourse of world history is a discourse of the history of Man "exiting" a merely natural life, and it is a history which, so it seems to the European, has gone furthest on the way to the end in and from Europe. In the first volume of this study, we saw how this understanding entered a crisis condition in the twentieth century. Today, I will suggest in this volume, it is worn-out and exhausted.

III

The history of Europe's self-understanding will always have been connected to the fate of this classic philosophical discourse of world history as a history of Man. The first thing that we find, however, is that this classic discourse was originally also religious.

And then there was Marx. For the first time in the history of the world (if there is such a history) philosophical history was elaborated and projected "scientifically", without recourse to religion, indeed against religion ("the criticism of religion is the prerequisite of all criticism" (CHPR, p. 3)). It was told against the mystical and metaphysical conceptions of all previous histories of the world, and in fact against the "national" character of the cosmopolitanism and universalism that such histories always retained. Geophilosophical cosmo-nationalism becomes, for the first time, geopolitical and international – a stamp on world history that, as we shall later in this book, survives still today – even if we are not Marxists.

And yet, despite the turn from religion to science, the *archeo-teleo-eschatological* horizon remained fundamentally intact in Marx's text, still under its shadow. On the other hand, a completely new guiding hand begins to show itself as central to this historical story: it becomes a story of democracy.

All State forms of politics are, Marx argued, forms of democracy: they are all the creation of the people, the *demos*. Democracy thus appears as "the essence of every political constitution" of "socialised man" (CHPR, p. 31). The history of the world becomes the history of a movement away from "primitive communism" or "primitive democracy" into a class-conflict ridden history of "man in society" towards the end of democracy, its proper end. As Engels put it in his Preface to the 1888 edition of the *Communist Manifesto*, insisting that it was an idea "that belongs to Marx", history begins with "the dissolution of primitive tribal society, holding land in common ownership", and the subsequent history of man in society has been "a history of class struggles" (CM, p. 48). But this is also a history of the State becoming increasingly not merely formally but actually democratic, and hence, as Marx puts it, "according to existence and actuality is *returned* to its real ground" (CHPR, p. 31), thus producing "a really *rational* state" (CHPR, p. 96), a movement which ultimately culminates in the dissolution of the democratic State form altogether and the realisation of a communist society in which there is no institution or apparatus of the State in society at all. As Lenin puts it "under Socialism much of 'primitive' democracy will inevitably be revived, since, for the first time in the history of civilized society the *mass* of population will rise to taking an independent part, not only in voting and elections, but also in the everyday administration of the State. Under Socialism *all* will govern in turn and will soon become accustomed to no one governing" (SR, p. 124). The departure and return to the origin in a higher form is the end, the "rational result" (CHPR, p. 39), of democracy as the form of self-organised humanity coming (back) to itself.

Without doubt, this history is *without God*. Heidegger suggests it remains a faith, a religious faith in the sense of a bond of profound trust, but I think Wittgenstein was right to stress (as Heidegger in fact did too) the central place of science to this faith, making of it a faith without faith, without a trace of a religious sensibility. Rush Rhees, one of Wittgenstein's students and friend, recalls a conversation on this point:

> Wittgenstein said that Marx's attitude towards economic developments and towards changes in culture or in way of living was always that of a 19th century scientist. He said this partly in comment on the view we often heard, that Marx's work put forward something like a religion. "There is nothing religious in Marx's writing; not a trace. He thinks of the world as one great system, in which everything – past, present and future – can be known. Something we don't know is something still to be known, or still to be discovered. It is all determined by laws of the system; and whatever unanswered question we take, it is only a matter of time before the scientific answer is given and demonstrated. So Marx sees it. – I (Wittgenstein) keep wanting to ask, "Aren't you ever in a position in which [you feel] you must say, 'We just don't know what will happen.'?" The most primitive level of religious belief could be expressed in something like Job's "The Lord gave, and the Lord hath taken away; blessed be the name of the Lord". But Marx saw in the 19th century progress of production the permanent law of human history. (WPC, p. 60)

Not a trace of a religious sensibility for sure; but more than just a trace of the mystical and metaphysical conception of human history that had guided earlier writings on universal history, writings that were both philosophical (Greek) and religious (Christian). As Rhees notes, Wittgenstein "would not have said Marx was a scientist" (WPC, p. 60), even if his universal history was supposed to be philosophical and scientific. No less than in Rousseau, Kant or Hegel, human history is, for Marx, the progress of reason, the movement towards an ideally rational result. And for Marx, just as much as for Kant or Hegel, this history goes on (for the most part) behind the backs of its human actors. One cannot say that "God's plan for Man" is replaced everywhere by "Man's plan for Man". Indeed, the rupture in the history of the history of the world that Marx's text inaugurates (from a discourse that is philosophical and religious to one that is philosophical and scientific) would belong to an event that should (in Marx's view) bring to explicit consciousness and knowledge a truth about the movement of world history as a process of democratisation, which had hitherto been merely implicit. And where previously, when human powers alone proved "powerless to fulfil [his hopes] himself" he "looks to providence", so now, now when "the abolition of religion as the illusory happiness of the people is the demand for their real happiness" (CHPR, p. 3), the nudging finger that can assist in the creation of the circumstances in which that can be fulfilled lies with Marx's own "scientific" philosophy itself. The "secret" of the existence of the proletariat, that it "cannot emancipate itself without…thereby emancipating all other spheres of society" (CHPR, p. 10), is revealed to thought in the radical and anti-religious critique "of philosophy up to the present" (CHPR, p. 6). Speaking, as he typically did, of a coming revolution in Germany which would be a prelude to ("the near future" (CHPR, p. 7)) revolutions everywhere in Europe, Marx affirmed that "theory is capable of gripping the masses as soon as…it becomes radical" (CHPR, p. 7), and "as philosophy finds its material weapon in the proletariat, so the proletariat finds its spiritual weapon in philosophy. And once the lightning of thought has squarely struck this ingenuous soil of the people, the emancipation of the Germans into men will be accomplished" (CHPR, p. 11).

"Once" *the thought* and *the people* are together. It is a profoundly messianic moment in Marx's text, announcing the coming of a new "covenant of redemption", where God's promise becomes the Communist promise. In and through this event, "Germany [can] attain…a revolution which will raise it not only to the *official level* of modern nations, but to the *height of humanity* which will be the near future of those [other European] nations" (CHPR, p. 7). Marx too has his chiliastic expectations.

IV

And what actually took place, in the actual history of the world, when this projected unity became the project of actual politics, in Russia and not Germany, when the attempt to attain it became the cause of State politics in 1917? Totalitarian terror – and not only in Russia.

At the other end of the century, and shortly after the collapse of the Soviet Union, Derrida looked back at what he was tempted to call "the Marxist blow" [*le coup Marxiste*], an event defining the whole course of European politics and beyond in the twentieth century. It is a complex event:

> The Marxist blow is as much the projected unity of a thought and of a labour movement, sometimes in a messianic or eschatological form, as it is the history of the totalitarian world (including Nazism and fascism, which are the inseparable adversaries of Stalinism). (SM, p. 98)

Derrida's idea can be put like this. The Marxist blow is essentially two things at once: it is, *on the one hand*, the projected unity of systematic thought (Marxist "scientific" philosophy) and the spontaneous activity of industrial labour in struggle ("labour movement" translates "*movement ouvrier*" which is a less organised sense of workers' resistance to exploitation), a unity-to-come sometimes expressed in a messianic form, and sometimes in an eschatological form; and, *on the other hand*, it is the history of the becoming-totalitarian of a number of States, including in this Nazi and fascist totalitarianisms understood as the inseparable adversaries of Stalinism. The "Marxist blow" has to be understood with the first hand in view, and not just the second. Indeed, the two hands identified are being proposed as aspects of the same tragic event.

Derrida had an original and thought-provoking hypothesis on the two hands of this unfolding tragedy: the genesis of totalitarianisms of both left and right belongs to the effort finally to be rid of the spectre of communism. This effort is more or less obviously the cause of the anti-Marxist right. However, at issue, Derrida suggests, is an aversive fear of the ghostly apparition in both anti-Marxists and Marxists alike, again in two hands: on the one hand, the anti-Marxists ("all the old powers of Europe"), who see the spectre of communism as a demonic threat, and so want to do everything they can to *make it gone;* and, on the other hand, the Marxists themselves (including Marx), who also want, above all, to get rid of the spectre in the sense that they want to do everything they can to *make it real*, to bring about the projected unity that would "objectively" manifest the messianic or eschatological promise of communism that its mere spectre heralds. In other words, anti-Marxist and Marxist totalitarianisms are "reciprocal reactions to the fear of the ghost that communism inspired" – a fear that drove both into a "ruthless war" in which each sought the final elimination of the communist spectre (SM, p. 105). Each did so by ceaselessly seeking out whatever or whoever seemed to deviate from that effort, and, where either side attained political power, bringing about the unlimited extension of the political to the whole of social life as a result. The whole history of European politics, and not just European politics, since Marx and Marxists began to pursue a first-time-in-the-history-of-the-world geopolitical and international mission of the universal emancipation of Man has been shaped and misshaped by the horrors, disasters, crimes and wars that unfolded in that event, including the history of countries which strived to resist both communist and fascist rule in the name of representative and electoral democracy. No one escaped its force-field.

In the next part of this book, we will begin to explore Derrida's effort radically, to rethink the interest in emancipation or progress that universal history had framed hitherto. His focus in this regard is, in fact, on the inheritance of the promise of democracy, not the communist hope of the end of democracy. Moreover, his analysis bears on the quite general "modern" hope of realizing or attaining a final "end of history" or "end of politics", not just the communist variation. As we shall see, Derrida urges us to keep in touch with the promise of democracy by doing everything we can, not finally to *realise* (or approach) a conception of its ideal form but to respect "the being-promise of a promise": to *keep* the promise *as* promise, and not to conceive "complete" democracy in terms of a yet-to-be-attained final form or even a regulative ideal, whether of the State or *demos* or anything else. Indeed, the very idea of an ideal end in this case ruins the "complete" concept it wants to respect. Complete democracy, for Derrida, will not be an attained condition that will have finally rid itself of its messianic promise, finally exorcising the spectre of its "to come", but one which embraces that spectre as an ongoing, internal, and necessary haunting of democratic political life itself. To *be* complete it must be freed of all onto-theology, freed of all teleo-eschatology: it must *remain* incomplete, spectral, "to come".

In the final chapter of this book, we will also come back to Derrida's reading of the Marxist blow, where we will see it situated as drawing together three other blows to the Greco-Biblical or onto-theological understanding of "Man", blows identified by Freud as the upheavals wrought by the work of Copernicus, Darwin, and Freud himself. It is interesting to see that all three of these blows are in view in Wiggins's text on our contemporary "perplexity" (TIML, p. 91, p. 89, p. 124). Wiggins speaks from, as well as, to the trauma of those blows. He was writing in 1976, in the middle of the Cold War, and the ongoing Marxist blow leaves its mark on his text too. Continuing the analysis of "this difference between them and us" cited earlier, he turns from considering "what it was like to be alive then", to attempting to speak for and from our time and to say something about "what it is like to be alive" today. In a time after Darwin, it is a world that is also becoming increasingly Copernican:

> Unless we are Marxists, we are more resistant in the second half of the twentieth century than the eighteenth- or nineteenth-centuries knew how to be against attempts to locate the meaning of human life or human history in mystical or metaphysical conceptions – in the emancipation of mankind or progress, or the onward advance of Absolute Spirit. It is not that we have lost interest in emancipation or progress themselves. But, whether temporarily or permanently, we have more or less abandoned the idea that the importance of emancipation or progress (or a correct conception of spiritual advance) is that these are marks by which our minute speck in the universe can distinguish itself as the spiritual focus of the cosmos. Perhaps [save the word, it may be all we have left. SG] that is what makes the question of the meaning we can find in life so difficult and so desolate for us. (TIML, p. 91)

We might "envy" the certainty of their conviction, but Wiggins sees no possibility whatsoever for us going back, having now freed ourselves from that condition – not least since Marx we might add, and I will come back to that too. We cannot, he suggests, "unless we are Marxists", "hope [for] some relatively painless accommodation...between the freedom and the certainty" (TIML, p. 89).

Where does this lead or leave us? Writing in the late 1930s, and on the eve of the second terrible world war of European origin, the German philosopher Edmund Husserl wrote of "the radical life-crisis of European humanity" (CES, p. 2) and the "distress" caused above all by our "now unbearable lack of clarity" about "our own existence" (CES, p. 297). Husserl was clear that this situation was due in main part to what he calls the loss of "faith in the meaning of history" (CES, p. 13); a collapse of the sense that the facts of the world, and especially the facts of history, have a "teleological sense" and hence "have [something] more to teach us than that all the shapes of the...world...form and dissolve themselves like fleeting waves, that it always was and ever will be so" (CES, p. 7). He wanted to make one last try to save the old discourse of a historical "world" we no longer quite inhabit, or inhabit without quite inhabiting, to find a new way to articulate an epic discourse of "reason" "coming to terms with itself" (CES, p. 298), a new path towards a self-responsible rational humanity. But Husserl never finished his European-life-crisis book. It was not that the War intervened. Wanting to speak according to his "best lights" (CES, p. 18), the lights gave out. He simply never finished it.

And then came the War and the Shoah, and the lights went out across all Europe once again. For some time after that, and as the Cold War chilled world politics, any conviction that the facts of the world made teleological sense, a sense which was, as we have seen, founded first on an *a posteriori* conception of God, seemed ("unless we are Marxists") beyond revival. At around the same time as Husserl was writing about the Europe-crisis, Paul Valéry was doing the same, and affirming too that we no longer know where we are going. *The discourse of Europe's modernity* had become *a discourse of modern Europe's crisis*:

> Will Europe become *what it is in reality* – that is, a little promontory on the continent of Asia?
>
> Or will it remain *what it seems* – that is, the elect portion of the terrestrial globe, the pearl of the sphere, the brain of a vast body? (HP, p. 31)

Europe's assumption of its centrality to world history, Europe's promise, had always been a kind of pearly appearance. But Europe had *made itself* by *calling itself to appear* as just such an "advanced point of exemplarity" for global humanity (OH, p. 24), a missionary culture, justifiably imperial and colonial. This appearance was dissolving, and in the wake of the Second World War, it looked more than ever like a novel-like philosophical story rather than a rigorous philosophical history – religious or scientific. More and more, Europe's old modern spirit lay in ruins – dispirited, shattered, and exhausted. The classic discourse of philosophical history was a discourse of Europe's exemplary modernity. And here we reach a second summary point: in our time, that old modern discourse is falling apart.

V

How should this conclusion be understood? As I have suggested, there have been two main currents in the interpretation of the contemporary condition of Europe's old modern self-understanding. The first sees a Europe-crisis problem: a condition arising in the midst of the history of human self-realisation – the emancipation or progress of rational subjectivity – described by the *archeo-teleo-eschatological* default. The second sees an exhausted-Europe problem: a condition arising when the very idea of such a history of the human world – including the idea of a "world-crisis" as a recurrent feature of it – is losing its grip on our thinking and believing. Both currents accept that what is taking place is something like the "inner dissolution" of the old modern European default. However, while the Europe-crisis strand regards this as taking place within an ongoing movement of world history as the unfolding of the reason in Man in time, the exhausted-Europe strand sees it as taking place in a movement of increasing resistance to the very idea of such a history from within the world shaped by that idea. It is the latter that Wiggins's expresses in terms of what he calls our freedom to disbelieve in mystical or metaphysical conceptions of human nature and history – a freedom matched by a much-reduced clarity and considerably increased perplexity concerning the meaning of our existence.

The clarity and specificity that was had by people living in European societies in the time before our time belonged to the holding sway of (submission to) a "world". Today this is a world in accelerating dissolution or deconstruction – even as it becomes increasingly global and planetary. In this book, I will want to link this to what seems to me to be an unavoidable fact about the history of this wearing and growing world: namely, that it has been, inseparably, a movement of the effective democratisation (in the wide cultural sense that includes the prestige and progress of "scientific" ideas) of European societies, a movement freed up within the old modern world now falling apart. The idea of liberty or freedom was central to the discourse of the history of the world in the modern default: the history of the world simply is the movement of Man becoming rational and hence free, and Europe's modernity has, as Hegel stressed, been everywhere informed by the rising consciousness – call it confidence – that "*all* are free". That confidence, I want to suggest, does not just survive the problematic condition of the modern default. On the contrary, as folded into the idea that this calls for a set-up in society that properly recognises, as Kant put it (Kant, p. 99), both "the principle of *freedom* for *all* members of society" (simply in virtue of their being human) and "the principle of legal *equality* for *everyone*" (simply in virtue of their being citizens), it fundamentally drives it.

As Wiggins notes when he addresses the envy we might feel at the sense of specificity and certainty regarding the question of life's meaning for those at home in the modern default, our condition today is one in which that envy is easily outweighed by our wanting to "rejoice in our freedom to disbelieve in that which provided the contingent foundation of the specificity and certainty" (TIML, p. 89). Freedom is the watchword for all modern political thought, but Wiggins is in fact taking sides on a crucial question of just how "our freedom" should be conceived when he affirms that his view of this is "in outright opposition" to what John Gray has called a "paternalist" conception of freedom: one which claims to know how human lives should be lived if we are really to attain "true" freedom (IB, p. 9), and hence in outright opposition to a conception of freedom in terms of which one can hope for "some relatively painless accommodation...between the freedom and the certainty" (TIML, p. 89). It is our (still rather religious-sounding) "rejoicing in our freedom" as a freedom to disbelieve time-honoured authority that is the end of God's finger as the origin and principle – the *archē* – of world history, increasingly the end of the idea of Man and his teleology.

Our time – the time of the death of God – is, above all, as Samuel Beckett puts it, the time of "a time-honoured conception of humanity in ruins" (CR, p. 278).

Our new condition is thus one in which we have freed ourselves from, and resist "submission" to the old world of Europe's modernity, and the conception of Man and his history that belonged to it. A certain promise inseparable from the idea of freedom, an idea which, in some form, was also absolutely central to the old worn-out philosophical history, seems therefore *unexhausted*.

Circling back now to the stage of the history of philosophical history that we had reached at the close of the first volume, and which we have caught up with again here – the onset of the Second World War – I will now pick up that history after the War, and the world-wide Cold War that marked it. My guide at this stage in our philosophical history of Europe will be a text by one of the great European thinkers of freedom as a political concept, Isaiah Berlin, a text in which a newly refreshed conception of philosophical history makes its way into our time, and perhaps a refreshed conception of democracy as well: "Two Concepts of Liberty".

PART II
The Cold War

3

LIBERTY AND DEMOCRACY

The ends of men are many

– Isaiah Berlin

I

In the 1930s, Martin Heidegger had already described Europe as "caught in the pincers" of the USA and USSR (IM, p. 35). The image of two great powers encroaching on Europe resonated only more strongly as the Cold War began to frame the geopolitics of the post-War European world. Indeed, we tend still today to think of the Cold War as, fundamentally, a "superpower" conflict. Looked at in this way the Cold War is something that befell Europe in the struggle for domination by two rivalrous camps. And not just Europe, of course. No doubt because it was both "cold" and "nuclear" it could become genuinely global. Literally every country on earth – every man and woman on the planet – was caught up in it. And it was as distinctive in its temporal phase as it was in its spatial reach. It lasted at least forty years, four times as long as the two World Wars put together. Indeed, it would be naïve to think that it is not lurking in the twenty-first century too. While there is some justification for saying that the Cold War came to an end in 1989, regarding a war that was in itself spectral, its historical ends are not like a wall going up when the Wall came down, marking a time before and time after. The phase of its conflict has other rhythms and survivals.

Yet despite its planetary reach, the Cold War was arguably more intense in Europe than anywhere else, being defined by the circumstances, events and especially ideas of European origin. Two geographically non-European superpowers fought it, but geographical Europe was in some way its centre. These two powers were drawn to Europe. Moreover, while the Cold War can look like a face-off between two independent hostile powers, from the point of view of Europe it was a profoundly internal division. We tend to forget it, but Winston Churchill's famous "iron curtain" speech in 1946 is not only about the "front" of two confronting powers but also, perhaps above all, a description of the division of old Europe:

> From Stettin in the Baltic to Trieste in the Adriatic an iron curtain has descended across the Continent. Behind that line lie all the capitals of the ancient states of Central and Eastern Europe. Warsaw, Berlin, Prague, Vienna, Budapest, Belgrade, Bucharest and Sofia, all these famous cities and the populations around them lie in what I must call the Soviet sphere, and all are subject in one form or another, not only to Soviet influence but to a very high and, in some cases, increasing measure of control from Moscow. Athens alone – Greece with its immortal glories – is free to decide its future at an election under British, American and French observation. The Russian-dominated Polish Government has been encouraged to make enormous and wrongful inroads upon Germany, and mass expulsions of millions of Germans on a scale grievous and undreamed-of are now taking place. The Communist parties, which were very small in all these Eastern States of Europe, have been raised to pre-eminence and power far beyond their numbers and are seeking everywhere to obtain totalitarian control. Police governments are prevailing in nearly every case, and so far, except in Czechoslovakia, there is no true democracy. (Churchill, from his speech "The Sinews of Peace" given at Westminster College in Fulton, Missouri, March 5, 1946)

"True democracy" – by which he simply meant a regime in which the government is selected by an open electoral contest ("democracy" was famously "the worst" form of government for Churchill, "except for all the others") – would not last long in Czechoslovakia either, and aspirations there to wrest independence from "control from Moscow" were altogether smashed in 1968. We will come to the lifting of the iron curtain and the fall-of-the-Berlin-Wall event in the next chapter, but as we make our way into Isaiah Berlin's contribution to this history as part of a philosophical history, it is worth emphasising that, in his writings, the Cold War becomes, in effect, a rivalrous conflict and division over the inheritance of the European understanding of freedom as a political concept – a dispute that divides Europe from the inside (geophilosophically) as well as from the outside (geopolitically).

II

In 1958 Isaiah Berlin delivered his inaugural lecture following his election to the Chichele Chair of Social and Political Theory at the University of Oxford. The extended (and rather charmingly baggy) text of that lecture was expanded and later published in the same year as "Two Concepts of Liberty". That text famously examines two senses of the "protean word" liberty or freedom (he uses these interchangeably), two of the "more than two hundred" senses of liberty. He does not take it to be anything like an exhaustive treatment, nor significantly a final one. Nevertheless, he takes them as "central" for the simple reason that they have "a great deal of history behind them, and, I dare say, still to come" (TC, p. 121). In other words, these concepts are the ones that already (if somewhat implicitly) belong centrally to the history of European thinking about freedom as a political concept. Indeed, they more or less appear by name in Hegel's *Philosophy of History*, marking a basic distinction between Kant's conception of (universal) individual freedom, and Hegel's own conception of (universal) rational self-realisation (IPH, p. 41; less clearly translated at PH, p. 40). The discussion of "negative" liberty and "positive" liberty that Berlin pursues thus aims at participating in and continuing a discussion or conversation already underway, and the terms themselves both track and attempt to give focus to that conversation: he uses them "following much precedent", and his conversation partners, all of whom he takes issue with ("This will not do"), include (in rough order of appearance): Saint-Simon, Heine, Kant, Rousseau, Fichte, Schelling, Hegel, Marx, Hobbes, Bentham, Mill, Constant, Tocqueville, Locke, Smith, Jefferson, Burke, Paine, Lassalle, Condorcet, T.H. Green, Bradley, Bosanquet, William James, Helvétius, Plato, Herder, Spinoza, Montesquieu, Comte. It was "Constant, Mill, Tocqueville, and the liberal tradition to which they belong" that Berlin felt closest to, though never uncritically (TC, p. 165). Liberalism is not a political theory without a history, and with Berlin, its centre of gravity begins to shift: from a vision of a society of isolated individual citizens claiming their natural rights, to historically situated persons and groups pursuing their own ends without fear of intimidation or violence, especially State intimidation and violence. Berlin will call this new liberal vision "pluralism", and thinking in governmental terms will tie this more or less closely to democracy. However, as I hope to show in this chapter, Berlin's affirmation of "pluralism as an ideal" justis the thought of a democracy to come in a more culturally pervasive sense, and I will want to inherit it myself in those terms.

The question of the inheritance of the European philosophical tradition of thinking freedom as a political concept is transparently central to Berlin's undertaking in "Two Concepts of Liberty". But it was a heritage of thinking that belonged to a land that time forgot in the Oxford he was addressing in 1958: that place seemed to him "undisturbed in the Garden of Eden" as far as political thinking was concerned (TC, p. 118). It was a time when British philosophy had all but given up on trying to make sense of our time, philosophically. It was, as Heidegger would have said, and not unfairly, historically history-lacking. In a world of unprecedented political tensions – with a threat and risk of nuclear war hanging over every man and woman on earth – they were not, as philosophers, saying anything about our time at all.

And so despite the long and rich philosophical heritage he was engaging with and contributing to, Berlin, in Oxford, was virtually alone with this conversation. And given the unprecedented political history that was being lived through right then – a history which Berlin's theme attempted to address and clarify – this was little short of a disgrace for philosophy.

Berlin's text begins where it will end, with the recognition that human beings, in the world as it is, do, in fact, disagree "about the ends of life", and this is why there is politics and thinking about politics in the first place (TC, p. 118). Now, if you believe that such conflicts can be eliminated from human life, if that is your "faith", then you also see the possibility of an end of politics as such: the possibility that all the outstanding or ongoing political problems we face will be overcome, and after some great transformation, will be replaced by problems that are of a "technical" nature (TC, p. 118). This would be the faith of "saintly anarchists" (TC, p. 118), among whom we should include Marxists and Leninists who assume that the end (*telos*) of democracy as a political regime (as a specific State form) is also the end (*terminus*) of democracy as such a form: the State "withers away" and we pass into a condition of pure self-administration without the apparatus of a State. (More orthodox saintly anarchists won't want to wait for withering, as Berlin notes.) Berlin cites Saint-Simon's phrase about "replacing the government of persons by the administration of things", and calls this apparently idyllic outlook "utopian" (TC, p. 118). Berlin is among "those for whom speculation about this condition of perfect social harmony is the play of idle fancy", and that the idea of an end of politics is equally fanciful. This fanciful utopian faith is not, however, juvenile or thoughtless. As we shall see shortly, it belongs to what Berlin will call "the metaphysical view of politics" (TC, p. 171), a view rooted in a teleological conception of Man and history. Berlin's tilting against Marxists and anarchists in his opening words thus draws on a quite general characteristic of his thinking about political thinking. To borrow Geoffrey Bennington's signature figure (as I will throughout this book), it is an approach that is everywhere "opposed to metaphysical thinking, for which the end of politics is the end of politics" (*Scatter 1*, p. 243). Against this metaphysical construal, Berlin will affirm that there is, in fact, no end to politics, and hence that there will always be a task – a task as urgent as politics itself – for thinking about politics too (TC, p. 118). And yet:

> Nevertheless, a visitor from Mars to any British – or American – university today might perhaps be forgiven if he sustained the impression that its members lived in something very like this innocent and idyllic state, for all the serious attention that is paid to fundamental problems of politics by professional philosophers. (TC, p. 118)

Berlin finds this both surprising and dangerous. Surprising because, right then, "fanatically held" political ideas and doctrines were so deeply affecting so many people all over the world, and indeed many were being murdered as a result.

Dangerous because the absence of a culture of "rational criticism" regarding such ideas simply leaves the field open to those ideas acquiring "an unchecked momentum"; those who have been "trained to think" simply leave the field open to fanatics (TC, p. 119). Not only that, but if those same people do not pay serious attention to ideas of this kind – to genuinely powerful ideas – they leave themselves "at the mercy of uncriticised political beliefs" too (TC, p. 119). It is not just a critique of political ideas that is lacking but a commitment to self-critique, of wanting oneself not to be subject to unexplored convictions and commitments which otherwise we both possess and yet which remain "obscure to us" (TC, p. 121). Philosophers should feel particularly uncomfortable with this condition – and yet these subjects "worthy of examination" were...unexamined.

An unexamined life in a time of unprecedented global political turmoil. Berlin does not think that political conflicts are reducible to conflicts of ideas. But he does believe that what I have been calling philosophical history is internal to our actual history, "involved" in its vicissitudes, and hence in some way has to be taken up, has to become a theme for thinking, if we are to understand the conditions of our time, the "dominant issues of our own world". And in 1958 that included, above all, "the open war that is being fought between two systems of ideas" concerning "the permissible limits of coercion" of individuals in the name of emancipation and progress (TC, p. 121). The (geopolitical) Cold War was, for Berlin, a (geophilosophical) Open War over the meaning of human freedom.

And so he speaks of freedom, of liberty, and two senses of liberty whose differences from each other, subtle as they are, "have led in the end to the great clash of ideologies that dominates our world" (TC, p. 131), and have come "into direct conflict with each other" (TC, p. 132). Berlin's work aimed to make the study of these ideas, and the fundamental "conceptions of man" (TC, p. 128; p. 169) from which "they directly derive" (TC, p. 134), and which frame our whole thinking about "the ends of life", anything but "merely academic" (TC, p. 134).

In 1958, Berlin felt it was not, in Oxford, even that. Twenty years later he was not so alone with his subjects. When David Wiggins writes that we in our time are resistant to the classic "mystical or metaphysical conceptions" of human life and history that dominated the lives of Europeans in the eighteenth and nineteenth centuries (TIML, p. 91), and sees it likely that even as we might envy the specificity and their certainty of purpose "we want to rejoice in our freedom to disbelieve in that which provided the contingent foundation of the specificity and certainty" (TIML, p. 89), what he is opposing are precisely those conceptions of Man and the end of Man that have so deeply informed a history-producing political history in Europe. Those conceptions elaborated a movement of the history of the world as the emancipation or progress of Man towards the proper end of Man with Europe at the head; an end of history in the self-realisation of a universally fitting human way to be; promising peace, freedom and well-being without political conflict. Marxism was its last survivor. Among those with whom Wiggins associated his own work in moral phenomenology, and the affirmation of "the plurality and mutual irreducibility of things good" that he takes to belong to the "broad stream of modern philosophy" that he then participated in, was Isaiah Berlin (TIML, p. 127). Berlin first among those.

III

Berlin's contribution to that European conversation has given rise to fairly endless academic discussion – fine-tuning, over-turning, under-mining, and so on – typical of university writing in our time. But Berlin was not simply engaging in a piece of concept analysis, nor was he backing just one of the senses as the proper or *bone fide* one. Berlin himself later regretted giving the impression that his modest affirmation of "negative" liberty – the freedom to pursue possibilities of being, of not being forced, not being interfered with by others in this regard – made it look like he saw nothing admirable in "positive" liberty – a "perfectionist" idea of self-mastery where the authority of a higher self (typically conceived as a fully rational self) makes its way against the naïve decisions and pleasures of a lower self. He regretted that his affirmation of a life marked by a "measure of 'negative' liberty" as belonging to a "more humane ideal" than the one that "positive" liberty promoted (TC, p. 171) suggested that he saw nothing of value in perfectionist ideas of freedom: he certainly did see value in them. Nevertheless, Judith Shklar, whose work I will want to reckon with as we go along in this book, and who explicitly identifies her own "liberalism of fear" as "inspired by Berlin's negative liberty", is right to insist that "it cannot be denied...that [Berlin's] very clear demarcation of negative liberty is the best means of avoiding the slippery slope that can lead us to its threatening opposite" (LF, p. 28). But the great threatening opposite is not perfectionism *per se* – the idea of an attainable and better but as yet unattained condition for me or for us – but a specifically paternalist and authoritarian claim by another or others that they possess the truth about me, that they understand better than I do what are or should be "my duties", "my real interests", "my goals", or who claim insight into the way for me to be that I too would choose if only I had overcome some disabling irrationality or some other impediment to judgement – which they have attained (and by implication my higher self could attain), and which for my own good, "in the name of some remote...ideal", I am forced to conform (TC, p. 171).

As we shall see, Berlin's point is not that there are no virtues to "positive" liberty but that a life without what he cautiously calls "a measure of 'negative' liberty" does not just deprive me of much that I have actually "found to be indispensable to it": it is a life that is not sufficiently mine to live. Indeed, and note the fresh, and in fact rather Nietzschean, conception of man that is making its way here, a life without this measure of "negative" liberty is not sufficiently mine to live as an "*unpredictably self-transforming* human being" (TC, p. 171, emphasis mine). The choices I make about my life, and "the fundamental moral categories and concepts" that have come down to me as the encumbered, historical, social self that I am, are a part of my being, part of my sense of who I am, and "part of what makes [me] human" (TC, pp. 171–2). Losing sight of the importance of the "negative" sense of liberty is to lose sight not simply of an idea that is important or historically significant but to part of what makes *this* human life – and the historical shape and shaping of its moral universe – mine, and mine as the unpredictably self-transforming human being that I am.

At the end of this book, I will look more closely at this new conception of Man as an unpredictably self-transforming being, and I will argue that Berlin does not construe it in the classically liberal terms of a self-legislating autonomous subject. Instead, Berlin conceives the self as fundamentally and from the start run through by a cultural and social inheritance – right down to its inherited resources for self-critique and self-transformation. Moreover, while I have individuated this description of our ordinary encumbered subjectivity to (each, any and every) me, avoiding the slippery slope that Shklar warns against is not about giving (each, any and every) me an unrestricted right to do as I please. On the contrary, political liberalism, in all of its major variations, has always understood that its principal political ambition, the optimisation of freedom for all, *equality in liberty*, is not its maximisation for (any) me. As Shklar puts it, "every adult should be able to make as many effective decisions without fear or favor about as many aspects of her or his life as is compatible with the like freedom of every other adult" (LF, p. 21). Again, the antipathy to paternalist government, what Kant calls "the greatest possible despotism" (Kant, p. 74), is not an individualist and libertarian demand that there be no "restriction of each individual's freedom" (Kant, p. 73). On the contrary, such restriction is *necessary* to the kind of social condition championed by political liberalism. As Kant puts it, "restriction of each individual's freedom so that it harmonises with the freedom of everyone else" just is "right" (Kant, p. 73). And for Kant, as we shall see in more detail later in this book, progressing ever closer to the optimal condition – where each, any and every human being has the greatest possible, and hence necessarily limited, freedom to make his or her own way in life ("*the ends of men* as individuals" (Kant, p 91)), just is progressing ever closer to the (in Kant's view, providential) *telos* of human history ("*the end of man* as an entire species" (Kant, p. 91)). No, the condition at the far end of the threatening slippery slope is about a form of restriction that is the demand for obedience from (each, any and every) me to *someone else's* conception of what a properly shaped life should look like, a form of individual and social life in which "*the ends of men* as individuals" are themselves prescribed. In the name of some supposedly fully rational or fully human way of being – an ideally rational or human configuration of the moral and political universe – "real" freedom (so the story goes) is fully realised only in that attained individual and social condition; that condition of self-realisation is the *telos* of human history as the realisation of "rational" freedom.

All politics, and every conception of political freedom, is, as Berlin puts it "bound up with our conception of man, and of the basic demands of his nature" (TC, p. 169). The classic modern European conception of political freedom is elaborated through the idea of the history of Man as rational theomorphic subjectivity: of the emancipation or progress of Man thus understood towards its proper end. This is what Berlin calls "the metaphysical view of politics" (TC, p. 171), and in the end, it encompasses Kant just as much as it (more obviously) does his successors, especially Hegel and Marx. For Berlin, however, and I am sure he is right about this, among these three only Kant's conception retains and preserves within it what Berlin calls "the empirical view of politics" (TC, p. 171): namely, the recognition that "the ends of men are many" (TC, p. 169). According to Berlin, Kant's successors transform his (Kant's) conception into "something close to a pure totalitarian doctrine" (TC, p. 152). However, for Berlin the seeds of this transformation also lie already in a certain "rationalism" in Kant's philosophy, making his account both the greatest historical expression of political liberalism, and also the troubling point of departure on the slippery slope:

> Kant came nearest to asserting the "negative" ideal of liberty when (in one of his political treatises) he declared that "the greatest problem of the human race, to the solution of which it is compelled by nature, is the establishment of a civil society universally administering right according to law. It is only a society which possesses the greatest liberty...with...the most exact determination and guarantee of the limits of the liberty [of each individual] in order that it may co-exist with the liberty of others – that the highest purpose of nature, which is the development of all her capacities, can be attained in the case of mankind". (TC, p. 153)

And yet despite the statement of "orthodox liberalism" that this contains, Berlin thinks Kant's own rationalism installs a reading of "the exact determination of the limits" of individual liberty that leaves "the door opened wide to the rule of experts" (TC, p. 152) such that "in the name of reason" very many "personal aims" may "at least in theory" be "ruthlessly suppressed to make way for the demands of reason...on the assumption that only rational ends can be the 'true' objects of a 'free' man's 'real' nature" (TC, pp. 153–4). The idea of "rational self-direction", rather than an historically and endlessly thought-provoking description of a flourishing human life becomes "the *a priori* assumption" for condemning "various personal aims" as "non-rational", and hence only a narrow sense of the many and (as Kant stressed) often conflicting and idiosyncratic "ends of men, as individuals" that "knowledge derived from experience of what men are and seek" shows up as actual will be "approved" as permissible by a zealous Kantian legislator of the "exact determination" of liberty in a national civil order based on "right" (TC, pp. 152–3).

We will come back to this fork in the road inside the skull of Kant when we look at the legacy of his thinking on the proper form of an international civil order based on "right", with reference to the form and formation of the European Union. However, the point, for now, is quite how difficult it is, as Shklar emphasised, to hold on to a "clear demarcation" of "negative" liberty that keeps the slippery slope at bay. As Berlin acknowledges "the freedom which consists in being one's own master" and "the freedom which consists in not being prevented from choosing as I do" seem to be "concepts at no great logical distance from each other" (TC, p. 131). The logical distance can seem great when one affirms Kant's revolt against paternalism: "no one can compel me to be happy in accordance with his conception of the welfare of others, for each may seek his happiness in whatever way he sees fit" (Kant, p. 74). But the gap starts to close once one stresses that the subject of happiness is a "rational" subject, and hence a subject that (it is supposed) cannot but resonate subjectively to an objectively or ideally rational form of individual and social life.

Nevertheless, even the conceptual difference is and remains significant for Berlin: without the "frontiers" of rules of protection "within which men should be inviolable" we are left in a condition where we are exposed to the limitless extension of the political that belongs to totalitarianisms of left and right: "when a man is declared guilty without trial, or punished under a retroactive law; when children are ordered to denounce their parents, friends to betray one another, soldiers to use methods of barbarism; when men are tortured or murdered, or minorities are massacred because they irritate a majority or tyrant" (TC, p. 166) – *this* is the threatening situation at the end of the slippery slope, "the opposite pole" of the one in force where those who believe in "negative" liberty enjoy political success: "the [latter] want to curb authority as such. The [former] want it placed in their hands. That is a cardinal issue. These are not two different interpretations of a single concept, but two profoundly divergent and irreconcilable attitudes to the ends of life" (TC, p. 166).

For Shklar this is all that is needed for the "very clear demarcation of negative liberty from…its threatening opposite" (LF, p. 28). However, she acknowledges too that Berlin wants to make one further step in defence of a politics that calls for some measure of "negative" liberty, a defence she thinks there is "no particular reason to accept" (LF, p. 28): namely, a view of and commitment to what Berlin calls "pluralism of values" (TC, p. 172). I think Shklar is wrong to think this step is superfluous, and in the next section, I will begin to explain why.

IV

For Berlin the two senses of liberty as a political concept are "on the face of it" not so very different from each other, "no more than negative and positive ways of saying the same thing" (TC, p. 132): both senses are about "holding off something or someone" from "trespassing on my field or asserting their authority over me" – holding off something or someone from interfering with or dominating me (TC, p. 158). (Interestingly, among the various things that Berlin conceives as something that I might be dominated by are "fears" (TC, p. 158). We will come back to this shortly with reference to Shklar's work.) What has really pulled the two liberty traditions apart, belongs more to history than to logic. Indeed, Berlin is clear that "negative" liberty defenders can, in certain circumstances, become just as dangerous as their "positive" liberty counterparts: the transformation or shift or "sleight of hand" from thinking that people sometimes need to be coerced for their own good, to thinking that since it is for their own good they are not really being coerced is something that "can no doubt be perpetrated *just as easily* with the 'negative' concept of freedom, where the self that should not be interfered with is no longer the individual with his actual wishes and needs as they are normally conceived, but the real man within, identified with the pursuit of some ideal purpose not dreamed of by his empirical self" (TC, p. 134, emphasis mine). Shklar supposes that "what Berlin calls 'positive liberty'...is the freedom of one's higher from one's lower self" (LF, p. 28). But that picture of the self can belong to *either* concept. "As a matter of history", the "positive" concept has "lent itself more easily to this splitting of personality into two"; but that splitting is, logically speaking, not its special preserve, and I think Berlin's fundamental insight is not about the distinction between "negative" and "positive" liberty, but something that will inform a quietly developing contrast between "monism" and "pluralism" as political ideals that emerges at the end of his text: namely, that the "road to one ideal" can *always* also "lead to its contrary" (TC, p. 162), to a nightmare.

"To preserve our absolute categories or ideals at the expense of human lives" (TC, p. 171) – and that ultimately means being willing to slaughter human beings on the "altars" of those ideals or in their name (TC, p. 167) – is, for Berlin, simply inhumane, and yet it is "an attitude found in equal measure on the right and left wings in our days" (TC, p. 171). Berlin's (as Shklar nicely puts it) "metapolitical" commitment to the pluralism of values is, I will suggest, his attempt to find a way to help reduce the likelihood of this unhappy outcome: to give societies ballast against the *always possible* tendency of political activists of all kinds to threaten, harass, bully, and ultimately torture or even murder human beings who they regard as standing in the way of the realisation of the ideals – of liberty or social justice or equality or fraternity or whatever – that they strive for, and whose realisation will, they believe, lead to a future in which political "conflict" can be brought to an end (TC, p. 168).

It is against any splitting of the self as a justification for coercion that Berlin resolutely cleaves to what he calls the "empirical" view of politics – which takes and accepts human beings and their idiosyncrasies as it finds them. He opposes this to what he calls "metaphysical" views which coax us towards some more ambitiously normative conception of what, to cite Jürgen Habermas, "it is reasonable to expect" is "*not* allowed" in a properly ordered political set-up. Conceptions such as this, as Bernard Williams puts it, bridling at Habermas's formulation, "situate [themselves] a great deal nearer – too near indeed – to the moral than the facts" (IBWD, p. 15). (Habermas's finding room in Kant for such "reasonable" expectations of the behaviour of *national* citizens – behaviour that they should come to see as the proper behaviour of their rational civil self – will be in view again when we look at his reading of Kant's conception of the proper form of an *international* civil order in the European Union.)

Berlin's ambition to avoid a conception of the many ends of men that winds up making a moralistic "assessment" of the value of these ends as such ("save in so far as they may frustrate the purposes of others" (TC, p. 153)), receives its primary argumentative support from a "metapolitical" assumption or belief: namely, as Shklar puts it, "the belief that there are several inherently incompatible moralities among which we must choose, but which cannot be reconciled by reference to a common criterion" (LF, p. 29). The thought here is that human moralities, while they all seem (empirically, anthropologically) to be informed by "moral categories and concepts" that are humanly familiar, do not all give the same weight of significance to any particular category or concept in their formation: we have tables of values. Berlin himself insists that "liberty is not the only goal of men" (TC, p. 125), not "a sacred, untouchable value" (TC, p. 126), and recognises that "the bulk of humanity has certainly at most times been prepared to sacrifice [liberty] to other goals: security, status, prosperity, power, virtue, rewards in the next world; or justice, equality, fraternity, and many other values which appear wholly, or in part incompatible with the attainment of the greatest degree of individual liberty" (TC, p. 161). The choices we make – how we weigh or differentially value familiar human values – might thus result in a "loss of liberty" but "a gain in justice or in happiness or in peace" (TC, p. 125). But Berlin's core claim against any and every political activist who supposes that their ideals would, if universally observed, lead to "some future perfection" (TC, p. 170) or "some perfect state" (TC, p. 168) in which no "empirical self" (at least no sane one) would actually will what was (by the activist's lights) "*not* allowed", a condition in which "the diverse ends of men would be harmoniously realized", and hence "the possibility of conflict" would be "eliminated from human life" (TC, p. 169), against all this Berlin's core claim is that this is not only a vision of "a wholly imaginary future" (TC, p. 171), but is "demonstrably false" (TC, p. 169).

There is and can be, he argues, no possible arrangement in which some ideal or final harmony of values is achieved: attaining one goal is strictly incompatible with other equally valid goals. Recognition of "the fact that human goals are many" thus also involves coming to terms with the plurality of humanly intelligible but mutually incompatible selections among values "not all of them commensurable" and which will remain "in *perpetual* rivalry with one another" (TC, p. 171):

> Neither political equality not efficient organization nor social justice is compatible with more than a modicum of individual liberty, and certainly not with unrestricted *laissez faire*; justice and generosity, public and private loyalties, the demands of genius and the claims of society, can conflict violently with each other. And it is no great way from that to the generalisation that not all good things are compatible, still less all the ideals of mankind...Conflicts of values may be an intrinsic, irremovable element in human life. To admit that the fulfilment of some of our ideals may in principle make the fulfilment of others impossible is to say that the notion of

> total human fulfilment is a formal contradiction, a metaphysical chimaera. (TC, pp. 167–8)

And again:

> If, as I believe, the ends of men are many, and not all of them are in principle compatible with each other, then the possibility of conflict – and of tragedy – can never wholly be eliminated from human life, either personal or social. The necessity of choosing between absolute claims is then an inescapable characteristic of the human condition... The extent of a man's, or a people's, liberty to choose to live as they desire must be weighed against the claims of many other values, of which equality, or justice, or happiness, or security, or public order are perhaps the most obvious examples. (TC, pp. 169–70)

Freedom itself is not, then, the only or even everywhere the "sole" or even "dominant" criterion for deciding between different actions (TC, p. 169). On the other hand, if (and here we can see Wiggins is spot on concerning what matters here) "the plurality and mutual irreducibility of things good" that Berlin identifies in his "metapolitical" point is to be recognised and respected then a "measure of 'negative' liberty" *must* be part of a humane political set-up as a precondition of lives led in pursuit of the good (TC, p. 171).

Shklar thinks liberalism can "do without" this "metapolitical" idea and claims that "the liberalism of fear" which she defends "in fact does not rest on a theory of moral pluralism" (LF, p. 29). That may be so, but she would be wrong to think that her own "conception of man" – the one that sees it as a near human universal to want to be rid of politically motivated "cruelty and the fear it inspires" (LF, p. 29) – altogether escapes "the possibility of conflict, and of tragedy" that Berlin supposes "can never wholly be eliminated from human life", never eliminated everywhere decisions between different actions have to be made, which is everywhere.

Shklar acknowledges that "a minimal level of fear is implied in any system of law, and the liberalism of fear does not dream of an end of public, coercive government" (LF, p. 29). What someone can fear from the operations of the State (or, indeed, any other very powerful agencies) that this liberalism wants to prevent are thus only fears that are "created by arbitrary, unexpected, unnecessary, and unlicensed acts of force and by habitual and pervasive acts of cruelty and torture performed by military, paramilitary, and police agents in any regime" (LF, p. 29). These unacceptable fears do not even begin to cover all fears, so Shklar's liberalism of fear would want to prevent or eliminate only a special subset:

> To be alive is to be afraid, and much to our advantage in many cases, since alarm often preserves us from danger. The fear we fear is of pain inflicted by others to kill and maim us, not the natural and healthy fear that merely

> warns us of avoidable pain. And, when we think politically, we are afraid not only for ourselves but for our fellow citizens as well. We fear a society of fearful people. (LF, p. 29)

But if fear is as pervasive as Shklar's anthropology suggests, and perhaps it is, then how and who is to decide or determine what the frontiers are between a fear of fear that is regarded as inappropriate for political prevention because it is "natural and healthy" or implied by "coercive government" and a fear of fear that is appropriate for political prevention because it is neither of these? I'm sure that no tribunal, no panel of experts – however transparent, pluralistic, representative and democratic it is – that is set up to judge whether someone's fears are "reasonable" fears would or could immunise us from the "*summum malum*" of the cruelty that someone can reasonably be afraid of from operations of the State and other powerful agencies. On the contrary – and this is what Shklar misses entirely in Berlin's "metapolitical" insight that the road to one ideal can always also lead to its contrary – such a tribunal or expert panel will also threaten to create them; will always also be open to abuses of power.

Shklar sees the "dispersion of power among a plurality of politically empowered groups, pluralism, in short, as well as the elimination of such forms and degrees of social inequality as expose people to oppressive practices" as the best way of limiting the damage that belongs to the possibility of abuses of power (LF, p. 28). No doubt she is right about that. But this institutional pluralism is not the metapolitical pluralism that Berlin wants us to acknowledge and which requires acquiescence to what he takes to be the (for some maddening) truth of the "crooked timber of humanity" (TC, p. 170): namely, that no single ideal, no "faith in a single criterion" of a properly ordered individual or communal condition, could, if realised, immunise human life from the possibility of conflict and evil. The politics of the liberalism of fear cannot, any more than any other political programme, remedy or radically immunise society against abuses of power, and if zealously pursued by powerful institutions it could "*just as easily*" provoke it. What Shklar calls "damage control" is indeed a central political objective for a society that wants to make abuses of power less likely, and Berlin's claim is that this "entails" creating and protecting a "measure of 'negative' liberty" (TC, p. 171). But to pass into the terms that belong to Derrida's diagnosis of this situation, we have to accept that whatever we do to prevent abuses of power is "at once, immunitary *and* auto-immune" (FK, 45); or, more precisely, there is no immunity "without a *risk* of autoimmunity" (FK, p. 47). This claim will remain in the background as I attempt to tease out an understanding of Berlin's metapolitical "pluralism".

V

The distinction between "positive" and "negative" liberty is the theme of Berlin's thinking in "Two Concepts of Liberty". But that thinking presses into something far more enigmatic and obscure than that striking pair of long-standing, if still intractable and still to be thought, ideas of freedom. At the end of the essay "monism" appears (and appears only once) as a summary term for any political perfectionist ideal that holds that there is, finally, one ideal configuration of the moral universe, one ideal form of the good life for Man: a conception of that form of individual and social life in which human self-realisation is ideally attained, or attained with ideal adequacy; "some ultimate, all-reconciling, yet realizable synthesis" (TC, p. 171) which would bring political conflict to an end, and Man to himself in authentic self-realisation. The perfectionist ideal that Berlin will affirm in its place is radically opposed to what Stanley Cavell has called this "debasement" of perfectionist thinking: radically opposed to a "sense...of a final or perfected state that each is to attain or pursue" (PDAT, p. 121). Instead, it affirms what Cavell calls its "democratization", envisioning a perfectionism that "asks for each the right to seek a step toward an unattained possibility of the self" (PDAT, p. 131). As we shall see as this book develops, here we find a perfectionism that not only "happily consents to democracy", but which is "called for by the democratic aspiration" itself (CHU, p. 1). Indeed, it is a perfectionism that *applies* to democracy itself. As well as finding this theme in Emerson, Cavell finds it in Nietzsche too, and we will return to that connection in Chapter 5. As we progress towards that, I hope to show that Berlin's contrast between monism and pluralism as ideals also belongs to this new turn in perfectionist thinking.

Philosophical history in its classic *archeo-teleo-eschatological* form has either been monistic (there is a conflict resolving end-of-history), or has a monism in view (as an infinite task or an "idea in the Kantian sense"), or in some other way relates itself to monism as a rational ideal. These philosophical histories have been, in various ways and to various degrees, history-producing. Not because they actually relate the "real" movement of history, but because they have actually shaped our world: people believe them and have wanted to make it so that our actual history will have been part of that philosophical history – and not without (typically murderous) consequence for our actual history.

"Pluralism" is then posited by Berlin (and once again appears only once as a name for an ideal) as a kind of humane corrective to "monism", a "*more humane ideal*" because – whatever it is – it acknowledges that "human goals are many", that conflict is thus (tragically) unavoidable, that politics does not have an end, and hence cannot be used to justify "barbarities" in the name of "some future perfection" (TC, pp. 170–1).

Yet it is, he says, an "ideal" – and hence if not "some future perfection" it is nevertheless something as yet unattained, or at least something not so pervasively actual that one might appeal to some *status quo* (somewhere, anywhere) as simply exemplifying the humane corrective to monism. So what is pluralism as an ideal? Berlin does not (anywhere) go further on this than he got to through his thinking of "positive" and "negative" liberty. But taking as my clue Shklar's suggestion that Berlin's claim about "the pluralism of values" (TC, p. 172) – what she glosses as the assumption "that there are several inherently incompatible moralities", and Wiggins glosses as the affirmation of "the plurality and mutual irreducibility of things good" – is a "metapolitical" claim, I will try to say something more, taking it (I hope with justification) in a rather Derridean and Cavellian direction as I do so.

First, we might clear the ground a bit and try to identify what he does not mean by "pluralism" when he speaks of pluralism as a humane counter-ideal to monism. He may or may not be in favour of the following but he is not recommending them: the "pluralism" of institutions that protect "negative" liberty; the "pluralism" of societies with significant levels of ethnic and religious diversity; the "pluralism" of "anything goes" slackness characteristic of postmodern culture.

On the other hand, holding pluralism as an ideal certainly envisages a future world where recognition of the pluralism of values is socially lived in an everyday way: we might look forward to a time in which an understanding that political conflict is interminable because of the plurality of things good has attained a condition in which it "sinks to the level of a commonplace", to borrow a phrase from Heidegger (IM, p.10). That is to say, *as* an ideal, it projects *an ideal way in which we might be* with respect to which a contemporary perfectionist interest in emancipation or progress might take its bearings. And yet, it is resolutely non-utopian in the sense that what it does not project or promise or hope for is an end to conflict, politics, history, or perfectionist ambitions. *It is itself a perfectionist ambition.* But it is an odd one. It stands, as an ideal, as a yet to be attained but attainable condition, to use Emerson's formulation (TDAT, p. 120), and in that respect has something of the character of a "positive" liberty project of self-mastery for us. But this perfectionism says *nothing whatsoever* about what perfectionist ambitions might belong to such a world, it says *nothing whatsoever* about "what it is like to be alive then", it says *nothing whatsoever* about what people there will have "found to be indispensable to their life as unpredictably self-transforming human beings" – that is simply unpredictable, beyond knowledge, and we should not want to predict anything here either. In short, it projects a way in which we might be without projecting any specific way in which we might be. Derrida will call this a messianism without (determinate) messianism; Cavell will call it, simply, perfectionism democratised; an essentially "open-ended thematics of perfectionism" which does entirely without "essential definition" (CHU, p. 4). As a "metapolitical" ideal it takes no position on anyone's political or moral position, only that there should be this "measure of 'negative' liberty" for (each, any and every) one's own political-value position-taking (and opposition-taking) to be one's own.

Very importantly, it is an ideal that wants everyone to have a share of "negative" liberty, for everyone to be able to stand by the political-value position-taking that is "part of their being and thought and sense of their own identity" and "part of what makes them human" (TC, p. 172): free to be the political animal that they are, and not forced to conform to someone else's vision of the good life for Man.

Berlin, of course, sees the ideals of freedom and equality as in important respects incompatible rivals in anyone's political-value position-taking: more of one means less of the other, calling for compromises and trade-offs. However, pluralism as an ideal holds these political ideals together in an enigmatically mutually implicating way. Indeed, at one point Berlin describes this interminable exchange as one of the "foundations of liberal morality": "*equality of liberty*" (TC, p. 125). Unlike Richard Rorty, who, as we shall see in a later chapter, supposes that the two ambitions are simply incommensurable, and hence as requiring a basic choice – either social justice (equality) or private self-creation (liberty) – Berlin affirms that in affirming one we cannot but affirm the (incompatible) other. This does not retreat from the forever "non-ideal" vision of eternal compromises and trade-offs (as if there was, finally, a perfectly just equilibrium between them) but seeks to cultivate *a form of human life that measures its attained conditions in relation to its interest in keeping the future open to new ways to be*, and to do so without a *telos* of ideal adequacy as its "proper end".

Relating itself to attained conditions makes this politics fundamentally *timely* – speaking up for what, by your lights is, here and now, the right thing to do with respect to concerns with experienced inadequacies and injustices, and to do so without having to plaster that judgement with "the specious glitter of unmeaning promises" about building a new civilisation or attaining a finally just condition or whatever (TDC, p. 18), and, equally, without fearing that you might be put in jail for speaking your mind. However, since it has an essential openness to the unpredictable, it also maintains, wants to maintain, promises, an opening for *untimely* "arrivals" too, arrivals that are beyond anticipation: the new, the singular; the birth, as it were, of the one who is not the same as every other, as, indeed, every birth is.

"Pluralism" as a political objective or goal is, first of all, a metapolitical ideal. It calls for a set-up that is set against the "monistic" mind-set of old "modern" Europe and the metanarratives of Europe's modernity that are still exhibited today in the self-righteousness and good conscience of those, from both the left and right, who routinely condemn political opponents as morally wrong or even evil. Pluralism as a metapolitical ideal is not about political quietism, it is not about avoiding political disagreement or avoiding taking political stands, it does not make one (as Bernard Williams wonderfully puts it) "stare at our convictions with ironical amazement" (IBWD, p. 13). It is about a way for us to be, in which politics can be lived without its characteristically modern moralism. Williams (without reflecting on this but uncannily in the very passage in which he speaks of the often "obscure" historical conditions of our own political thinking) calls the mind-set to be attained: the mind-set of political thinkers who are "democrats" (IBWD, p. 13). And, indeed, I think another name for Berlin's "pluralism as an ideal" is simply – "democracy". Not the democracy of majorities who force their way on every other who thinks differently, but a "metapolitical" set-up in which political deliberations and decisions on matters of public concern want to optimise the inclusiveness of those deliberations (within the limits to "negative" liberty, the restriction of individual liberty, that this optimisation will always imply), up to and including deliberations on the metapolitical set-up itself. Metapolitical questions are also in themselves political questions in just the same way that the question "What is philosophy?" is a philosophical question. And like the latter, they are never over.

Disengaging our thinking about politics from monism does not eliminate all thought of "the end of conflict", but that theme is now folded back piecemeal into an ongoing history of political victories and defeats, rather than in relation to one finally attained and perpetual peace. On the other hand, pluralism as an ideal does frame a distinctive view of how, from our "political positions", we should view the end of any actual political conflict. Considering a political victory, Williams describes the scene:

> A very important reason for thinking in terms of the political is that a political decision – the conclusion of a political deliberation which brings all sorts of considerations, considerations of principle along with others, to one focus of decision – is that such a decision does not in itself announce that the other party was morally wrong, or indeed, wrong at all. What it immediately announces is that *they have lost.* (IBWD, p. 13)

VI

Democracy is a regular but largely unthematised theme of Berlin's essay. His main claim about it, and one that Shklar highlights, is that there is no "necessary connexion" between democratic government and the provision of "negative" liberty: "it is perfectly conceivable that a liberal-minded despot would allow his subjects a large measure of personal freedom". So he sees the relationship between them as "a good deal more tenuous than it seemed to many advocates of both" (TC, pp. 129–31). Indeed, he recognised that while a democratic government "may disarm a given oligarchy, a given privileged individual or set of individuals", it "can still crush individuals as mercilessly as any previous ruler" (TC, p. 163). Nevertheless, he thought that democratic government "may, on the whole, provide a better guarantee of the preservation of civil liberties than other regimes" (TC, p. 130). And this is what Shklar emphasises when she stresses that the institutional pluralism required by a liberal society will make that society "of necessity" a democratic one since "without the institutions of representative democracy and an accessible, fair, and independent judiciary open to appeals, and in the absence of a multiplicity of politically active groups, liberalism is in jeopardy" (LF, p. 37). This sense of necessity is not logical or conceptual but practical. Democracy in this strictly governmental sense ensures that there is "sufficient equality of power" – in conditions where the inequality of power between State and citizens is structurally so vast – to prevent an effective liberalism being wiped out. But she follows Berlin's main claim in seeing the relationship as an external one: "It is therefore fair to say that liberalism is monogamously, faithfully, and permanently married to democracy – but it is a marriage of convenience" (LF, p. 37).

This is all well and good, but with its focus on pluralism as opposed to monopolism of power this reading of democracy totally de-emphasises Berlin's concluding affirmation of what I am calling meta-political pluralism, pluralism as opposed to monism as perfectionist ideals, which opens another kind of thinking, still hesitant and subterranean, of democracy. It is, nevertheless, something one can see emerging in Berlin's own thinking too. In his "Message to the 21st Century", written in 1994, when the Cold War era seemed to be closing, it was the meta-political claim and not the battle of ideas over liberty that came to the fore in his last reflections on our time, emphasising that "the central values by which most men have lived, in a great many lands at a great many times – these values, almost if not entirely universal, are not always harmonious with each other" (MC). Once again, he describes the monist "champions" of one or another of these values, "sometimes very fanatical", as those whose political tendency is "to trample upon the rest, as the great tyrants of the twentieth century have trampled on the life, liberty, and human rights of millions because their eyes were fixed upon some ultimate golden future" (MC). The question, he asked, was "what is to be done" to "restrain" the monist champions. He frankly admitted that he had "no dramatic answer". But he saw the slow realisation that "the search for a single, overarching ideal" (an ideal that would deliver humanity from conflict "because it is the one and only true one for humanity") "invariably leads to coercion", as a happy development (MC). And when he tried to articulate what he thought of as the "*rationality* and *tolerance*" of a less "crushing" ideal that is making its way in our time in place of this old monism, he is drawn, as Williams was, to the idea of *democracy*, and to what he considered a justified optimism one can feel in view of the fact that "liberal democracy, despite everything, despite the greatest modern scourge of fanatical, fundamentalist nationalism, is spreading" (MC).

Rationality. Tolerance. Democracy. Two years earlier, Francis Fukuyama had also identified "toleration" as "the *chief* virtue in democratic societies" (EH, p. 305), and had affirmed too the "rationality" on which it "rests" (EH, p. 303). Derrida, and in the same year as Berlin, also invoked "a universal rationality" as indissociable from "political democracy" (FK, p. 19), and a "tolerance" that should be "in accord" with the thought of the "messianicity…beyond all 'messianisms'" that he takes to belong internally to the *promise* of democracy (FK, pp. 21–2). Of course, they are not all saying the same thing. A year earlier Derrida had, as we shall see in the next chapter, strongly criticised Fukuyama for bringing closure to the history of democracy in a new thought of the end of history that his (Derrida's) "messianicity beyond all 'messianisms'" wanted, precisely, to keep open. But there is something very, very deep in the fabric of our thought that is surfacing with these appeals to the co-belonging of a concept of universal rationality and the concept of universal tolerance inside the history of democratic politics. It is a co-belonging which, as Derrida noted, "makes its way from a Greco-Judaeo-Christian tradition", and hence is strictly inseparable from the becoming-European of a world (FK, p. 19). While Derrida will want to see an "uprooting" and "atheologising" of this tradition away from any given people (Greek-European) or any given faith (Judeo-Christian) (FK, p. 19), it nevertheless, carries the hope or promise of a political culture beyond the classic – and, we can now add, historically monistic – onto-theological or *archeo-teleo-eschatological* programmes that have riven the mainstream of the political history of modern Europe's (and thence the world's) history; beyond the classic narratives of the emancipation or progress of Man but without losing a perfectionist interest in emancipation or progress themselves.

In the spreading out of the European world, the thought of "pluralism as an ideal" is surfacing. We are seeing the emergence, in the wake of the tragedies of monist perfectionism in Europe, a new perfectionism making its way, a perfectionism connected in our time, explicitly so in Cavell's thought, to democracy. Berlin lived to see, and to welcome, a world in which liberal democracy was spreading. Fukuyama saw something even more conclusive: liberal democracy is not just spreading but is the "only viable option". In the next chapter, I will consider Fukuyama's conception of this option as our philosophical history moves to the end of the Cold War.

4

THE END OF HISTORY

Liberal democracy is spreading

– Isaiah Berlin

Liberal democracy is the only viable option

– Francis Fukuyama

[The triumph of] liberal democracy...has never been so critical, fragile, threatened, even in certain regards catastrophic

– Jacques Derrida

I

On November 4th 1989, half a million people marched in East Berlin to demand freedom of the press and freedom to travel. A plan was drawn up by the Communist Party leadership in the GDR for a new travel law that would allow free movement to all countries, with the State using passports and exit visas to control the flow. At 6 pm on November 9th, the daily press conference took place to announce the Party's decisions. Daniel Johnson, a very young reporter for *The Daily Telegraph* who had flown in the day before, remembers the occasion:

> We all trooped into a dreary hall at the international press centre in the Motzstrasse. The central committee spokesman was Günter Schabowski, the East Berlin party boss, who spoke for nearly an hour on live television. Most of the questions came from tame East German journalists and the wait for a chance to get the microphone was almost unbearable. It seemed like a non-event. (SMSW)

However, in the last seven minutes, questions started to be asked from foreign correspondents about the draft travel law. It was clear that passport and visa offices had already been told about the proposed changes, and that they would be implemented "without delay". A flustered Schabowski accepted that this meant "immediately". At 6.58 pm "a painfully thin, anxious young man in a slightly fogeyish three-piece tweed suit rose to his feet, microphone in hand", and Daniel Johnson asked what he took to be "the most obvious question that came to mind":

> "*Herr Schabowski, was wird mit der Berliner Mauer jetzt geschehen*?" ["Mr Schabowski, what will happen to the Berlin Wall now?"] Hundreds of thousands of Germans on both sides of the Wall were watching: they wanted the answer, too. Schabowski looked nonplussed. He announced that this would be the last question. He repeated my question to himself, adding that "the permeability of the Wall from our side does not yet and exclusively resolve the question of the meaning of this fortified state border of the DDR". It was somehow very German to ruminate at such a moment on the meaning of the Berlin Wall. But there was the rub. Now that I had used the fatal words "Berlin Wall", Schabowski could have seized the opportunity to make it clear that there was no question of opening the Wall that night. He could have explained what its rationale would be, now that people would no longer be shot for attempting to cross it. Instead, he hesitated. He stumbled over his words. He waffled about peace and disarmament for two of the longest minutes of his life. But he did not answer the question, because he had no answer. A wall between two halves of a country could have no "meaning" if the people were allowed to travel freely. It was over. (SMSW)

Hundreds gathered at the Wall that evening and began climbing it, dancing on it, and hacking great chunks out of it. They breached it from the eastern side – met with hugs and cheers from their fellow Germans on the western side. Shortly before midnight, somewhere in the chaos, a young East German, Angela Merkel, made it through the Bornholmer crossing. The division of Berlin, the division of Germany, the division of Europe, the divided world of the Cold War, it was all but over.

"To some extent", Johnson reflected, "the media made the message" (SMSW). And it continued to do so in what Derrida called "the new stage of geopolitics" (SM, p. 56) in which an international news media "made the message" as never before. And the basic message was not only the announcement of "the end of societies constructed on the Marxist model" but also "the end of the whole Marxist tradition" – and a new proclamation of "the end of history" (SM, p. 56).

The disappearance of the West's principal antagonist led many to anticipate the possibility of an end to global conflict. But others – others who were just as pleased, honestly delighted, to see the collapse of the totalitarian nightmare of Soviet Communism – anticipated no such coming end, expecting instead that the West would gather itself once more in new friend-enemy configurations. Against who? "China? Islam?", Derrida wondered aloud in 1990 (PF, p. 77). Following a series of four coordinated terrorist attacks by Islamists on the United States on the morning of Tuesday, September 11, 2001, the event going by the curious date-name "9/11" seemed for some time to have answered that question. However, what no commentators seemed to consider in the 1990s was that the old principal antagonist might just change into the generic uniform of an illiberal authoritarian...and start getting back up again. Reports of the triumph of political and economic liberalism, the alliance of multi-party democracy and capitalism, seem to have been greatly exaggerated.

No one articulated the post-Cold War euphoria in the West with more confidence and optimism than Francis Fukuyama in his classic text of philosophical history *The End of History and the Last Man*, written in 1992. It was not widely read in political science, his own discipline, perhaps in virtue of its ambition to pursue political-science history as philosophical history. But it was not much read by Anglophone philosophers either, perhaps for the same reason. On the other hand, perhaps it was also for the same reason that Derrida devoted a lengthy discussion to it in *Specters of Marx*. We will follow some of his reading of Fukuyama in this chapter. I will not give an exhaustive account of either text, but will focus on their respective conceptions of "complete" democracy, a key idea for both, and for our time.

II

In the immediate aftermath of 1989, it had become possible to think that geopolitical conflict was waning; liberal democracy seemed to have defeated all opposition, perhaps especially on its own territory. Fukuyama's text became the intellectual loadstar of this post-Cold-War "new world order". Derrida's response to it was, as we shall see, largely critical, but his opening comment was somewhat warmer than is likely remembered, and should give us pause:

> The book is not as bad or naïve as one might be led to think by the frenzied exploitation that exhibits it as the finest ideological showcase of victorious capitalism in a liberal democracy which has finally arrived at the plenitude of its ideal. (SM, p. 56)

And he later adds:

> It would seem neither just nor even interesting to accuse Fukuyama of the fate reserved for his book. One would do better to ask oneself why this book, with the "good news" it claims to bring, has become such a media gadget... And how it is that a discourse of this type is sought out by those who celebrate the triumph of liberal capitalism and its predestined alliance with liberal democracy. (SM, p. 68)

The precise content of "the 'good news' it claims to bring" will be a central question for Derrida in his criticism, but what is most striking about Fukuyama's text is the type of discourse in which it is announced: astonishingly, by "raising once again the question of whether there is such a thing as a Universal History" (EH, p. xiv). At a time in the history of philosophical history when it might have been thought impossible to do so, but at a time in political history when the flow of events were so dramatic, Fukuyama attempted to revive the classic form of *teleo-eschatological* philosophical history, and in particular (at least part of) Hegel's conception of its unfolding, claiming to see "a common evolutionary pattern for *all* human societies – in short, something like a Universal History of mankind in the direction of liberal democracy" (EH, p. 48).

From its "beachhead in Western Europe" (EH, p. 58), liberal democracy has been spreading worldwide, first to America and thence beyond, and, Fukuyama insisted, "there do not appear to be viable alternatives" to it (EH, p. 137). There are alternatives, of course, but it is not at all obvious anymore that we in the West can see a serious competitor:

> We who live in stable, long-standing liberal democracies face an unusual situation. In our grandparents' time, many reasonable people could forsee a radiant socialist future in which private property and capitalism had been abolished, and in which politics itself was somehow overcome. Today, by contrast, we have trouble imagining a world that is radically better than our own, or a future that is not essentially democratic and capitalist. Within that framework, of course, many things could be improved: we could house the homeless, guarantee opportunity for minorities and women, improve competitiveness, and create new jobs. We can also imagine future worlds that are significantly worse than we know now, in which national, racial, or religious intolerance makes a comeback, or in which we are overwhelmed by war or environmental collapse. But we cannot picture to ourselves a world that is *essentially* different from the present one, and at the same time better. (EH, p. 46)

With the fall of the Berlin Wall a more or less global public will have been faced with questions to which only post-War philosophers had devoted any serious attention – or rather, since "Oxford" (and all that suggests) had been mostly in the Garden of Eden during this time, questions which had hitherto belonged primarily to those philosophers who were still steeped in the classics of philosophical history. Post-War philosophers on the European mainland had, as Isaiah Berlin had in near isolation in Oxford, already raised questions about the end of History and the end of Man, and the relation of Marxism to both. And they had done so with "the totalitarian terror in all the Eastern countries" before their eyes (SM, p. 15). They did not have to wait for 1989 to think together questions of the end of Man and the end of historical Marxism. Many academics – uncomfortably too many – will have held fast to the idea that "totalitarian terror in all the

Eastern countries, [and] all the socio-economic disasters of Soviet bureaucracy" (SM, p. 15) was simply a Marxism "perverted", and not, as Derrida affirmed, the upshot of "perversions that some have been saying for a long time are precisely not perversions" (SM, p. 91). Nevertheless, the questions about the end of history, the end of Man, and the end of Marxism that had belonged for some time only to the reflections of philosophers (mostly) on the European mainland, their "daily bread" (SM, p. 14), were suddenly everyone's.

What Derrida saw, above all, in the new quasi-public discussion that followed the fall of the Berlin Wall, the collapse of communist rule across Central and Eastern Europe, and the dissolution of the Soviet Union, was the message that the Western media made: "what one hears, reads, and sees, what is most *mediatized* in Western capitals" (SM, p. 15). This phenomenal debate – this new media appearance of the thing – sold the situation as "the death of Marxism as the end of history", and the final victory of liberal capitalism and liberal democracy. "It proclaims: Marx is dead, communism is dead, very dead, and with it its hopes, its discourse, its theories, and its practices. It says: long live capitalism, long live the market, here's to the survival of economic and political liberalism!" (SM, p. 64).

As we shall see, Derrida had no intention of making "a belated-rallying-to-Marxism" in his Marx book, insisting that to do so "would have to have misunderstood quite badly" his own attempt to inherit and radicalise a *certain* spirit of Marxism (SM, p. 88). Nevertheless, he wanted to challenge an end of history being proclaimed in the name of an historically specific understanding of a particular form of democratic order (economic and political liberalism). And proclaimed at a time when its own actually attained order faced severe difficulties, and was fragile and exhausted even as it was becoming singularly hegemonic across the globe (a "new world disorder" (SM, p. 37)):

> This triumphant conjuration [of the death of Marxism] is striving in truth to disavow, and therefore to hide from, the fact that never, never in history, has the horizon of the thing whose survival is being celebrated (namely, all the old models of the capitalist and liberal world) been as dark, threatening, and threatened. (SM, p. 52)

We should stress the qualification "old" in this reference to models of capitalism and liberalism. On the first (capitalism), Derrida will assert that "there never was just…capitalism in the singular, but capitalisms plural" (SM, p. 59), and we have no reason to suppose that the various "old models" of capitalism with their irreducible differences and antagonisms to each other are the end of the historical line, with no possible, or indeed wholly unpredictable, variations and mutations to come. With regard to the second (liberalism), we should certainly say the same (and we will flag up, as Derrida did too, Fukuyama's stress on different movements within the history of political liberalism). Shklar's "liberalism of fear", for example, explicitly announces itself as a successor to, and "differing sharply" from the old "liberalism of natural rights" (LF, p. 26). Indeed, when Derrida positioned himself against those "who puff out there chests with the good conscience of capitalism, liberalism, and the virtues of parliamentary democracy" – the ones who celebrate the death of Marxism as the end of history – he immediately added that "parliamentary democracy" here is "a term with which we designate not parliamentarism and political representation *in general*, but the *present*, which is to say in fact, *past* forms of the electoral and parliamentary apparatus" (SM, p. 15; see also SM, p. 79). In Chapter 8, we will explore some of the changes in the form and formation of democratic politics that Derrida saw shaping up in our time, but he remained throughout a committed thinker of democracy and its future, even while he resisted attempts to anticipate a future finality for it. Indeed, as we have already seen, he seeks a way of inheriting the classic interest in emancipation or progress that ran through the classics of philosophical history without their messiano-eschatological foresight of an "ideal" end of history or end of Man.

However, what was not anticipated by philosophers in the 1950s or 1960s, what could not have been "calculated in advance" – and Derrida underlines Fukuyama's alertness to this – was the incredible speed at which the communist system collapsed. There are rhythms and events to history that no one can master (SM, p. 69). Equally unpredictable was the revival in our time of an unequivocal affirmation of the old discourse of Europe's modernity, a new teleo-eschatological philosophical history of the world. Unless we were Marxists, those discourses had unravelled in both their conceptual and historical credibility during the twentieth century. But suddenly, with the end of the Cold War and, as we will see in the next part of this book, with hopes of a European re-union based on principles of liberal democracy and the market economy (principles soon enshrined in the 1993 "Copenhagen criteria" which state that membership of the EU "requires that a candidate country has achieved stability of institutions guaranteeing democracy, the rule of law, human rights, respect for and protection of minorities, the existence of a functioning market economy"), that old modern discourse was once more, and especially in the work of Fukuyama, showing signs of life: the idea of the end of history was back on the table, and a philosophical history was once again being attempted:

> By raising once again the question of whether there is such a thing as a Universal History of mankind, I am resuming a discussion that was begun in the early nineteenth century, but more or less abandoned in our time because of the enormity of events that mankind has experienced since then. (EH, p. xiv)

Seeing "a worldwide liberal revolution" (EH, p. 39) overcoming "our pessimism" (EH, p. 3), it was back to Kant (who had anticipated "the achievement of a just civic constitution and its universalization throughout the world" (EH, p. 58)), and to Hegel (who also saw a constitutional state with rational laws as "the embodiment of human freedom" (EH, p. 60)), and to reviving "the notion that history is directional, meaningful, [and] progressive". Fukuyama stressed that this "notion" was "very foreign to the main current of thought of our time" (EH, p. 69). Indeed.

The astonishing "empirical flow of events" at the end of the twentieth century, with the rapid collapse of the Soviet empire, seemed to provide solid reason to reject our earlier twentieth century despair and pessimism, and to embrace the affirmation of the advent of "good news": "To Kant's question, Is it possible to write a Universal History from a cosmopolitan point of view? our provisional answer is yes" (EH, p. 126).

III

In Fukuyama's view, the universal history to be related in our time is not Kantian or Marxist but Hegelian – or at least a Hegelian history as filtered by Fukuyama via the work of Alexandre Kojève, the French-Russian philosopher who taught a highly influential series of seminars at the *Ecole Pratique des Hautes Etudes* in Paris in the 1930s. The text of those seminars was first published in French in 1947, and in English, under the title *Introduction to Reading Hegel*, in 1980. Taking the form of an account of the historical development of humanity based on a totally *non-economic* drive, "the struggle for recognition", Kojève's Hegelian approach, Fukuyama claimed, "is actually a very useful and illuminating way of seeing the contemporary world" (EH, p. 145): the struggle for recognition was, Fukuyama suggested, becoming "evident everywhere around us and underlies contemporary movements for liberal rights" (EH, pp. 145–6). Derrida would insist that "whether we like it or not, whatever consciousness we have of it, we cannot not be [the] heirs of [Marx and Marxism]" (SM, p. 91). With equal assurance, Fukuyama proclaimed that "whether or not we acknowledge our debt to him, we owe to Hegel the most fundamental aspects of our present-day consciousness" (EH, p. 59).

Derrida thought that Kojève's work was undeniably interesting (SM, p. 91), including him in the canon of the "*classics of the end*" (SM, p. 15). Derrida was, however, it has to be said, impatient with Fukuyama's "Hegel-Kojève *artifact*" (SM, p. 72), indignant even, calling his book a "grammar school exercise of a young, industrious but come-lately reader of Kojève" who "deserved better" (SM, p. 56). Derrida seemed to be especially affronted by Fukuyama's failure to do his homework on the classics of the end beyond his Hegel-Kojève synthesis: "it is a little as if he had never come across...a certain Marx...not to mention Nietzsche...not to mention Husserl...or Heidegger...not to mention a few thinkers who are even closer to us...not to mention a certain Hegel" (SM, p. 67). Perhaps. But Derrida, who confessed "the obvious limits" to his own "competence" (SM, p. 51) to speak on the history of Marxism, will stumble himself over the history of political liberalism. It is a history which, take it from me, whether we like it or not, whatever consciousness we have of it, we cannot but be the heirs. What a tangle of spirits!

IV

We will look at Derrida's reading of Fukuyama's treatment of the history of liberalism and liberal democracy later in this chapter, but to prepare for that I want first to explore something very central to Fukuyama's own conception of political liberalism that Derrida notes in passing but does not discuss at all: Fukuyama's identification and critique of a distinctively "Anglo-Saxon" liberalism, and the idea of "negative" liberty that it champions. As I have indicated, Fukuyama's account of an Hegelian universal history aims to show that the underlying development – the real driver of history – is the struggle for recognition. However, and still in Hegelian spirit, this is conceived as being, essentially, a struggle for "recognition of our freedom" (EH, p. 200). "Freedom" here is not the "negative" liberty idea of unimpeded choice or freedom from interference by others, but the "positive" liberty idea of attained self-perfection or self-mastery. The struggle for recognition as a struggle for freedom has as its political *telos* "the achievement of self-mastery in the form of democratic government" (EH, pp. 200–1). "Democracy is, after all, a matter of self-government" (EH, 218). There is a serious effort here by Fukuyama to challenge, in the name of a new "Hegelian" liberalism, the old "Anglo-Saxon" liberalism and its defence of "negative" liberty. It is not only a revival of philosophical history, but also the "positive" liberty tradition that Berlin had so vigorously criticised.

Central to Fukuyama's effort to revitalise this type of "positive" liberty ideal is a claim that the "negative" liberty tradition is based on a conception of political life that seeks (at least in principle) to exclude from its proper order something it both ought not to, and, in fact, could not exclude, something Fukuyama calls "*thymos*". What is "*thymos*"? And how does it bear on the struggle for recognition? Fukuyama summarises as follows:

> The desire for recognition may at first appear to be an unfamiliar concept, but it is as old as the tradition of Western political philosophy, and constitutes a thoroughly familiar part of the human personality. It was first described by Plato in the *Republic*, when he noted that there were three parts to the soul, a desiring part, a reasoning part, and a part that he called *thymos*, or "spiritedness." Much of human behavior can be explained as a combination of the first two parts, desire and reason: desire induces men to seek things outside themselves, while reason or calculation shows them the best way to get them. But in addition, human beings seek recognition of their own worth, or of the people, things, or principles that they invest with worth. The propensity to invest the self with a certain value, and to demand recognition for that value, is what in today's popular language we would call "self-esteem." The propensity to feel self-esteem arises out of the part of the soul called *thymos*. It is like an innate human sense of justice. People believe that they have a certain worth, and when other people treat them as though they are worth less than that, they experience

> the emotion of *anger*. Conversely, when people fail to live up to their own sense of worth, they feel *shame*, and when they are evaluated correctly in proportion to their worth, they feel *pride*. The desire for recognition, and the accompanying emotions of anger, shame, and pride, are parts of the human personality critical to political life. According to Hegel, they are what drives the whole historical process. (EH, pp. xvi–xvii)

The Anglo-Saxon "negative" liberty tradition, which understands freedom "as something like the simple absence of restraint" (EH, p. 148), "does not attempt to define any positive goals for their citizens or promote a particular way of life as superior or desirable to another", and this leaves us, Fukuyama insists, "unsatisfied" (EH, p. 160): it leaves out "much of what we find satisfying in our lives" (EH, p. 190). This is because it frames its politics exclusively in terms of reason and desire; the reason of economic calculation and the desire for comfortable self-preservation and prosperity. This kind of politics can only take us so far in understanding the history of the world – it can explain "the process of industrialization, and a large part of economic life more generally", but no more (EH, xviii). According to Fukuyama, however, this will be just one of two pillars in a capitalist liberal democracy, the capitalist part. The other pillar, the choice of liberal democracy is, Fukuyama, supposes, and supposes fairly I think, relatively obscure to Anglo-Saxon liberalism. Even if there is a stated preference for it in a marriage of convenience that can help to ward off political tyranny, there is, Fukuyama notes, "no economic rationale for democracy; if anything, democratic politics is a drag on economic efficiency. The choice of democracy is an autonomous one" (EH, p. 205). Fukuyama's neo-Hegelian narrative posits this latter choice as devolving precisely from what is left out of the Anglo-Saxon picture: from a *thymos*-embracing vision of a liberal society: "undertaken for the sake of recognition and not for the sake of [selfish] desire", and hence as arising independently, "out of *thymos,* the part of the soul that demands recognition" (EH, p. xviii).

The "higher understanding of modern liberalism that tries to preserve the *thymotic* side of the human personality rather than exiling it from the realm of politics" thus aims, in part, to overcome what one might call the motivational deficit that seems otherwise to belong to political liberalism (EH, p. 191). There is a "vacuum at the heart of Lockean liberalism" filled only by "the open-ended pursuit of wealth" (EH, p. 160). And this "filler" of "prosperity" is thin, shallow and spiritless: it is, as so many have thought, from Hegel, to Husserl, to Hitler and beyond, the spiritless (and basically English) spirit *par excellance*, and it is, on its own, deeply unsatisfying.

Fukuyama attempts to overcome this problem not with a new motivational filler but a new "higher" understanding of the history of liberalism in terms of a wider and much longer history of *thymotic* politics. Recognition, for Fukuyama, ultimately resolves into two basic forms, "two basic manifestations" (EH, p. 182). The first, and the one that marks most of human history, is the politically "highly problematic" passion of *megalothymia* – the desire to be "recognised as superior to other people" (EH, p. 182). But it has another form too, its opposite: "its opposite is *isothymia,* the desire to be recognized as the equal of other people" (EH, p. 182). For Fukuyama, the Anglo-Saxon tradition of Hobbes and Locke can be understood as attempting "to overcome *megalothymia*" simply by ridding social and political life "of its *thymotic* part" altogether. This is central to the historical creation of the conditions of the first pillar, economic modernisation (liberal capitalism), but, as should now be clear, it seems to have nothing essential to say about political modernisation (liberal democracy), and for Fukuyama, it simply can't.

On the other hand, Fukuyama does not think that a *thymos*-including development might just be tagged on, as a second pillar, to this early liberal understanding of political life. For Fukuyama, as we shall see, the Anglo-Saxon liberalism that underpins the development of the first pillar belongs just as much inside the history of the struggle for recognition as democracy does, inside the movement towards a self-consciousness that "all are free", and hence towards the development of increasingly *isothymotic* politics – the "positive" liberty struggle for rational self-mastery that would conclude in the realisation of fully implemented liberal democracy. Fukuyama countersigns Hegel's signature schema of universal history as a history of the progress of reason and freedom:

> The unfolding of Universal History could be understood as the growth of the equality of human freedom, summed up in Hegel's epigram that "the Eastern nations knew that *one* was free; the Greek and Roman world only that *some* are free; while *we* know that *all* men absolutely (man as *man)* are free." For Hegel, the embodiment of human freedom was the modern constitutional state, or again, what we have called liberal democracy. The Universal History of mankind was nothing other than man's progressive rise to full rationality, and to a self-conscious awareness of how that rationality expresses itself in liberal self-government. (EH, p. 60)

"From its beachhead in Europe" liberal democracy is spreading out, the last stage at the end of political history as the realisation of "positive" liberty in the ideal of *isothymotic* politics.

V

It is certainly true that a kind of willed motivational deficit – the upshot of resistance to tyranny – is a characteristic feature of Anglo-Saxon liberalism. But there is a problem with Fukuyama's treatment of this tradition. By treating non-Hegelian liberalism as exclusively a matter of the early liberalism of natural rights, Fukuyama opposes to Hegel an historically truncated conception of its history, identifying its early Anglo-Saxon formation (Hobbes and Locke) as a stopping point of its own (non-Hegelian) development. This is a peculiarly un-Hegelian idea that leads him to neglect, at the very least, Berlin's own problematisation of Anglo-Saxon "negative" liberty liberalism, and his development of a successor liberalism of the pluralist ideal. Berlin really doesn't think one can make good sense of political history in terms of struggles for "negative" liberty alone, and those who have most vociferously demanded the latter belong anyway, Berlin says, to "a small minority of highly civilized and self-conscious human beings" (TC, p. 161).

Berlin's own affirmation of the pluralist ideal – and the non-elitist (non-self-splitting) form of democratised perfectionism which that champions – is intended as a corrective of that minority view. But it is intended equally as a "more humane" corrective of every monist perfectionism too. In the very effort to protect itself from external subversion, in the very effort to *immunise* itself from whatever threatens it, every perfectionism risks self-destroying *autoimmunity*. (I am drawing on concepts of immunity and autoimmunity that, as we shall see, Derrida will deploy in his account of political defence mechanisms to flesh out Berlin's idea here, I hope justifiably.) The pursuit of Berlin's "pluralism as an ideal" is not immune to autoimmune disaster either, since nothing is – but it is, Berlin thinks, in a better position than any other perfectionism to resist it. Fukuyama's vision of fully implemented liberal democracy as the end of political history does not escape this logic either. Seeing history as unfolding towards that supposedly final and universal form, this vision of the end of Man and the end of history in a final perfection, is as vulnerable to autoimmune disorders as any other. Illiberal *megalothymia* can always break out. We are seeing this almost everywhere in our time.

Fukuyama is not entirely blind to this kind of problem, recognising, for example, that "liberal democracy could...be subverted internally...by an excess of *isothymia* – that is, the fanatical desire for equal recognition" (EH, p. 314). But he regards this kind of possibility, the possibility of some kind of internal subversion, as an unfortunate eventuality that can befall a liberal democracy, not as an essential risk internal to every politics pursued in the name of an ideal order, whether that order is conceived as still to come or now (more or less) attained. Fukuyama's selection of evidence of *megalothymia* from the "empirical flow" has no hesitation fingering "those tyrants who have risen among us like Hitler, Stalin, or Saddam Hussein" (EH, p. 190). Moreover, as Derrida noted, Fukuyama "cannot deny, without inviting ridicule", "all the violence, all the injustices" that are still all around us in our contemporary twin-pillared capitalist and liberal democracies. And Fukuyama does not deny them. However, what he cannot acknowledge without having to unpick everything is that the "tyrannical and dictatorial manifestations of what he calls '*megalothymia*'" that we see in the capitalist liberal democracies (SM, p. 64) are not external subversions of an *isothymotic* ideal but autoimmune possibilities internal to it. The recent upsurge in MAGAphilia is a *megalothymia* just as much as the ambition to forge a "new American century" was at the end of the Cold War.

Fukuyama's evangelical book, his announcement that "good news has come" (EH, p. xiii), became a "media gadget" gift for those who wanted to use it to proclaim at the time that, with the collapse of the Soviet empire, the end had indeed been attained, that the "good news" is that we have now made it to the end. However, as we shall see, the good news that has arrived is not, in Fukuyama's actual book, the celebratory claim that the end has arrived. Fukuyama's vision is a *teleo-eschatological* messianism: it announces only what this world promises as its political finality, as yet unrealised. On the other hand, his vision of the end is not simply removed from the new world order that so happily embraced his book. The Hegelian vision of the end that he endorses is not only the Hegel he finds in Kojève, but, as Fukuyama himself openly acknowledges, the Hegel of an originally "Christian vision of a free and equal society" (EH, p. 199). It is not a negligible feature of an apparently scientific text that its formation is rooted in that religion. Derrida does not let it go:

> The model of the liberal State to which [Fukuyama] *explicitly* lays claim is not only that of Hegel, the Hegel of the struggle for recognition, it is that of a Hegel who privileges the "Christian vision". If 'the existence of the State is the coming of God into the world', as one reads in [Hegel's] *The Philosophy of Right* invoked by Fukuyama, this coming has the sense of a Christian event. The French Revolution would have been the event that took the Christian vision of a free and equal society, and implanted it here on earth… This end of History is essentially a Christian eschatology. (SM, pp. 60–1)

This point re-situates Fukuyama's geophilosophical considerations about universal history within the context of the geopolitical developments we can see in our time. And a point to note above all here is that rather than seeing Fukuyama's text as simply announcing a coming end of global conflict, it should be seen as participating in something like an ongoing war, a war in which the three great religions of the Book still have a massively determining role in contemporary geopolitics. This is a geopolitics now centred on the Middle East, where each participant simultaneously mobilises the most archaic and the most modern forces. Fukuyama explicitly acknowledged that we live in a time of the rise of "religious fundamentalism…within the Christian, Jewish and Muslim traditions" (EHO, p. 13). But the garb of scientific objectivity cannot hide that Fukuyama's philosophical (hi)story is fully part of this geopolitical scene. Fukuyama's vision of the world at the end of history is a vision of the Christian European world writ large. In the terms of the three parts of the world that belongs to Christian spiritual geography, the realms of the sons of Noah – Ham (Africa), Shem (Asia) and Japheth (Europe) – what most marks our time is Japheth's realm enlarging or spreading out across the whole globe, what, as we shall see in more detail in Chapter 8, Derrida called "globalatinization" (FK, p. 11). It may have attained a condition of near-global hegemony, however, its triumphalism is not only premature but belongs more to an ongoing conflict than testimony of its coming end.

Derrida was left stupefied by Fukuyama's calm avoidance of so much that is actually going on in the world that would contradict the "good news" story of the "empirical flow of events" towards fully implemented or "complete" liberal democracy. There is still a history of the world to be told, but less than ever is this the story of the movement of world history towards a final end of Man.

On the other hand, calling Fukuyama's new optimism into question does not have to recoil to mid-twentieth century despair. Indeed, I will follow Derrida in wanting to see a new chance for the classical interest in emancipation or progress – and perhaps even for an exemplary Europe that can "band together" against *both* "the politics of American global dominance" *and* "Arab-Muslim theocratism" (LLF, p. 41) – by affirming a conception of democracy which, unlike Fukuyama's, does entirely without the idea of a final end. To orient ourselves towards this fork in the road over the idea and future of democracy, I want to pick my way through Fukuyama's reading of the history of liberalism in Europe and Derrida's concerns with it.

VI

Derrida does not spend much time engaging with Fukuyama's Hegelian-Kojèvean history of political liberalism. He picks up Fukuyama's thread on this theme twice, but on both occasions, there is a cursoriness that forecloses a discussion that could have been more fruitful.

As Derrida notes, Fukuyama's book claims to bring a "positive response" to the question "whether a 'coherent and directional History of mankind' will eventually lead 'the greater part of humanity', as Fukuyama calmly, enigmatically, and in a fashion at once modest and impudent calls it, toward 'liberal democracy' (p. xii)" (SM, pp. 70–1). Fukuyama focuses on the history of political modernity, and it is on this theme that his account differs most strikingly from classical Anglo-Saxon liberalism and its view of modern history, outlining "a very different way of reading the historical process" that leads to liberal democracy (EH. p. 189), and providing a very different "reason for its choice" (EH, p. 181). Importantly, it will also claim to reveal the "real meaning" of liberalism in a way that remains, Fukuyama argues, totally unthought "in the Anglo-Saxon tradition" of Hobbes and Locke, the tradition in which political liberalism is, in fact, historically rooted (EH, p. 145).

As we have seen, for Fukuyama that older liberal tradition conceives "civil society" in terms of the operations of two "parts of the soul", reason and desire (EH, 145). This liberalism, "the liberalism of natural rights", has as its "prototypic product" a "self-understanding of liberal society" composed of atomised individuals: the "*bourgeois* individual" who is "primarily preoccupied with his own material well-being, and is neither public-spirited, nor virtuous, nor dedicated to the larger community" (EH, p. 145). On this conception "a state's legitimacy" is nothing over and above "its ability to protect and preserve those rights that individuals possess as human beings" (EH, p. 156); "a constitutional regime providing safeguards for the citizen's fundamental human rights" (EH, p. 158), rights "to life and property" (EH, p. 159), rights, especially, to pursue activities that deliver private (and thence hopefully – via a "hidden hand" – societal) prosperity. "His own self-preservation and material well-being" is all that really matters, and the individual is "interested in the community around him only to the extent that it fosters or is a means of achieving his private good" (EH, p. 160). It is a vision of society "in which all public-spiritedness" is either missing or (since it typically is not) is understood as ultimately motivated by private self-interest (EH, p. 161). As Shklar puts it, on this conception of "society composed of politically sturdy citizens", its optimal condition is one "composed solely of rights claiming citizens. In all cases, therefore, the liberalism of natural rights regards politics as a matter of citizens who actively pursue their own legally secured ends in accordance with a higher law" (LF, pp. 26).

The Anglo-Saxon liberal State is characterised by Fukuyama as seeking to overcome tyranny and *megalythomia* by "banish[ing] *thymos* from political life" (EH, p. 190). And it does this by granting and protecting individual rights, rights these individuals can claim to possess "naturally" in virtue of their humanity. How then does the *thymos*-affirming "higher" liberalism of Hegel differ from this classical liberalism? How does a liberal state "recognize" all human beings universally on a *thymos*-including Hegelian account? Fukuyama is unequivocal: "it does this by granting and protecting their *rights*" (EH, p. 202).

This is a fascinating moment of Fukuyama's analysis. For, as he acknowledges, at this point the Lockean liberal State and the Hegelian liberal State that supposedly goes beyond it "sound virtually identical" (EH, p. 203). And suddenly one might wonder if there is any great difference between the Lockean and Hegelian positions at all. Fukuyama is not content with that thought, and he attempts to tease out this apparent difference-without-distinction by fundamentally re-thinking the history of modern liberalism. The idea is not that Lockean liberals happened to arrive at the same conclusion as later Hegelians. On the contrary, to get things right here according to Fukuyama, we have to see that the whole history had always been Hegelian. In Europe and America, as a matter of historical fact, the economic pillar was set in place first, and set on Lockean liberal foundations, but, and this is Fukuyama's key claim, "their self-understanding had never been purely Lockean" (EH, p. 203). The first pillar (economic liberalism, a competitive market economy) may be autonomous from the second pillar (political liberalism, liberal democracy) but the struggle for recognition belongs to the entire course of political history; again, "the desire for recognition, and the accompanying emotions of anger, shame, and pride, are parts of the human personality critical to political life. According to Hegel, they are what drives the whole historical process" (EH, p. xvii). It is the development of "the achievement of self-mastery" (EH, p. 200) characterised by a "positive" liberty story of human self-realisation going on inside but behind the back of its thin and unsatisfying "negative" first steps. Here, in full, is the passage where Fukuyama's Hegelian history meets and comprehends the earlier Anglo-Saxon development:

> In what way can we say that modern liberal democracy "recognizes" all human beings universally? It does this by granting and protecting their *rights*... Popular self-government abolishes the distinction between masters and slaves; everyone is entitled to at least some share in the role of master. Mastery now takes the form of the promulgation of democratically determined laws, that is, sets of universal rules by which man self-consciously masters himself. Recognition becomes *reciprocal* when the state and the people recognize each other, that is, when the state grants its citizens rights and when citizens agree to abide by the state's laws. The only limitations on these rights occur when they become self-contradictory, in other words, when the exercise of one right interferes with the exercise of another.
>
> This description of the Hegelian state sounds virtually identical to the Lockean liberal state, which is similarly defined as a system for protecting a set of individual rights. The Hegel specialist will immediately object that Hegel was critical of Lockean or Anglo-Saxon liberalism, and would have rejected the notion that a Lockean United States of America or England constituted the final stage of history. He would of course be right in a certain sense. Hegel would never have endorsed the view of certain liberals in the Anglo-Saxon tradition, now primarily represented on the libertarian Right, who believe that government's only purpose is to get out of the way of individuals, and that the latter's freedom to pursue their selfish private interests is absolute. He would have rejected the version of liberalism that viewed political rights simply as a means by which men could protect their lives and their money or, in more contemporary language, their personal "lifestyles."
>
> On the other hand, Kojève identified an important truth when he asserted that postwar America or the members of the European Community constituted the embodiment of Hegel's state of universal recognition. For while the Anglo-Saxon democracies may have been founded on explicitly Lockean grounds, their self-understanding has never been purely Lockean. (EH, pp. 202–3)

For Fukuyama, the two-pillared history of liberal democracy is not an Anglo-Saxon beginning (first pillar) followed by an additional implicitly Hegelian supplement (second pillar), but, and throughout, a temporality – and teleology – of the development of rational recognition internal to human history as such.

That Derrida reads Fukuyama's central line of argument about the history of modern liberalism rather awkwardly is evident from his brief comments on the passage I have just quoted at length, which he comes back to twice. The first time points up a misreading of Fukuyama's appeal to Kojève that will continue into the second.

> After having distinguished between the Anglo-Saxon model of the liberal State (Hobbes, Locke) and Hegelian "liberalism" that pursues first of all "rational recognition", Fukuyama distinguishes between two gestures by Kojève. When the latter describes the perfection of the universal and homogeneous State, he is depending too much on Locke and on an Anglo-Saxon model criticized by Hegel. On the other hand, he is right to affirm that postwar America or the European Community constitutes "the embodiment of Hegel's state of universal recognition" [p.203]. (SM, p. 61)

There is a lot one might object to in this rapid summary. Fukuyama certainly does want to distinguish Anglo-Saxon and Hegelian liberalism, but the problem explored in the passage from *The End of History* just cited arises from a point of their near indistinguishability. That indistinguishability is going to be questioned by "the Hegel specialist" – who is not pointedly Kojève but any imaginary Hegel scholar – who would want to insist on distinguishing the two (as Fukuyama had just done and was continuing to do). That distinguishability is then restored with reference to an "important truth" that does derive from something specifically in Kojève: a corrective reminder that the unfolding historical reality was, despite the Lockean character of its founding, already not only Lockean through and through, and was, when properly understood, already on the way to a Hegelian state of universal recognition. In other words, the Anglo-Saxon development was already something other than and more than it appeared to itself. For example, "the fact that the American Founding Fathers did not use the terms 'recognition' and 'dignity' did not prevent the Lockean language of rights from sliding effortlessly and invisibly into the Hegelian language of recognition" (EH, p. 204).

The reference to Fukuyama wanting to find an "important truth" in Kojève's affirmation of the end of history embodied in contemporary America and the member states of the European Community returns in Derrida's second comment on this passage. Here, Derrida acknowledges something of Fukuyama's commitment to an internally Hegelian history, this time going right back to the emergence of the idea of *thymos* in Plato, and the Anglo-Saxon (failed) effort to exclude it. However, the "important truth" from Kojève is now taken as a straight affirmation by Fukuyama of the attained arrival of the end of that history in America and the member states of the European Community – and that is not a credible reading. Fukuyama's reading of Hegel's "dialectic of desire" is, Derrida asserts,

> presented, with an imperturbable confidence, as the continuation of a Platonic theory of *thymos*, relayed all the way up to Hegel, and beyond him,

> by a tradition that would pass by way of Machiavelli, Hobbes, Locke, and so on, despite so many differences and disagreements among all these political thinkers. The Anglo-Saxon conception of modern liberalism would also be exemplary in this regard. It would in fact have sought to exclude all this *megalothymia* (characteristic of Stalin, Hitler, and Saddam Hussein [p. 190]), even if "the desire for recognition remains all around us in the form of *isothymia*". Any contradiction would be cancelled once a State has succeeded in conjugating what Fukuyama calls the "twin pillars", that of economic rationality and that of the *thymos* or the desire for recognition. This would be the case, and *the thing would have already happened*, according to Kojève at least as he is interpreted – and seconded by Fukuyama. The latter credits Kojève with having "identified an important truth when he asserted that postwar America or the members of the European Community constituted the embodiment of Hegel's state of universal recognition" [p.203].
>
> Let us underscore the words "important truth". They give a pretty good translation of the sophisticated naivete or the crude sophism that impels the movement of such a book and sets its tone. They also deprive it of any credibility. (SM, p. 62)

Derrida's reconstruction of the Hegelian history recounted by Fukuyama here is again faulty. For Fukuyama, the "contradiction" (the exclusion of what was not excluded) was only ever merely apparent, and depends entirely on a history of political liberalism that he rejects (one damn pillar after another). According to Fukuyama, what is needed to see the contradiction as merely apparent is the perspective of "a higher understanding of modern liberalism" (EH, p. 191): namely, one where the Anglo-Saxon development takes place not before but within the history of the struggle for rational recognition – a history which unfolds in stages and which slowly brings into view a final form of political existence in "the universal and homogenous state" ("universal" because it grants recognition to all citizens simply on the basis of their humanity; "homogenous" because it abolishes the distinction between political masters and slaves in conditions of *isothymia*). Derrida, however, cites Fukuyama's affirmation of Kojève's "important truth" to suggest that the post-War societies of America and Europe which rest on the "two pillars" of economics (liberal capitalism) and recognition (liberal democracy), not only *herald* that end, but *attain* it.

Derrida takes the "important truth" that Fukuyama wants to endorse as a claim to cognisance of the "observable event" of a political reality in America and Europe that would mark the actual arrival of the end of history in those places (SM, p. 62). But Kojève's point about America and Europe in the twentieth century is actually drawn on by Fukuyama as part of an historical claim about the totally unattained – but still Hegelian – condition of early liberalism in the eighteenth and nineteenth centuries, and its movement into the twentieth century. The "important truth" was that a Lockean grounding was in reality part of an ongoing Hegelian process. Moreover, with regard to the post-War world,

Fukuyama does not think America and Europe have realised the Hegelian ideal either, even as they embody its principles. As Derrida in fact acknowledges, for Fukuyama, "contemporary democracies face any number of serious problems" (EH, p. xxi), and there are various ways in which Fukuyama thinks it falls short of the Hegelian ideal, and fails adequately to embody its principles.

Derrida's charge that the book lacks "any credibility" depends on his reading Fukuyama as wanting his cake and eating it: Fukuyama's wanting to assert both that the end of history has actually arrived (the "important truth") and that it is a yet to be attained ideal ("serious problems"). As we have seen, Fukuyama certainly regards it as without serious competitor. But the only thing he claims to have actually arrived at is an understanding or consciousness of the teleology of history and its ideal end. That is what has actually happened, as it were. And Derrida might have recognised a certain credibility to this – to see what is attained in reality as "a heralding sign or promise" (SM, p. 63). For Fukuyama, the becoming-actual of liberal democracy in certain parts of the world (with all its actual defects) is the unfolding outcome in our time of a long-run history which heralds or promises an ideal end in the universal and homogenous state which could not be improved on. Where it is not actual it is ideal, and where it is actual-but-not-ideal…it is still ideal. That's Fukuyama's credible claim: not that "today's stable democracies are without injustice and serious social problems" but that "the ideal of liberal democracy could not be improved on". The problems we still see today are, in his view, a matter of "incomplete implementation" of the "principles of liberty and equality" not a "flaw in the principles" (EH, p. xi). And he pleads that we do not get "sidetracked" by pointing to all the terrible things and shortcomings that still make our own history one of ongoing injustices (EH, p. 13).

VII

The assertion by Kojève that Fukuyama says contains an "important truth" was even more boldly expressed by Kojève elsewhere when he claimed that world history had effectively ended in 1806: the principles of liberty and equality that emerged in the wake of the French Revolution "represented [for Kojève] an end point of human ideological development" (EH, p. 66). But far from reading this as a simple record of the "observable event" of the attained end of history, Fukuyama stresses that what has been attained belongs only to the realm of ideas or consciousness – the emergence of certain principles – and is as yet incomplete in the real world. So Fukuyama carefully distances himself and Kojève from what he calls Kojève's "intransigent" assertion (EH, xxi). One has to read through "layers of irony" to see the point of the "important truth" (EH, p. 66).

But Derrida does not want to be fobbed off with pleas not to get sidetracked, and insists against Fukuyama that he (Fukuyama) has to sideline "all the evidence that bears massive witness to the fact that neither the United States nor the European Community has attained the perfection of the universal State or of liberal democracy, nor have they even come close" (SM, p. 63). Well, Fukuyama did not claim it had attained perfection, and I'm not sure what the criterion would be for "coming close" either. You would have to be a pretty poor witness of observable events not to recognise that they have come closer to it than some other parts of the world, and perhaps close enough for Fukuyama, quite reasonably, to suppose that real – if always fragile and reversible – progress was being made in the movement to the end. Indeed, at the time Derrida wrote his text on Fukuyama there was also "all the evidence" that developments for the better had begun to take place elsewhere too – evidence that Derrida personally bore witness to when he was imprisoned by the Czechoslovakian police State and said to himself "This barbarism could last for centuries…" (SM, p. 70). Derrida had absolutely no regrets about the passing of Soviet Communism. No qualification needs to be made, no regret needs to be sounded, concerning "the actual collapse of those totalitarian states…that gave themselves the figure of Marxism" (SM, p. 70), the passing of the "totalitarian terror in all the Eastern countries" (SM, p. 15), the "totalitarian monstrosity" (SM, p. 88) whose power had been sustained "at the cost of millions and millions" of lives and lives lived in fear (SM, p. 30), and whose "terrifying failures" (SM, p. 91) and "cadaverous rigour" (SM, p. 105) was not a mere "perversion" of Marx but the "deployment of an essential logic present at the birth" (SM, p. 91), a logic that meant Derrida would want to produce an inheritance for us (for a generation whose world had been, as we have seen, shaped and misshaped by the history of the Marxist "*coup*") that could and should effectively disassociate itself from "*almost everything*" in its political legacy (SM, p. 89, emphasis in original). And doubtless, Fukuyama would feel considerable sympathy with that thought.

In the end, it is really all about the sense of an end. The head-to-head between Fukuyama and Derrida over the facts about democratic progress belongs ultimately to a very intimate difference between them over their understanding of democracy and its ideal concept – and of Derrida's fundamental concern that Fukuyama's conception, no less than "almost everything" in Marx, *deprives it of a future*. This is the real root of the differences between them. And there is, Derrida thinks, a "spirit" of Marx that needs to be retained if our own understanding – and cultivation – of democracy is not to share the tragic fate of Marxist orthodoxy.

The crux here is between a commitment to a democratic *teleology* in Fukuyama that cannot but risk autoimmunity in its own *megalothymia*, and, on the other hand, a commitment to a democratic *promise* in Derrida which claims that there is no ideally adequate or finally "complete implementation" of liberty and equality that would be immune to disorder or abuse of power. It is not that Derrida thinks that democracy, properly thought, escapes the risk of autoimmunity: absolutely nothing does. (Derrida is anything but an optimist in this respect.) Rather, his claim is that there is a certain kind of hospitality to autoimmunity in democracy, which is a genuinely good thing. This is a trait that he finds expressed most continuously and most radically in "a certain spirit" of Marxism, and this is what, in his view, we should want to preserve and cultivate in its political legacy, even as we extract ourselves from "almost everything" in it; namely, a will to self-critique that never ends:

> To continue to take inspiration from a certain spirit of Marxism would be to keep faith with what has always made of Marxism in principle and first of all a radical critique, namely a procedure ready to undertake its self-critique. This critique wants itself to be in principle and explicitly open to its own transformation, re-evaluation, self-reinterpretation. (SM, p. 88)

Derrida conceives this Marxist spirit as internal to the "ideal" concept of democracy itself. As the commitment to public deliberations and decisions over matters of public concern, democracy must be understood as having its content applied to itself, as part of its own ideal content. That is to say, democracy itself, as an undeniable "matter of public concern", retains within itself (as part of its "ideal" identity) the ongoing promise of self-critique, and hence bears within its "ideal" content a certain void: a space left open for "something that remains to be thought and to come" (OH, p. 78).

This is a concrete commitment to democratic critique as self-critique which never ends, and which it wants never to end, and hence for which, *pace* Fukuyama, there is no last word, no final end, no complete or ideal implementation – but only an imminent and ongoing promise. Derrida finds a passing moment in Fukuyama's text that (along with some confusion) attests to this when he (Fukuyama) states that the "current trend toward liberalism...*promises* to be victorious in the long run" [EH, p. 212 emphasis added]" (SM, p. 66).

It is for this reason, and not because he supposes the concept to outline some ideal future in which it would have finally been perfected and implemented, that when Derrida speaks of democracy; and its ideal concept he speaks of it as an elliptical expression for "democracy to come":

> The expression "democracy to come" takes into account the absolute and intrinsic historicity of the only system that welcomes in itself, in its very concept, that expression of autoimmunity called the right to self-critique and perfectibility. Democracy is the only system, the only constitutional paradigm, in which, in principle, one has or assumes the right to criticize everything publicly, including the idea of democracy, its concept, its history, and its name. Including the idea of the constitutional paradigm and the absolute authority of law. It is thus the only paradigm that is universalizable, whence its chance and its fragility. But in order for this historicity – unique among all political systems – to be complete, it must be freed not only from the Idea in the Kantian sense but from all teleology, all onto-theo-teleology. (R, pp. 86–7)

Democracy, by granting (promising) free-speech, free-assembly, free press, free travel, an electoral calendar, where the possibility of change in government is never excluded, and so on: this form of political organisation is the only one that calls for its own critique, admits to its own revisability, and its openness to challenge in its present institutional or constitutional and legal set-up. Here "autoimmunity", self-destroying, becomes a source of perfectibility rather than suicide, though the latter is not and is never excluded: the election by a democratic majority of fanatics who present themselves as democrats but then, in its name, suspend or destroy it, always remains a standing threat. America, Hungary, Turkey, India, Russia have all shown signs of such an unravelling in our time. And, of course, as we shall see in some detail in Chapter 6, Brexit Britain has given rise to its own brand of fanaticism and democratic foot-shooting too.

Equality and freedom (including freedom of speech, freedom of the press, and so on) remain central concepts here, and again as "promises". Like Berlin, Derrida conceives these principles as incommensurable ideals facing each other, demanding calculations and trade-offs of one against the other, with no "ideally adequate" equilibrium or implementation. However, and again like Berlin, he also conceives their mutual co-implication as implicit in the modern affirmation of universal freedom. The "*all* are free" of modernity, already means "all are *equally* free" and thus draws political equality into anything we are willing to think of as freedom. Hence, while remaining incommensurable values, "equality is not *always* an opposing or rival term *beside, facing,* or *around* freedom, like a calculable measure...beside, facing, or around an incommensurable, incalculable, and universal freedom. Not at all. As soon as everyone...is...free, equality becomes an integral part of freedom" (R, p. 49).

The thought of "equality of liberty" that founds liberalism thus also founds the "all" of the *demos* of a democracy as the ones who should share equally in this universal freedom. But we have already seen that democracy as majority rule (democratic government) does not in the least exclude the radical loss of liberty, for one, some or, indeed, (nearly) all. As Berlin puts it "if I commit suicide, am I the less dead because I have taken my own life freely?" (TC, p. 164). It is, I think, with the threat of this (bad) kind of autoimmunity in view that Derrida's description of democracy as "democracy to come" insists on a very specific condition required for an understanding of democratic history – the coming-to-be-democratic of a regime – to be regarded as "complete": it must be "freed from all teleology, all onto-theo-teleology" – and hence, in Berlinian terms, freed from every monism of the proper end of history or the end of Man. Calling for democracy *without* such ideal end is thus not the "indifferent" (metapolitical) position that Fukuyama takes it to be (EH, p. 160), but (politically) position-taking. Complete democracy (which must not be confused here with the idea of a final form of ideal adequacy) implies the interruptability of every heading, implies that the possibility of *another* heading is always possible. It is a politics freed from, and opposed to, all teleology of a final end.

A politics freed from all teleology is not just hospitable to "pluralism" in a democratic society (a social space open to diverse ways in which one can be) but, equally importantly, to its own way of being a regime: it is a regime that *is* one only insofar as it is not *one*. That is, a democratic space that really is one – a democratic space worthy of the name – wants to remain open to unpredictable self-transformations up to and including its own. Democracy on this model *is* "democracy to come"; that "messianism without messianism" which keeps hold of and cultivates the promise of "this eschatological relation to the to-come" but does so with respect to "an alterity that cannot be anticipated" (SM, p. 65). There is an "indifference" to content here but it is not "an *attitude* of indifference" (SM, p. 73). Rather it is an "affirmative thinking of the messianic and emancipatory promise *as* promise: as *promise* and not as onto-theological or teleo-eschatological program or design" (SM, p. 75).

We will come back to this in detail in the final part of this book. But it should be clear already that what is at stake here is the difference within the thinking of the history of democracy between every monism that wants or anticipates a determinate end (*telos*) of democratic politics, and one which wants there to be no end of democratic politics, wants politics to have a future for us (where that "us" is also open to development, transformation and re-politicisation). As I have indicated, this "empty" promise is anything but an empty promise.

The disagreements between Derrida and Fukuyama thus finally turn on their respective conceptions of "complete" democracy. As I say, in the end, it is all about the end. For Derrida, what matters most is freeing the political space from a certain desire for its own projected completeness, a teleological "end of politics" that would be an end of Man. Such an end is precisely what Fukuyama has in view with his "ideal" end of history in the "complete implementation" of the values of equality and liberty in a liberal democracy. For Derrida any such projection of an end – whether "in the Kantian sense", which means it is an inexhaustible regulative norm through which one only ever (endlessly) approaches an end, or some more substantive conception of an in-principle attainable condition of ideal adequacy – is necessarily hostile to the unpredictable arrival beyond anticipation, and dangerously hospitable to the "tyrannical and dictatorial manifestations of what [Fukuyama] calls '*megalothymia*'". It negates the "spirit" of ongoing critique as self-critique which gives democracy its life, its chance, its future – and which Derrida finds in a spirit of Marxism that he wants to save. In short, unless we can keep that spirit alive, the drive to the end (*telos*) of democracy effectively drives us only to the end (*terminus*) of democracy. Interrupting that drive to the end – striving (endlessly, in every here-and-now) to keep the future of democracy open to its own unpredictable self-transformations, its open-ended perfectibility, its openness to unknown democratic friends to come – this, somewhat paradoxically, turns out to be the best way of maintaining rather than negating its promise (see Bennington, 2007). Democracy, to attain completeness, to be the "democracy to come" it promises, requires the empty promise of a messianism without content – and not the "good news" that the end is in sight, still less that it is attained.

VIII

In Fukuyama's references to "members" of (what was then) "the European Community", it was really only the nationally attained order of each, the attained liberal democratic order of each nation, that was under consideration (for better and worse). What he never seriously considered at that time was that the (then) European Community itself constitutes a development of the increasing democratisation of European life and politics. In the next part of this book, I will look at this extraordinary development in post-War Europe: from the European Coal and Steel Community of five western European nations, to the European Community of 12 western European nations, to the enlarged European Union of 28 (now 27), including many of the central and eastern European nations that had been cut adrift by the Iron Curtain. However, I will not do so only with the post-War developments in view. As I have indicated, before being a political construction, it had been already a philosophical projection. To understand the development of the European Union in our time I want to step back into the philosophical opening of its practical commencement.

I will begin that step back, once again, to Nietzsche, and to his anticipation of the integration of the old nations of Europe into a league of nations or (old model) Swiss-style "federation". Nietzsche's practical interest in this federation only goes so far, leaving it to "future diplomats" to sort out its proper order (HH, p. 344). As the history of the formation of European institutions has shown, however, this is no small task. Not least because some of those "diplomats" of integration might have designs of their own in view, seeking not merely to form a Federation of States, but a supranational Federal State. That Federal State idea is a profoundly "modern" conception of the rational *telos* of European integration. It should, I think, be resisted, and taking my cue from a surprising twist in Nietzsche's tale of European political development, I will defend a rational-*telos*-interrupting alternative. This alternative was first framed, in fact, some one hundred years before Nietzsche came on the scene, and by an unlikely figure in this context. At that point in the discussion, as I reach forward to a vision of European political integration worth constructing beyond a still-too-modern Federalist *telos*, I will step back again, back to the thinker who did more than anyone to give strength and speed to the modern thought of the rational *telos* of Man: back to Kant, and to an even more surprising twist in his own tale of Europe's "modern" promise.

PART III
European union

5
BECOMING EUROPEAN

The democratisation of Europe is a resistless force

– Friedrich Nietzsche

I

The conception of democracy as "democracy to come" that Derrida defends is itself prefigured in the work of a thinker who is often thought of as one of democracy's most critical opponents: in the work of Nietzsche. As we saw briefly in the opening chapter, Nietzsche conceives the history of Europe's modernity as inseparable from the coming-to-dominance of "democrats", their "democratic taste" and "modern ideas". Most people today would regard this, not unreasonably, as basically a good thing. Nietzsche does not entirely demure from that: he too has his disgust for, and is anything but nostalgic for, the "good old days", the old-world-order of Christian ecclesiastical power. And he conceived the "democratic Enlightenment" as an effort "in grand fashion" to weaken that world-order (BGE, p. 4). He also regarded the movement of democratisation as, in any case, a "resistless force" (HH, p. 329). However, as we shall see in detail in this chapter, what he sees in the unfolding historical reality of "the democratic movement in Europe" is the spreading out a version of itself that is deeply problematic: the transformation of Europeans (and those who live in the lands where Europe's influence predominates) into "stunted little animals", herd animals. In what he called the "misarchism" of its flight from the Christian ecclesiastical power and the divine right of Kings of the Middle Ages, the promise of democracy was being compromised within the very space in which it was being freed up.

And yet, for Nietzsche, it is not all over for Europe or its democratic movement. The "levelling" mediocrity of "modern" democratic taste may be, increasingly, our reality, but that very historical reality has within itself (and not simply opposed to it), its own "beyond": a democratic desire which is, within all of this, already the opposite of all of this. In *The Wanderer and his Shadow*, Nietzsche articulates this conceptually by defining democracy in a way that sounds exactly like the opposite of a herd animal society. It is a political regime that wants and tries, he says, "to create and guarantee [for its citizens] as much independence as possible in their opinions, way of life and occupation" (HH, p. 344). This is something he affirms as a foundation for a European culture that has been genuinely freed from the Middle Ages and the power of the Church. But he affirms this in a distinctively futural way. When he speaks of this democracy, he says, "I speak of democracy as of something to come" (HH, p. 345). This other democracy, this democracy to come, is as far as possible from herd animal egalitarianism, where individuals are reduced to organs of the community, but is very close to Berlin's pluralism as an ideal, Derrida's messianism without messianism, and Cavell's perfectionism democratised: it is a society that wants to welcome the fact that the "ends of men" are both many and fundamentally unpredictable – and that wants a political order that promises this in the three-fold sense he outlines.

Nietzsche embraced the possibility of such a development for European democracy, not, however, as an end in itself (as I will – but only as a no-end in itself) but because it opens the space for a few exceptional people – he will call them "real philosophers" – to emerge who ultimately promise something even more ambitious. Once again, these real philosophers, like the old ones, will articulate the possibility of a brighter future for all humanity – and, once again, first of all, for Europeans: a future beyond the shadow of the death of God. As Nietzsche anticipated that some would, I will stop short of his more exalted vision.

Beginning where we are, however, what, if anything, is happening now that offers hope for a cure for Europe's all-at-sea-sickness? There is, Nietzsche thinks, a more or less unstoppable process underway in the very democratic movement in Europe that created that sickness in the first place, a movement that points beyond its currently attained democratic-herd-animal condition: namely, the overflowing of national democracy (and the nationalist deformations of European subjectivity which that cultivates) towards a new supranational order in Europe, and a newly cosmopolitan (if in certain respects still nationally shaped or inflected) European subjectivity to come.

Running the irresistible programme of the process of democratisation of Europe into a future projection, Nietzsche predicted the emergence in Europe of an increasingly dominant and prosperous "middle class" with more interest in "novelty and experiment" than it had piety for the "historic memories" of the old nation-states (HH, p. 344). In this context of a weakening sense of national belonging and hence also a weakening of historic national rivalries, the next "practical result" of European democratisation would be, Nietzsche predicted, the development of political preferences which would "inseparably connect" "home" and "foreign" politics in Europe in a way that would make the former far less beholden to destructive upheavals from the latter. In what might be called, institutionally speaking, a kind of (old model) Swissification of Europe, Nietzsche predicted: "a European league of nations within which each individual nation, delimited by the proper geographical frontiers, has the position of a canton with its separate rights" (HH, p. 344). Nietzsche is among those who anticipated the coming into being of what today is making its way in the (still fragile and unstable) form of the European Union.

The experience of the disastrous interplay of home and foreign politics – the tendency of foreign politics (war) to devastate any chance of democracies delivering sustained prosperity at home – was certainly a powerful motivation in the post-War process of European integration and the post-Cold-War formation of the European Union. Developing in a relatively continuous ("neo-functionalist") way from the institutions of the European Coal and Steel Community, formally established in 1951 by the Treaty of Paris, and signed by the governments of Belgium, France, West Germany, Italy, the Netherlands, and Luxembourg, it became the European Union by name in 1993, with the Maastricht Treaty, signed by the by-then twelve member states of the European Community: the six founding members plus Denmark, Greece, Ireland, Portugal, Spain, and the United Kingdom. It has since undergone considerable enlargement, with a further sixteen countries, including many from the former Soviet bloc, joining by 2013. Even if not single-handedly, the European Union has been central to delivering over half-a-century of peace to an historically war-torn continent, and has achieved levels of political and economic integration that would have seemed miraculous at the end of the Second World War.

In 2016, the UK held a referendum on its own membership of the EU, which came down decisively (if not overwhelmingly) on the Leave side. In many respects, the UK hardly deserved to be a proper member anyway, often seeking an "opt out" from key developments. That being said, it had also been a significant architect of integration, perhaps especially of the single market and its "four freedoms" (the free movement of goods, capital, services, and labour), and of enlargement. Britain took its sovereignty into the Union, and argued a lot, but also contributed a lot. Whether it can effectively "take back control" by leaving remains to be seen.

The watchwords for the EU's development, the words one finds affirmed again and again in the treaties that have brought it into being, are and for nearly its whole history have been: "ever closer union among the peoples of Europe". These are beautiful vague words. And questions concerning their practical realisation, their political translation, are internal to the Union's history too. Today they are often supposed to affirm a quite specific political sense: a post-national movement towards supranational government, a process with its *telos* in the formation of a Federal or quasi-Federal State, with a European central government. That interpretation, however, tends to obscure that this kind of federalist political project (and any supranational institutions that it gives rise to) is ultimately in service to what is, first of all, a cosmopolitan hope between "peoples" (plural): the hope to promote conditions of mutual trust and understanding among them.

Of course, one might think that the best – indeed, perhaps the only rational – way of bringing that about would be through the formation of something like a Federal State or a kind of United States of Europe. But that's a different question. In the next chapter, I will tackle that question head-on, but there is no doubt that the Federal State idea has been a powerfully guiding ambition for many. The alternative – a considerably less State-like formation, a Federation of States or United Europe of States – is regarded by federalist-minded people as (in Jürgen Habermas's words) "weak" and "sterile" in comparison (BNR, pp. 314–5): a mediocre ambition at best.

Mediocre. From the Latin "*mediocris*", meaning of middle height or degree, and somewhat crazily derived from "*medius*", meaning middle, and "*ocris*", meaning rugged mountain. In relation to persons, the mediocre are, in any case, a certain kind of "people of the middle". Indeed, precisely the kind that Nietzsche thinks the "English" are. On the other hand, "people of the middle" are precisely the kind of people who Nietzsche thinks *all* Europeans are – or at least all the Europeans who are on his mind when the future of Europe is on his mind. So, what was on Nietzsche's mind, when he turned his mind to Europe?

People of the middle were on his mind. This will be Nietzsche's figure for the peoples he thinks of as the major Europe-producers, the ones who have spread their own spirit, or something of their own spirit, beyond their own national borders and across the whole, most effectively making a mark on the whole *as* a whole. They are the Germans, the French, and the English. However, as we shall see, he will think each of these very differently in this figure. And this raises a topic that I have deliberately left in some kind of suspension hitherto. The Europe whose self-understanding is the theme of this book is the "Europe of the nations", and there is only so long one can speak about Europe as such and as a whole without stumbling into its internal diversity, and wondering whether there is such a whole. Of course, there is more than one kind of diversity inside Europe. But if any diversity has indelibly marked its geography, whether its physical geography or what Husserl called its "spiritual geography", it is national differences. Discourses on such differentiation are typically a mix of the funny and the hopeless. Descriptions of "national character" are the stuff of fantasy, and are probably best avoided. Nietzsche does not only not avoid them, he revels in them, and no national peoples that he discusses come out too well. I think most readers today would find such an attempt by an English writer mostly insufferable: it is all too likely to descend into a speech by Bertie Wooster ("Temperamental blighters, these Frenchmen" (RHJ, p. 212)), or (more likely in English academia) a studied exercise in self-loathing. Impossible.

And yet, doubtless, it is in some way already happening and unavoidable, right here, right now. This will have been an English book on Europe. I cannot step outside the thing. Nietzsche makes no attempt to hide his own German belonging as he surveys the culture of the people of the middle. Fortunately, since he is hard on everyone, the reader is not left with a sense of insufferable parochialism or (self-congratulatory or self-loathing) exceptionalism, and he (mostly) gets away with it.

Nevertheless, his account is still German. Indeed, as I hope to show, the very fact that he turns his mind to Europe at the very moment and in the very movement in which he turns his mind to Germany is a very German turn of mind. Moreover, the figure of Europe as "the middle" and its people as "the people of the middle" is itself a German variation of a European invariable. The figure of Europe: what is it? Derrida, in some part an outsider to all this, summarises the not-simply-national formations of this figure that he has seen:

> In its physical geography, and in what has often been called, by Husserl for example, its spiritual geography, Europe has always recognized itself as a cape or headland, *either* as the advanced extreme of a continent, to the west and south (the land's end, the advanced point of a Finistère, Europe of the Atlantic or of the Greco-Latino-Iberian shores of the Mediterranean), the point of departure for discovery, invention, and colonization, *or* as the very center of this tongue in the form of a cape, the Europe of the middle [*milieu*], coiled up, indeed compressed along a Greco-Germanic axis, at the very center of the center of the cape. (OH, pp. 19–20, emphasis in original)

Derrida italicises an either/or between the figure of the advanced extreme and the figure of the middle, between a Europe of the sea and a Europe of the land. This stressed disjunction will, as we can see in this passage, and as we will discuss further in this chapter, typically get thought in terms of a rivalry between (mostly French) Latinity and Germanity over the inheritance of Greece as the origin of Europe. But there is a west/south alternative within the first figure that Derrida does not stress: *either* Europe of the Atlantic *or* Europe of the Mediterranean. If England or (I would prefer to say in this context) Britain lies anywhere in this figure of Europe it will be in this western "Atlantic" region – a region from which it might "spiritually" spread itself not only eastwards, into the continent, but also westwards, right across to the other side of the "pond". It is a European median figure that one can lose sight of. Nietzsche, within the German figure of a Europe of the middle, does keep a certain middle "England" in his sights. Indeed, he finds it situated in his time right in the middle of that (German) Europe of the middle. As we adventure with Nietzsche into the theme of European integration and its future-producers, I will keep an eye on this "England" too. I preserve an interest in it, and do so (I hope) as a good European. Right ho! Off we go.

II

As we have seen, Nietzsche is a thinker of democracy as something yet to come. He is also a thinker of Europe as something yet to come, a thinker of Europe as having a future not just in some already well and widely anticipated "tomorrow", but from a distance that looks beyond that horizon towards "the day after tomorrow". And Nietzsche is not just predicting a happy outcome for this Europe, but wants to contribute to making it so. He writes from some kind of "today" with the untimely ambition that the day after tomorrow will belong to *him*.

Nietzsche's time-horizon-busting speech for the future of Europe takes its bearings from the movement of modern political democratisation which was beginning to dominate Europe in his "today", and which was blowing apart the Europe of "the good old days" (BGE, p. 157). As we shall see, he finds very little to cheer in that development. Nevertheless, he sees in its unstoppable unfolding the potential for the creation of a European configuration beyond its present configuration, and in particular, beyond what he regards as the stupidly nationalistic configuration which most marks its "today". Nietzsche reads inside its present form a movement towards the democratisation of Europe itself, and the creation of a European political unity beyond petty nationalisms. This remains to come, but it is (he thinks) beginning: a feeling and desire is already underway among the most cultured Europeans. And it expresses an emerging spirit in Europe of a Europe that "*wants to become one*" (BGE, 169, emphasis in original).

Like Kant a little over one hundred years earlier, Nietzsche himself has a feeling that a new political order will emerge out of the old world-order of the Europe of the nations: a new and unprecedented European political union. Unlike Kant, however, Nietzsche does not see this development as an unambiguous good. This movement towards the integration of Europe will not, he thinks, produce free modern citizens in republican States living together in peace, but rather, and for the most part, will only accelerate the worst: the most repellent "levelling and mediocritizing" of European peoples, making Europeans into serviceable herd animals, "weak willed highly employable workers". The general trend of European democratisation is simply a movement towards the production of a type that is, as he puts it, "prepared for *slavery* in the subtlest sense" (BGE, p. 154).

On the other hand, this movement is not simply a linear story of ever greater-levelling among the peoples of Europe. The same democratic conditions may also, although "involuntarily", pave the way for something Nietzsche thinks really is worth hoping for, something newly promising. They are also the conditions for producing "a new supra-national and nomadic type of man"; people "detached from any *definite* milieu" who will have as their distinction "a maximum of the art of and power of adaptation" (BGE, pp. 153–4). And some among these new Europeans could eventually form "a new caste" that can "rule" this newly integrated European space. Ultimately, Nietzsche thinks that the process of democratisation will give birth to a new "synthesis" of old European spirits (plural) (BGE, 170); a new type of cosmopolitan "plant 'Man'" (BGE, p. 54) capable of bringing Europe under the domination of a new spirit (singular). While democratisation thus brings about conditions for slavery in the "subtlest sense" for most Europeans, he also thinks it will likely bring about something like its exact (and hence equally subtle, or as he puts it "spiritual") opposite too:

"the breeding of *tyrants*" (BGE, p. 154), a new ruling spiritual hegemony. It is a new single will to form and forge a new kind of Man on the foundations of the process of democratisation, a new kind of Man in the democracy to come.

So, even though it is predominantly a movement of weakening and levelling, it is also a process in which, in virtue of their "unprejudiced schooling" (having liberated themselves from the deformations of a narrowly national formation), and as a consequence of the "tremendous multiplicity of practice, art and mask" made available to them in the new synthesis of spirits, "strong individuals" can emerge in Europe once more, "stronger and richer than has perhaps ever happened before" (BGE, p. 154. These will be the Europe-producers among the "Europeans of the day after tomorrow" (BGE, p. 128; see also BGE, p. 124). And as I say, even if Nietzsche is in some sense predicting these events, he is also participating in it, sending himself off in a future-producing way: "the day after tomorrow belongs to me", says Nietzsche (AC, p. 114). Nietzsche, here and now, elects to speak to these friends of the day after tomorrow, who, he insists, he "as yet knows none" (GM, p. 135). But, as Derrida notes, he sends himself off to speak to those unknown friends *so that there may be such friends*, to "form and forge", to "conjure" them at a distance of time of who knows how long, in writings that "produce an event" "here and now" out of the possibility of its own "will have been" a speech to these friends: "a *teleiopoetic propulsion*...produces an event, sinking into the darkness of a friendship which is not yet" (PF, p. 43). Once again, a messianism without determinate messianism.

Europe's modern self-understanding had been framed by a profoundly *archeo-teleo-eschatological* philosophical discourse of universal history: a movement of the history of "Man" from primitive and savage animality to rational and civilised humanity, with European humanity at the head. In Nietzsche's writing on Europe, another philosophical (i.e. epic) discourse of European humanity makes its way. And it makes its way through a new hidden hand, a new cunning of reason that belongs within the tidal wave of "the democratic movement in Europe" (BGE, p. 153). It is into this wave that Nietzsche sends an untimely message-in-a-bottle, gathering the forces that belong to "we good Europeans" of today towards the unknown friends of Europe the day after tomorrow. And yet, despite everything, it is still a universal history, and even a "beyond modern" variation of the old European discourse of Europe's modernity: "I'm glad to hear that our sun is moving rapidly towards the constellation of *Hercules*, and I hope that the people of this earth will act like the sun. With us in front, we good Europeans! –" (BGE §243).

III

As a preliminary to following Nietzsche's discussion of the Europe-producers, I want briefly to raise the question: why Europe? Why the emphasis on "we good Europeans"? In his insistent opposition, in a newly united German nation, to the rising nationalist appeal to "we good Germans", why wouldn't Nietzsche say, simply, "we good *whoevers*"? One might want to excuse Nietzsche by referring to the "context" of his times: the world was not so big then, the horizon for his thinking was European because his world was. But that is nonsense. Nietzsche's work is peppered with non-European references, and often, typically even, with great admiration. Nietzsche certainly thinks that Europe has been a site of "great things" (BGE, p. 13) – but he does not think that Europe has a monopoly on that at all: Asia and Egypt are mentioned in the same breath. So why the initial limit to thinking the newly cosmopolitan plant "Man" to come to the indefinite but definitively European *milieu*? Is it white racism? Eurocentric parochialism? Modest pragmatism? My suspicion is that it is, above all, German.

The German question ("What is Germany?") casts a profoundly determining shadow over Nietzsche's reflections on Europe. My basic hypothesis is that when Germany thinks itself, it thinks itself in an essentially European horizon, a European horizon that it invents and projects (there is, after all, no "natural reality" of a European space) as the immediate context of its own spiritual destiny. Germany will not have been alone in this, nor even the first to do so. Indeed, no European peoples have ever been able entirely to do otherwise: there is an *agon* of (not only but especially national) projections internal to Europe's cultural identity. Nevertheless, there is, I think, a peculiar intimacy between the German question and the European question, or at least a distinctive shaping of both in that relation.

We know how difficult it is to comprehend how the horrors of National Socialism could possibly belong within German history except as an absolute aberration. But with the invitation to think Europe as a German thing, I do not mean this to imply that we must always be on our guard against what Habermas has called a "fatal" temptation for Germany to "succumb to power fantasies" of achieving "'semi-hegemonic status'" in Europe (LT, p. 18). No, the European horizon is just as visible in Habermas's own call for Germany finally to give up those fantasies as some kind of repentance for its indulging them. Habermas may make a more welcome gesture when he says "that it is in our [German] national interest to permanently avoid" them, since not doing so leads only to "catastrophe" (LT, p. 19). However, his call for rapid steps to be taken towards the formation of a "supranational democracy" at the European level, and the crossing of "the red line of the classical understanding of [national] sovereignty" that this would entail (LT, p. 14), is fully part of this German story insofar as Germany's own national interests are conceived as inseparably connected to that distinctively European future. These intertwined fates belong, I think, to "the German question", making it at once entangled with what Habermas calls "the European question" (LT, p. 18).

There is a wonderful illustration of this mutual implication in a "New History" of Germany by Hagen Schulze which draws explicitly on the Nietzschean contribution that we will be exploring. Writing shortly after the second German unification, in 1990, Schulze maintained that, in fact, the German question had now finally been answered:

> For the first time in history, the German nation state is "fulfilled in the present," as Ernest Renan said with reference to France. Nietzsche once observed, "The Germans are from the day before yesterday and the day after tomorrow – *as yet they have no today*" [BGE, p. 154]." This was so in his day because from the time the idea of a nation state was born at the beginning of the nineteenth century, the nation and the state were always two different things. The early nationalists dreamed that they might recreate the medieval empire, a vast territory including Bohemia and northern Italy, but led by Germans. Later, many people regarded Bismarck's Small German state as only a down payment on a Great German empire, which they would own in the fullness of time. The Weimar Republic was torn apart in a struggle to undo the Treaty of Versailles and restore the pre-1919 eastern border, while the partial nation that was the Federal Republic declared it politically imperative to re-establish the frontiers of 1937.
>
> In other words, the form of the state at any given moment was never enough; it was always just a provisional solution, a way station *en route* to a utopia that could be attained either through force of not at all. This was why the expression of German nationalism and the search for identity took their particular neurotic forms. That phase of German history is now over. As of October 3, 1990, the Federal Republic of Germany is the only conceivable form that a state for the German nation could take; it has no legitimate competition whatever in the minds of its citizens. For the first time, the question once posed by Ernst Moritz Arndt – "What is the German fatherland?" – now has an unambiguous and lasting answer. (GNH, pp. 336–7)

That would seem to be it then. Not quite. Turn a couple of pages, to the final page of this "New History", and this "unambiguous and lasting answer" suddenly begins to look a little more like just one more "way station" towards a new version of the old answer:

> As long as no corresponding institutions legitimated by democratic elections are available on a European level, there is no alternative to [the German nation-state] in sight. (GNH, p. 340)

In other words, an alternative to the German nation-state as the proper sphere of German life is in sight, and in fact already available today on the horizon of tomorrow – and it belongs "on a European level". In that democratic event's coming, Germany might then really finally become what it is already beginning to be: "a necessary part of the European system, even as a future major power" (GNH, p. 338).

Schultz is hopeful that "Germany's ties to Europe will hold it steady" (GNH, p. 340). This is a common and totally understandable theme in post-War Germany, alive as it is to the anxiety that Germany might, once more, as Habermas puts it, try to create a "German Europe instead of a Germany firmly integrated 'into Europe'" (LT, p. 19; see GNH, p. 340). This distinction between the Germanisation of Europe and the Europeanisation of Germany might seem to mark a break from the old anxieties surrounding the German question. Indeed, we tend to welcome the second and fear the first. However, it may be a distinction without much of a difference, especially if the Europeanisation in view is already something of a German projection. Even in political terms, it may not always be a significant contrast. Indeed, the more fearful version, which Nietzsche thought was already happening in certain respects (BGE, p. 156), can amount to almost the same thing as the welcome one, precisely by its stemming German nationalist tendencies within a finally united (if German projected) Europe. And the more welcome version, which Schultz and Habermas affirm, can amount to the same thing as the more fearful one when the German nation and its interests "holds the keys" to the success of the EU "in its hands" (LT, p. 16) as a "major power" (GNH, p. 338).

"Europe" and the idea of a "European Union" may be something of a German thing, but of course it is not only a German thing. Not only has it never long remained an uncontested German thing – other becoming-Europeans will have their own ideas – but as the French philosopher Philipe Lacoue-Labarthe has stressed, the German way of styling "Europe as a whole" is something whose development was "essentially induced by the French one" (HPP, p. 79). There is a fascinating tête-à-tête between France and Germany here, what Lacoue-Labarthe calls "a mimetic rivalry" that is played out in relation to the question of "the imitation of the Ancients" (HAP, p. 90). With both players conceiving Greek antiquity as the point of origin of a movement of world history that unfolds into Europe's modernity, Lacoue-Labarthe identifies two distinctive models of self-identification, French and German respectively, which are forged through the appropriation of that heritage, and through that the future of Europe. France, on the one hand, returns to Greece through "Latinity": the Roman and Renaissance imitation. The Germanic world, on the other hand, "situated beyond the *limes*" of Latinity, is faced with the choice, in Alfred Bäumler's words, "to be either the anti-Roman power of Europe or not to be" (HAP, p. 91). Germany finds its voice in this struggle over the appropriation of the Greeks, aspiring to create itself thereby *as* the "the creator of a Europe that will be more than a Roman colony" – and to do so through the inheritance of "an altogether different Greece" (HAP, p. 91). This other imitation finds its decisive expression in Winckelmann's famous invocation to the Germans to imitate the Ancients "in order to make ourselves inimitable in turn". In this "*Kulturkampf*" with French neo-classicism and republicanism (Greek-Roman-Christian-revolutionary), it became necessary for Germany "to 'invent' a Greece which had up to that point remained unimitated…which would allegedly be at the foundation of Greece itself… What the German imitation is seeking in Greece is the model – and therefore the possibility – of a pure emergence, of a pure originality: a model of self-formation" (HPP, p. 79).

One might begin to summarise all of this by recalling the Delphic Oracle's reply to Zeno: "Take on the colour of the dead" – which Zeno interpreted as "study the ancients"; repeat them. And then we have two models of self-formation: either the Latin model which is to do what they did in the sense of becoming like them in your ways (*paidea/humanitas*), or the German model which is to do what they did in the sense of becoming yourself in your own ways (autochthonous *Bildung*).

In his discussion of the German sword-in-the-tree called "Nothung" that cuts through Wagner's *Ring* cycle, Stephen Mulhall invites us to follow something of Nietzsche's claim to see "the Wagnerian representation of Wotan's overthrow...as itself the refounding of a new, non-Christian [ie. non-Latin, SG] culture that might run counter to the philistinism of contemporary *Germany* by reconnecting *Europe* to its sources in Greek culture" (SAS, p. 22, emphasis mine). Mulhall speaks here about Germany/Europe and its genealogy, not in political terms but philosophical terms: through its Greek philosophical origin. Germany, attaining itself in this appropriative way – through the authentic repetition of the inimitable rather than the mere imitation of the classics – would enable Europe too to attain to "the innermost course of its history" which, as Heidegger will insist, was "originally 'philosophical'" (WP, p. 31). Nietzsche came to think that "late Wagner" had lost his way and had begun to "preach *the road to Rome*" in his *Parsifal* (BGE, pp. 171–2). "Is this still German?" asks Nietzsche pointedly, and with barely disguised disgust, in a rhyme that closes the "Peoples and Fatherlands" chapter of *Beyond Good and Evil*. And he closes the rhyme by asking again "– Is this still German? – Reflect! And then your answer frame:– For what you hear is Rome – *Rome's faith in all but name!*" (BGE, p. 172).

But this Franco-German duo are not the only major players, not the only "great cantons" of Europe (HH, p. 344). Geophilosophically speaking there is an invariable, if sometimes set aside, third hand in this drama of the modern European political, a third party in the form of that most semi-detached of European places: Britain (what Nietzsche, like most who do recall it and do not set it aside, calls "England"). Always announcing a European Brexit of one kind or another, always ready to oppose itself to a "Continental" Europe that is itself (primarily) the divided German/French Europe, Britain too will have its say. I cited Mulhall's remarks on the sword-in-the-tree called "Nothung" a moment ago in part to help prepare to get this into view: for he goes on to note that the British Arthurian legend embodied in the (not actually the) sword-in-the-stone called "Excalibur" represents a myth of British national identity "that is historically constructed (and repeatedly reconstructed) in opposition to the very aspects of Northern European culture...with which [Wagner] proposes to reconstruct German life and values" – and hence, we might now say, with which he proposes to reconstruct European life and values (SAS, p. 22). Britain has never been wholly cut off from its Continent, nor always – in fact, rarely – omitted in practical considerations of European life and values. It remains the case, however, that both the philosophy and the politics of modern Europe has often exhibited a rather binary aspect: it is primarily a French and German affair over who will be (or will have been) the "creator of a Europe" (HAP, p. 91).

Nietzsche is a notable exception here: his own experimental "synthesis" of the "European of the future" (BGE, 170) is more or less entirely composed of a Germano-Franco-Britannic trio of Europe-producers, although with a significant debt to the Jews in Europe as well.

It will be an oddly framed synthesis, however, since what Nietzsche wants to *reject* in what belongs to everything "English" in the Europe of his time is...almost everything. Nevertheless, as we shall see, here, once more, almost everything is not everything. I will examine Nietzsche's take (down) on the English in the next chapter, and take special note of what, in the production of the new synthesis, takes on the colour of the English there. But we might already imagine an exemplary Britain in the "mimetic rivalry" we have been following. Unlike Germany, Britain had been (mostly) Romanised. But there was a decisive break with Rome. And it came (not with a religious revolution but) with the demand of an English King not to be dictated to by an overweening and corrupt foreign authority. (He wanted a divorce.) One might wonder if the modern "English" model of liberty as a political concept has its own corresponding and commendable form: not as "sovereignty" (of "the people"), and not a fantasy of "autochthony" (of "the people") either but, perhaps, freedom as "non-domination" (of *whoever*). "Take back control", as it was decisively expressed in the Brexit campaign of 2016. With respect to the mimetic *agon*, this would also imply a third way: that one can learn from the ancients – or indeed any other – but without thereby feeling oneself obliged to imitate them. Indeed.

Nietzsche's experimental synthesis turns out to be (largely) Germano-Franco-English and not exclusively Germano-French. But, if we ask why Nietzsche is so interested in a specifically European future, why he is the thinker of "we good Europeans" and not, say, "we good *whoevers*", we can simply say: Nietzsche is fundamentally a philosopher of Europe because, first of all, he is fundamentally...a German philosopher. And we other Europeans still have a lot to learn from him – up to a point.

IV

Europe is the name of a privileged site for Nietzsche, a site of "great things" (BGE, p. 13 and GM, p. 135). But it is now, in a time that is doubtless still our time, a site of degeneration and decay: those with a nose to smell it, those who have some reverence for its history, are aware, Nietzsche says, that the existence of European humanity has become something "indecent, dishonest, deceitful", marked now by what he labels its "feminism, weakness, cowardice" (GM, p. 135).

Most today are likely to see Nietzsche's hopes for a new ruling tyranny in Europe as a mark of political failure, and are equally likely to think that the advance of feminism within the democratisation of Europe is a distinctive mark of its political success. I know I do. By "feminism" Nietzsche will likely be thinking primarily of a movement that would encourage equality for women within the terms of a "modern" conception of progress: so that women might come to resemble men, taking the position that had been hitherto been reserved for men, or males first, in that supposedly universal history. Nevertheless, Nietzsche is aware that his own words are "bound to make a harsh sound and not easy for ears to hear" (BGE, p. 106). It is a massive provocation against the prevailing political tide. The idea that the most important, leading and governing principles of society should be based on what we have in common, and hence governed by appeals to what is in the best interest of the community, revolts Nietzsche who sees in it a quasi-religious bond forged through its hostility to all authority beyond "faith in the community as the *saviour*" (BGE, p. 107). He recoils against everything that crowds out anyone who aspires to be "set free from the crowd" (BGE, p. 39), recoils then, especially, from what he perceives as the obscene self-righteousness of "modern" men, "progressives", especially socialists, who are so fundamentally convinced that their values are on the side of the angels.

These "men of 'modern ideas'" seem so sure that they "manifestly *know*... what is good and evil" (BGE, p. 106). We (and I am not simply outside the thing) strive in our politics for equality of rights and the alleviation of suffering. So a counter-recoil against Nietzsche's recoil is not only an understandable reaction: it can seem an overwhelmingly just reaction. I will come back to this, but for now, I will for my part tolerate Nietzsche's hostility towards the mainstream – the middle – of European politics. And I will tolerate this because I also accept Nietzsche's assessment that the general direction of Europe's current "democratic era", and the various ideals (left and right) one finds there of a community that really *is* one because it finally is *one*, really is increasingly hostile to the pluralist promise of democracy as democracy to come (a promise I will not give up on).

Nietzsche's hopes lie in the thought that the movement of levelling democratisation is not terminal for Europe. Indeed, in stark contrast to the new faithful who see in their own projected democratic "tomorrow" a "final goal", Nietzsche sees democracy as "a link in a chain" (HH, p. 329), and anticipates something "reserved for Europe" as its other future, "the day after tomorrow": a process of self-overcoming which may last as long as the two-thousand year-long movement of the becoming-European of European humanity that went before it. The old Greco-Christian world, the old European world, "must now be destroyed" says Nietzsche. Indeed, he thinks "we are standing on the threshold of this very event" (GM, p. 135). But this old-Europe destruction, for Nietzsche, holds out a new still-European promise. What is happening? Specifically this: we are, in our time, coming to realise that the world-understanding that belongs to Europe's dominant heritage, the idea that there is an underlying moral world-order and an irreducibly divine or providential significance to the whole of human life and history – this "*logos*" which was believed to *be* objective reality, and believed to be there to be known by a rationally adjusted mind – this cognitivist idea has been exposed as a dogma that we can no longer believe. Or better: it has exposed itself as such, devalued itself. God is dead, and we have killed Him.

> Christian truthfulness...finally draws its *strongest conclusion*, its conclusion *against* itself; this will occur when it asks the question: "*What is the meaning of all will to truth?*"...There is no doubt that from now on morality will be *destroyed* through the coming to consciousness of the will to truth: this is the great drama in a hundred acts which is reserved for Europe over the next two thousand years, the most fearful, most questionable and perhaps also most hopeful of all dramas. (GM, p. 135)

The destruction of the cognitivist idea, the destruction of the Europe of this idea, would indeed be a massive event. The Greco-Christian conception of Man as theomorphic rational animality supplied us with a sense of ourselves as the centre of cosmic significance, with European Man as the centre of that centre, the advance-guard of human self-development. Europe called itself to appear as a site of "great things" as a result – but its own "modern" spirit, what Nietzsche calls the "democratic enlightenment" that breaks with the old authorities, serves only to decapitate Man, leaving us with no way of giving content to the idea that what gives life a meaning or purpose is something real and objective – no way of making sense of the idea that living a good life is a matter of adjusting one's beliefs to how things are, a matter of attaining an anterior truth or meaning about the world and Man. Hence the madman seeing us increasingly "straying through an infinite nothing", in a world that is no longer a world, and, in fact, leaving Europe with an experience of its own history that in our time appears, more and more, only as a series of disasters and crimes.

In the Preface to *Beyond Good and Evil* Nietzsche once again identifies our time as a threshold – a time in which what he calls this moral-cognitivist "foundation-stone" for Europe will be revealed as "a grotesque", "a nightmare" from which Europe must recover and so learn to "breathe again", a recovery from "the most dangerous of all errors" (BGE, p. 14). And the grotesque monster here is, once again, not one European idea among others but "Plato's invention of pure spirit and the good in itself" (BGE, p. 14). But, lest the Europe we encounter today be thought as through and through Greek, he immediately continues:

> But the struggle against Plato, or to express it more plainly and for "the people", the struggle against the Christian-ecclesiastical pressure of millennia – for Christianity is Platonism for "the people" – has created in Europe a magnificent tension of the spirit as has never existed on earth before... European man feels this tension... (BGE, p. 14)

"European man" must overcome himself, send himself in a new direction and can do so: for "with so tense a bow one can now shoot for the most distant targets".

And the "good Europeans", have "the arrow, the task and, who knows? The *target*..." (BGE, p. 14)

Who knows... But wasn't "modern man", the man of European modernity, meant to be the one who broke from the past and forged a new way of sovereign self-legislation? Why do we need to look forward to "we Europeans of the day after tomorrow" (BGE, p. 128) when we already have democratic modern (I mean rational, scientific, egalitarian) Europeans of today? Those for whom the day after tomorrow belongs are those among us who experience democratic modernity, not as "progress" towards a glorious future of equality and a new "brotherhood" (BGE, p. 107), but those (those brothers? those friends?) who, when they encounter this democratic taste, feel (Nietzsche says) "one more kind of disgust than other men do" (BGE, p. 109). "Modern ideas", "democratic taste", the whole "democratic movement" is the movement that understands itself in terms of its disgust with Europe's old Christian order, the divine right of Kings, and so on. Nietzsche shares that disgust. He too thinks that the time in which Christian Europe could achieve anything "worthwhile" is decisively past (BGE, p. 93). But Nietzsche insists that these modern men and their modern ideas are really not so very different from their predecessors after all. On the contrary, living still in the shadow of the dead God, "the democratic movement inherits the Christian" (BGE, p. 107). Hence Nietzsche's extra feeling of disgust is directed towards the taste of those who approve and promote democratic taste, and especially their "faith in the community as the *saviour*".

Nietzsche's thinking is thus directed most aggressively against that movement in our time – a movement marked for him most prominently by "the brotherhood fanatics who call themselves socialists" (BGE, p. 107) – which is the faded hang-over of European Christianity, its morality of good and evil, and equality before God. Nietzsche's extra disgust is disgust at modern man himself and the "herd-animal morality" that has "broken through and come to predominate" in modern Europe (BGE, p. 106), quasi-religiously bound together by their "profound mistrust" of old (theistic, Greco-Christian) authorities.

So egalitarian liberals and socialists of the democratic enlightenment, the inheritors of Christian morality, are in reality "*levellers*" (BGE, 53); tamers of the European promise, not its great liberators from dogmatic tradition and superstition. On the other hand, as I have indicated, Nietzsche retains a hope: "the greatest possibilities of man are still *unexhausted*" (BGE, p. 109). Just as "the Bible and the Greeks" was the source of a certain European greatness, so also it will be out of that legacy that Europe can forge a vital future for itself, and remain something to come: a Europe beyond its modernity. And it will involve nothing short of a new conception of Man. For Nietzsche, that is to say, the primary "target" (*qua* goal) is not a new political construction, but, rather, as we shall see, a new philosophical conception. The task is a task not simply for "politicians of the future" but, finally, for what he calls "philosophers of the future" (BGE, p. 52): those concerned, above all, with the meaning of Man, and with creating (*being*) a new meaning of Man.

The old Greco-Christian philosophical anthropology is decisively turned by Nietzsche but it is not abandoned in its universal mission. Philosophy, European philosophy, was and had always been the site of thinking not a regional Europeanness but a universal humanity. And history is then grasped in terms of the unfolding of this distinctive form of life towards its proper end. In the movement of its own de-moralising deconstruction, Nietzsche turns this towards a new variation, proposing a specifically non-metaphysical and non-theistic variation of the old metaphysical and theistic conception: "man is the animal *whose nature has not yet been fixed*" (BGE, p. 69) and "in man, *creature* and *creator* are united" (BGE, p. 136). Man gives himself a meaning through what Nietzsche regards as "artistic fashioning", through a movement of *auto-teleiopoesis.* In reality, according to Nietzsche, Christianity attempted this too, for example with the ascetic ideal. But what did they achieve in their work on "the boldest animal" (BGE, p. 136)? Since Nietzsche, it has been hard to ignore the possibility that what they achieved was – an "abomination", an "abortion": the herd-animal man of the democratic enlightenment.

In the last part of this book, I will try to think a little more boldly about the created creature that we are. For now, we are concerned with the way in which Christianity, as "Platonism 'for the people'", had provided a defensive bulwark against a nihilistic anxiety about the meaning of our life that we – the type that human beings are – can never simply be free from. Europe had forged itself on the ground of that Greco-Biblical foundation stone: its onto-theological *teleo-eschatology* imbued human life and history with meaning. Nietzsche offers a distinctive interpretation of Europe's modernity in that connection: the movement of resistance to the hegemony of Christian ecclesiastical authority (resistance to the power realm of Christendom) that takes place through democratic enlightenment (political democratisation), this movement is not a new era of progress but of Greco-Biblical Europe in decline, and of a nihilistic anxiety on the rise. Nevertheless, as we have seen, despite that reading of the movement of the death of God into our time, Nietzsche still conceives those developments as potentially belonging to a step forward, and a fresh understanding of Europe's promise to the world. Let's follow him – if only for a while.

V

In the throw of the inner dissolution of the Greco-Christian world, Nietzsche sees the chance for a new ambition for the philosopher: from realising (so far as that is possible) an objectively ideal individual and social condition of Man under the guidance of the philosopher King (or Party, or the People), to creating a new meaning of being human. An honest self-overcoming for the animal that is artistically self-creative.

There is a way of interpreting Nietzsche on this shift of ambition which might be especially attractive to those who have altogether lost confidence in the kind of responses to our condition that European politics has provided: one might think that the Nietzschean project of self-overcoming is now simply dissociated from a political and social project. Nietzschean overcoming, one might think, is an exclusively personal and individual affair. This is one way of taking Nietzsche's relentless criticisms of the communalism of the modern movement of democratisation, and his emphasis on being a "friend of solitude".

In the "Introduction" to his book *Contingency, Irony, and Solidarity*, Richard Rorty encourages this "privatized", "individualized" construal of Nietzschean propaganda: Nietzsche's challenge to we moderns is for us to give up on political ideals of social transformation (give up on getting rid of exploitation, for example) and to become a private work of art all on your own (CIS, pp. xiii–xvi). In order to set this kind of reading aside, and to get back to Nietzsche's Europe to come, we need to hold on to the fact that Nietzsche does not simply celebrate and cultivate the possible emergence of a new kind of individual, or a new kind of genius – though, as we have seen, he has hopes that a Europe to come can open the space for extraordinary people to make their way again – but, especially, a new kind philosopher: "real philosophers" (definitely not academics) (BGE §205). At issue, are people willing to take on the absolute maximum of responsibility, "the most comprehensive responsibility" (BGE, p. 67): responsibility, that is to say, for the meaning of Man as such, responsibility for the meaning of our being. And this means that "they have more to do than merely know something new – namely to *be* something new, to *signify* something new" (BGE, p. 166). This makes of these philosophers, for Nietzsche, a class or "caste" among the good Europeans who – in a grand Platonic tradition – "should *rule*" (BGE, p. 112). While it belongs to the overcoming of onto-theological metaphysics – a movement in which ideas of "knowing the essence" of Man claimed by metaphysics is displaced by the inventive creating of a new creature – Nietzsche's arrow is also very political.

The Nietzsche that Rorty champions, by contrast, will insist that the upheaval that is needed is not a shift from ideals of communalism to a new ruling tyranny, but a shift from the public and political to the personal and private. This conception of Nietzsche fits very neatly with something else that Rorty wants to foreground in his elaboration of the outlook of what he calls the "contemporary liberal ironist". This might be called the "postmodern" interpretation of the condition of Europe beyond modernity: we postmodernists, for Rorty, are sceptical about "the whole idea of finding a comprehensive outlook that would hold [private] self-creation and [public] justice, private perfection and human solidarity, in a single vision" (CIS, p. xiv).

Nietzsche would be seen, on this understanding, as situated on one side of a divide between (on the one hand) those old modern philosophers like Kant, Hegel or Marx who see the project of self-realisation and the project of achieving a just society as fundamentally the same (*teleo-eschatological* or onto-theological political) project – a "metaphysical conception of politics" that attempts to unite a striving for human perfection with a sense of community – and (on the other hand) those postmodernists who see that whole Greco-Christian project as one which simply sacrifices self-realisation in the name of the solidaristic community.

What we need, Rorty suggests, is to "drop the demand for a theory which unifies the public and the private" and be content with the thought that "the demands of self-creation and of human solidarity are equally valid yet forever incommensurable" (CIS, p. xv). The basic incommensurability here is this: there is no way of simultaneously respecting the demands of public virtue and of private virtue. One can only choose a path of either "the general good" of the community or the path of one's own good. It is, as Rorty puts it, a choice between "speaking the language of the tribe and finding our own words" CIS, p. xiv). It is because one cannot do both things at once: that we cannot fulfil the task of constructing a unified theory (or way of life) in which we square public solidarity in a community and private fulfilment for an individual. That old modern project should be abandoned.

The distinction between public and private goods – between communal and individual fulfilment – is not, I believe, peculiar to modern political thought. But, and rather more interestingly, it belongs to what we might call the classic European idea of the political as such, and to the concept of *res publica* – the idea of public things, or distinctively public affairs – which dominates that European idea of the political. Rorty's postmodernist is the one who has given up an idea of justice that was central to the Platonic tradition in European politics: that justice in one sphere can only be brought about where there is justice in the other – that realising a just society can only be achieved where that society maximises individual flourishing too. On that view, justice in one sphere must be essentially compatible with justice in the other. After all, both aim at the same thing: justice. And the voice of justice must be at one with itself. ("Justice just is justice", as G.A. Cohen liked to say.)

Rorty's postmodernist retains the distinction between spheres but gives up on that old hope of achieving a conception that can unify justice in both spheres at once. In fact, Rorty does not give up on the idea of the univocal voice of justice altogether but places it entirely on only one side of the old distinction: he distinguishes "the vocabulary of justice", which is communal, from the "vocabulary of self-creation" which is individual. He supposes that as long as one stays within a single vocabulary one can get along fine. The only radically abyssal question – left to each individual – is the choice between incommensurable vocabularies: social justice in a community or self-creation for an individual. Nietzsche, for Rorty, makes propaganda to side with the latter.

It is significant, I think, that Rorty will distinguish the voice of justice and the voice of self-creation, as if justice has nothing to do with how things are at an individual level. Nietzsche, like Plato (which is really to say, like the entire European tradition), does not tolerate that idea. Justice cannot be confined to the sphere of the social. As we have seen, Nietzsche recoils in disgust from what he calls the "community as *saviour*" idea so loved by those moderns with a democratic taste. The fundamental feature of such a taste in politics is, for Nietzsche, a dogmatic, and essentially Christian, insistence on the value of what is common to us all. This sounds, precisely, *just*, at least as far as the social dimension is concerned. Nietzsche is clearly hostile to that. So on Rorty's, reading he must be one of those who opts for self-creation instead. But Nietzsche refuses to accept that justice only applies to the social domain. Like Plato, he does not think that the question of justice is indifferent to the outcome for individuals. However, for Nietzsche, unlike "the old socialist Plato", the voice of justice is *not* univocal: "Equality for equals, inequality for unequals" – that would be the true voice of justice", says Nietzsche reciting a Greek voice lost to Europe's too-Latin modernity (TI, p. 102).

We have seen that, for Nietzsche, so-called political progressives, the egalitarian liberals and socialists of the democratic enlightenment are, in reality, "levellers". In terms of justice, one can put it like this: that "modern" democratic movement is not, for Nietzsche, simply against justice, but it is entirely one-sided, and hence its sense of justice remains, as it were, radically unjust. We need also to acknowledge, justice would demand that we acknowledge, the inequality of unequals. That too needs to be equally respected.

Nietzsche will have no hesitation in distinguishing "the best" from "the rest". But his point about justice which subtends recognition of any social and cultural "order of rank" is not itself separated in a quasi-aristocratic way. It is not that we have equals here, who can be treated equally, and special ones, the few, the unequals, there, who should be given special treatment. On the contrary, Nietzsche's point about justice is universal (indeed, one might say democratic): insofar as we are all equals, then we should be treated as such. But insofar as we are all unequals, then we should be treated as such too. This is not an incommensurability of social justice and personal fulfilment, but an incommensurability within justice itself: an irreducible aporia within "the true voice of justice". How to live with that irreducible aporia – how to live with a sense of justice that constantly demands adjustment without a last word on a finally just end – that is a question of politics. And it is to that question I will now turn.

VI

For Nietzsche, as we have seen, the movement of political democratisation in Europe that unfolds from the French Revolution holds within its formation the possibility for the creation of a European configuration beyond petty nationalisms. And Nietzsche sees the trajectory of this democratic movement as having two major outcomes: subtle slavery, on the one hand, and the unintended emergence of a spiritual tyranny led by "real philosophers", on the other. But all of this presupposes Europe overcoming its national dis-integration, and thus opening the space for the newly cosmopolitan Europeans of the future. Even in Nietzsche's day that overcoming did not seem so distant. In fact, it was, he felt, already happening:

> Thanks to the pathological manner in which nationalist nonsense has alienated and continues to alienate the peoples of Europe from each other; thanks as well to the short-sighted and swift-handed politicians who have risen to the top with the help of this nonsense, and have no idea of the extent to which the politics of dissolution that they practice can only be

> *entr'acte politics*, – thanks to all this and to some things that are strictly unmentionable today, the most unambiguous signs declaring that *Europe wants to become one* are either overlooked or wilfully and mendaciously reinterpreted. The mysterious labor in the souls of all the more profound and far-ranging people of this century has actually been focused on preparing the path to this new *synthesis* and on experimentally [*versuchsweise*] anticipating the Europeans of the future. Only in their foregrounds or in hours of weakness (like old age) were they "fatherlanders". (BGE, §256)

These path-breakers are those whom Nietzsche calls (and includes himself among) "we good Europeans". And he immediately provides a little list. "I am thinking about people like such men as Napoleon, Goethe, Beethoven, Stendhal, Heirich Heine, Schopenhauer…, Richard Wagner and the later French romanticism of the forties…and I specially mention Delacroix, the nearest related to Wagner" (BGE, p. 170).. A fairly reasonable mix of German and French souls here – though not an English one in sight, yet.

Nations may, anyway, seem to fade into the background here: "it is the soul of Europe, the one Europe, that presses and yearns upwards and outwards through their multiple and tumultuous art" (BGE §256). However, what is at issue in the "one" to come is a "synthesis" of the old plurality. And, as I have indicated, in the "Peoples and Fatherlands" chapter of *Beyond Good and Evil*, where Nietzsche sorts the wheat from the chaff, and selects what to inherit and what to leave behind, it is from national souls that are already reaching beyond themselves into, and producing, a trans-European space – the souls of the Germans, French, and English, along with the already trans-European Jews – that he makes his own experimental anticipation of the Europeans of the future.

In this respect, Germany, the nation Nietzsche regards as the most stupidly nationalistic (because so promisingly European) of the silly European nations, remains, exemplary:

> More than anything else, the German soul is multiple, it originates in different places and is more piled up and pieced together than actually constructed… As a people composed of the most enormous assortment and combination of races, perhaps even with a preponderance of the pre-Aryan element, as a "people of the middle" in every sense, the Germans are more incomprehensible, comprehensive, contradictory, unfamiliar, unpredictable, surprising, and even more frightening than other peoples are to themselves (BGE, p. 155, trans revised as Cambridge)

The Germans: first among others as a "people of the middle". A "people of the middle [*Volk der Mitte*] in every sense". In every sense? What senses of "middle" are there for a people to have? Two stand out, anyway. One can think of them as being like the water of the main stem, a confluence place where water from other streams meet and mix; but also as inhabiting the spatial centre, the geographical

Mitte. The German example will set the European standard – only in every respect more so than any other nation: they are the middle of the middle, the very centre of the centre, the central case, the exemplary instance. And so the soul of Europe, itself manifold, of diverse origins, more pieced together than constructed, itself composed of an assortment and combination of peoples, thus finds its exemplary middle people in one part of itself... in the Germans. They are the European people who already have this internal variation within themselves, who "have the most neighbours" as Heidegger puts it repeating the figure, making them central for all thinking of the Europeans of the future.

There will be a lot of chaff in the German case too, however, and some of it, as we shall see in a moment, genuinely sickening. Nevertheless, while Nietzsche takes Germany to be, presently, the main carrier of nationalist excesses – exemplary too, therefore, in its failure to be more boldly European, i.e. more authentically German – he takes this multi-sourced German soul-characteristic as giving rise to a truly German distinction: the capacity not for "profundity" (the customary – and not wholly false – attribute) but what he calls (basically citing Hegel) "development". This is the capacity to exist as a movement of becoming. "The German himself *is* not, he *becomes*, he 'develops'" (BGE §244). And this German-self-discovery is itself becoming the first "ruling concept" already at work in a Europe-producing way: contributing to a becoming-European spirit through an effective "Germanization of all Europe" in this regard (BGE, p. 156). As Europe Germanises in this dimension, it will henceforth be increasingly a question of *becoming European*, where that is precisely not *being European* (as such) at all, or being such only in the sense of being in a condition (a self-relation) that has always belonged more to Germany than any other European peoples (especially the French apparently): of always holding open "the question" of what it is, of always eluding "*definition*" (BGE, p. 155).

Nietzsche accepts that a new becoming-European subjectivity in this German mode would largely displace the "outmoded feelings", the nativism and atavism, of national belonging, but he does not think it entirely eclipses them (BGE, p. 152). On the contrary, Nietzsche recognised that even "good Europeans" (himself, for example) would occasionally lapse into "atavistic attacks" of "fatherlandishness". On the other hand, he expects that this sort of thing would be increasingly short-lived, and the Europeans of the future would be quickly "restored to reason" (BGE, p. 152). That is to say, their national belonging would be a much reduced and far less influential feature of their subjectivity, and its "good Europeanism" (BGE, p. 152).

Perhaps because of Germany's newness as a nation, fatherlandishness has had a particularly monstrous expression among the Germans: anti-Semitism. And when Nietzsche turns to consider "what Europe owes to the Jews", he is especially critical of his own people, proposing with a smile that a practical remedy to Germany's difficulty accommodating its Jewish population might be "to throw the anti-Semitic hooligans out of the country" (BGE, §251). That would not finally settle the matter, since it only deals with the "excessive" anti-Semitism that is officially frowned upon anyway, whereas the real problem is a "universal" German instinct (BGE, §251). Nietzsche confesses and asks forgiveness for having not been able entirely to "escape this illness" himself (BGE, §251). Nevertheless, for his own reformed part, having come fully to accept that the Jews "are *not* working and making plans to...control Europe", Nietzsche regards Europe's debt to the Jews to be immense and ongoing (BGE, §251). On the other hand, the Jews are also conceived by Nietzsche as ("like the Russians") external to Europe: "a thinker who has Europe's future on his conscience will, in every sketch he draws of this future, consider the Jews, like the Russians, to be the most certain and probable factors at present in the great play and struggle of forces" (BGE, §251). The Jews live in but are not wholly of Europe for Nietzsche. Even so, however, Nietzsche thinks that what still "glows" in Europe, as the light of its old Greco-Christian world darkens, is due above all to "the grand style in morality, the horror and majesty of infinite demands, infinite meanings, the whole romanticism and sublimity of the morally questionable" that it has learned from the Jews (BGE, §250). Germany may have given Europe a new governing idea with "development" – but its greatest national stupidity, anti-Semitism, should, Nietzsche insisted, have no future at all.

Writing in a time before that stupidity became an unprecedented horror, and "the thirst for some place where they can be settled" (BGE, §251) drove so many of the surviving European Jews to support the establishment of the state of Israel in part of Mandatory Palestine (a British administered part of the defeated and collapsed Ottoman Empire), Nietzsche could still hope that the Jews in Europe would find respect in a Europe to come where their "spirit and spiritedness" could become more radically integrated into European culture, and to be of Europe "at last" – and to help thereby to form and forge a "new caste to rule Europe", the "breeding" of which he "takes *seriously*" as the *real* "European problem" (BGE, §251).

Nietzschean eugenics was doubtless a gift of sorts to the Nazis, among others – others who also included "progressive", left-wing eugenicists. But this temptation belongs to a path-breaking history that does not have to gather itself in such an attempt. Nietzsche writes of his "good Europeans" "experimentally [*versuchsweise*] anticipating" the future Europeans. His text frequently plays on the similarity of the terms *Versuch* (attempt or experiment) and *Versuchung* (temptation), and in the next chapter, I will continue to follow his tempting attempt to forge this "new synthesis" of the people of the middle, and its practical-institutional expression in European political integration. But I will do so as someone who takes the path established by the "mysterious labour" that has made its way through Europe over the last two hundred years without Nietzsche's eugenicist attemptations. One can take his synthetic breeding plans seriously without taking them literally. Moreover, and not altogether fortuitously, this thought experiment will, in fact, take us back to the "English", at least for a while. And as I indicated at the end of the last chapter, that will take English me back to "the great Chinaman of Königsberg" (BGE, §210), back to the old Scot Kant.

6

A UNITED EUROPE OF STATES

Out of the crooked timber of humanity, no straight thing was ever made
– Immanuel Kant

I

Nietzsche's Germanised Europe of the future is not German through and through. Or, rather, Europeans will become German through and through only in the sense that their still-multiple European souls will have each taken on something of the colour of German "development". Indeed, the European souls of the new synthesis will still think of themselves as national: it is the overwhelming intensity of their national feeling that will have been overcome. Europeans will have got over the aggressive, xenophobic nationalism of Europe today, and in that respect will most resemble the "good Europeans" of Europe's history, those whose "mysterious labours" will have best prepared for their arrival. Nietzsche will often refer to such historical figures as "European events" in contrast to national ones (BGE, p. 159). These are figures (another list) "like Goethe, like Hegel, like Heinrich Heine, [and] Schopenhauer" (TI, p. 79), all of whom avoided, for the most part, over-identification with a "fatherland" – and in this case who were all German.

Exemplary Germans among the people of the middle. Indeed, Nietzsche suggests that there is a greater chance of greatness that is due to the Germans than even the French in view of the fact that "we… are still closer to barbarism than the French" (BGE, p. 171). The French get a pretty good run for their money nevertheless, and have also given a French colour to the whole of Europe: "the European *noblesse* (of feeling, of taste, of manner – in short, taking the word in all its higher senses) – is France's work and invention" (BGE, §254). France also has "three claims" to superiority in spiritual culture over any other Europeans.

The first two claims over-Europe are their capacity for artistic passion and their moralism. The third, however, is most important to me: "at the core of the French there is a half-successful synthesis of north and south" (BGE, §254). In other words, Nietzsche's own attemptation of a new synthesis is already in development there: "in France there is still a predisposition to understand and accommodate those rarer and rarely satisfied people who are too far-ranging to find satisfaction in any fatherlandishness, and know how to love the south in the north and the north in the south, – the born Mediterraneans" (BGE, §254). Born Mediterraneans. Europe of the Mediterranean? No. The German for the Mediterranean is *Mittlemeer*, but that is not what Nietzsche wrote. He wrote that the French are the born *Mittelländler*. They are the born people of the middle place.

The French like the Germans are people of the middle – although the former perhaps more secretly than the latter. Indeed, the best of the French "have the *ambition* to hide themselves" and "keep themselves well hidden" (BGE, §254). Like Henri Beyle who "ran with a Napoleonic tempo through *his* Europe, through several centuries of the European soul, as a pathfinder and discoverer of this soul" (BGE, §254). Henri who? This is *Stendhal* – who took his pen name from the German city of Stendal, birthplace of Winckelmann, and hometown of a woman called Wilhelmine with whom he fell in love. Stendhal called her "this soul of the north".

France is not everywhere praised, however. "It is", Nietzsche says, "a coarsened and stultified France that thrashes around in the *foreground* these days, – it recently celebrated a real orgy of bad taste combined with self-admiration at Victor Hugo's funeral" (BGE, §254). It is also prone, dare I repeat it, to a southern "temperament" that "bubbles over from time to time" (BGE, §254). Moreover, while the French overtly do their best to "ward off spiritual Germanization", they are actually quite unable to do so (BGE, §254): France can't resist being "impregnated" by Germany – which in turn "needs to impregnate". The genius in each thus "look to each other like men and women; but they also misunderstand each other, – like men and women" (BGE, §248).

For the most part, then, the *agon* over the future of Europe in Nietzsche's new synthesis is a French and German affair. Indeed, despite the shortcomings of France "these days", Nietzsche stresses that they too, like the Germans, "understand things that an Englishman will never understand" (BGE, p. 168).

II

Ah, the English. Although, as I have indicated, the English do appear in Nietzsche's synthesis, it is by no means clear why he mentions them at all in that regard. It is an unlikely event, in any case, since no English figures figure as European events – or rather they only appear when what is at issue is a less exalted point of European "feeling", the point where, for example, "the same European destiny that in Beethoven knows how to sing found its way into words", and "into words" with "Rousseau, Schiller, Shelley, Byron" (BGE, p. 159; see also BGE, p. 165). There are lower points on this scale. Indeed, in this context the German composer Schumann gets the worst write-up: with him "*the voice for the soul of Europe*" is positively in danger – "sinking into a merely national affair" – but Nietzsche's talent for uncharitableness to his fellow Germans does not outweigh the respect he has for those not-simply-German Germans he most admires. Again, the mark of being not-simply-national Europeans, the mark of the exemplary people of the middle, is credited above all to the Germans – with a somewhat secret French companion given a ride.

On the face of it, then, England is not going to be a great contributor to the new Europe. The English are, Nietzsche thinks, "a race of former Puritans" (BGE, p. 139) who are clever enough to make Sundays so "boring" that people positively look forward to going back to work on Monday (BGE, p. 94). We (and I say "we" here deliberately) are "clumsy" and "ponderous", our literature is "impossible" (even Shakespeare takes a hit (BGE, p. 134)), and our special vice is "cant", i.e. pietistic whinging and whining – and he's surely right about that (BGE, p. 138–9). We cannot "dance", indeed Englishwomen, despite being "the most beautiful doves and swans" on earth, can hardly "*walk*" (BGE, p. 165). We are marked by our "profound averageness" (BGE, p. 166). The major English "philosophers" of Nietzsche's time, the utilitarians, are quintessential "herd animals" preaching "one morality for all", and hence are fundamentally detrimental to the "higher men" and their task of building on the future made possible by the process of democratisation. Utilitarians may think that this "English happiness" (the "happiness of the greatest number" is, Nietzsche says, simply "the happiness of England") is the "true path of virtue" but is, in reality, the worst kind of levelling of individual differences: "what is right for one *cannot* by any means therefore be right for another" (BGE, p. 139). (He makes this point again, more clearly, with the thought that "they generalize where generalisation is impermissible" – i.e. over individuals (BGE, p. 101).) In short, since the future rulers are responsibility-maximising philosophers, the English contribution is absolutely minimal: "they are no philosophical race" ("it was against Hume that Kant rose up"), and "what is lacking in England" is "real power of spirituality" and "real depth of spiritual insight" (BGE, pp. 164–5). We are, in sum, on the list not of European events but of the most contemptible: "shopkeepers, Christians, cows, women, Englishmen and other democrats" (TI, p. 92; see also BGE, p. 97). There is a certain exemplary representativity of everything awful about modern Europe…in the English. For Nietzsche, the "profound averageness", "modern ideas" and "democratic taste" of the English is precisely what "the *German* spirit has risen against in profound disgust" (BGE, p. 97). It is hard to imagine we will have any part in Europe's future beyond modernity. We have "mediocre minds" and are "mediocre spirits" (BGE, §253).

But wait! These mediocre spirits what are they up to? "The spirit of respectable but mediocre Englishmen – I mean Darwin, John Stuart Mill, and Herbert Spencer – is starting to come to prominence in the middle regions of European taste" (BGE, §253). The mediocre Englishmen [*mittelmässiger Engländer*] gaining ground in the middle regions [*in der mittleren Region*]. The English too are "Mediterraneans" of a sort. We too are some kind of people of the middle who dominate the middle, currently occupying, Nietzsche says, the very middle of the middle.

So, in fact, we have three singular people of the middle: the Germans who are people of the middle "in every sense"; the French who, somewhat hidden, are "born Mediterraneans"; and, finally, the English who, most encrypted of all, are the "mediocre" spirits who dominate "the middle regions". But according the English such an honour (of sorts) is not the end of Nietzsche's English honouring. For Nietzsche immediately continues his identification of the mediocre English as ground-gainers in the middle regions by giving them leave to do so: "In fact, who would doubt the utility for *such spirits* to dominate for a while? [*In der That, wer möchte die Nützlichkeit davon anzweifeln, dass zeitweilig* solche Geister *herrschen?*]" (BGE, §253, translation mine, emphasis in original). What a turn up for the books. I will exploit this.

Nietzsche's reasons for giving the English-type spirit a temporary priority in the movement towards the new Europe to come are basically practical and pragmatic: working towards a new Europeanism will be safer in the hands of "mediocre spirits" instead of the "exalted spirits" of the French and German type who have a tendency to "fly off", not knowing and not keeping to the "rules" (BGE, pp. 165–6). English "narrowness, aridity and industriousness" is thus better suited to "dominate" in our time "for a while", even though we are utterly incapable of "being able…to *be* something new" (BGE, p. 166).

Well, thank you. But having been given the floor by Nietzsche (for now), I would like to repay the compliment and suggest right off that what "English spirits" suppose that Europe needs today, and any day they can see thereafter – and I will confirm this in detail – really is Nietzsche's vision of a Europe that wants to become one through the formation of a European federation of States. We Europeans (if you don't mind an English spirit speaking in this name) are, we "English spirits" think, a unity only of the singularly different: we can be drawn together as *one* (spiritually) precisely because we are not *one* (spirit). *We are the community that is not One.*

This idea is fundamentally at odds with the other major conception of European integration, and the interpretation of "ever closer union", that I introduced in the last chapter. That interpretation is the one that conceives economic and political integration as the movement towards the formation of a supranational federal State, to put it in German; a great European Republic, to put it in French; a European superstate, to put it in English. Instead, English spirits would urge a (genuinely) more modest (moderate, mediocre) interpretation. "Ever closer union among the peoples of Europe" simply means: cultivating supranational institutional conditions in which war, conflict and mutual antagonism between the nations of Europe become increasingly less likely – and the arrival of the good Europeans of the future overwhelmingly more likely.

Europe becoming one. This is, first of all, a cosmopolitan hope of harmony and peace among peoples, not a project of levelling harmonisation or a single European government. Not a United States of Europe, but a united Europe of States. And what does it lead to for the people of this place? They are not citizens of nowhere, but not just citizens of a nation either. It will lead to the formation of a new kind of cosmopolitan plant "Man", Nietzsche says: people with an "increasing independence of any *definite* milieu".

Milieu. Mid-Lieu. Middle Place. People of the middle without a *definite* middle. These are the European to come, in the Europe of the *milieu*.

But they are not, even in this new figure of the old German figure, One; even unto the spiritual figure they configure for the cape or headland that they all share without sharing. Moreover, while many Europe-producers hitherto have found the attemptation to make Europe One hard to resist, they have succeeded only in making it less so. Indeed, the greatest "English" anxiety is that success for the more exalted and amalgamating federalist interpretation of a Europe to come will be just such a failure. Europe could become as J.S. Mill (one of Nietzsche's "respectable but mediocre Englishmen") had supposed China (in his time) to have become: namely, "stationary" rather than "progressive":

> What has hitherto preserved Europe from [becoming another China]? Not any superior excellence in the [European family], which, when it exists, exists as the effect not as the cause; but their remarkable diversity of character and culture. Individuals, classes, nations, have been extremely unlike each other: they have struck out a great variety of paths, each leading to something valuable; and although at every period those who travelled in different paths have been extremely intolerant of one another, and each would have thought it an excellent thing if all the rest could have been compelled to travel his road, their attempts to thwart each other's development have rarely had any permanent success, and each has in time endured to receive the good which the others have offered. Europe is, in my judgement, wholly indebted to this plurality of paths for its progressive and many-sided development. (OL, p. 71)

Mill (thankfully) stresses cultural diversity and not racial superiority in his estimation of the cause of whatever comparative excellence one can find in Europe. Like Nietzsche, then, he stresses the "unlikeness" of Europeans to each other (OL, p. 70). (As a matter of fact, Mill only ever mentions three European nations by name in *On Liberty*; once again the German, French and English examples are the only Europe-examples.) On the other hand, and despite other intriguing Mill/Nietzsche similarities – notably on democratic "levelling" (OL, p. 72) – there is a striking unlikeness in their respective ways of configuring Europe in its singular identity-without-single-identity. While Nietzsche maps Europe in terms of a "Europe of the middle" figure, in Mill's text it is a "Europe of the Atlantic" figure that gathers the plurality: each nation presented as something like a distinctive "point of departure for discovery, invention, and colonialization" (OH, p. 20). Not only do the Europeans "continually" make "new inventions" (OL, p. 70), but through road and path extension efforts, something akin to colonial domination (extending control over other countries) is "at every period" attempted in over-Europe operations too. This overreaching is obviously part of Nietzsche's picture, though it is not so clear why his people of the middle are so keen not to stay coiled up in their own land. On a "Europe of the Atlantic" picture, by contrast, heading out, not staying put is part of the programme.

For Mill, and once again like Nietzsche, each European nation ultimately benefits from the "great variety" of headings of the other nations, but they do so only on condition of the failure of particular national efforts at overall over-Europe domination. (Mill did not think that this point holds everywhere that such domination was attempted by European nations. He generally supported European countries extending control over other countries where he considered those other places not yet ready for "civilised" forms of self-government. But if there is a good to be received from others, any others, I cannot see how what Kant rightly called the "whole litany of evils" resulting from colonialism could anywhere be thought an acceptable or respectable way to deliver it (Kant, p. 106).) What is achieved through the singular ways that each has "struck out" is not valuable for that nation alone: when (and because) they are not simply overwhelmed, every nation can receive and draw in "the good which the others have offered", even if it is itself transformed (for example, Germanised) in the process of that development. In short, what is valuable for Europe overall is not a development in which the European community comes ever closer to being One; on the contrary, Europe's own best-becoming depends entirely on its people and peoples remaining gathered as a developing Many.

In the end, for Mill, plurality is Europe's irreducible excellence, its "many-sided development", its "remarkable diversity", the insistent mark of what is valuable in Europe itself, a good overall that each nation has a hand in creating – and each has a hand in threatening ("each would have thought it an excellent thing if all the rest could have been compelled to travel his road"). The perhaps paradoxical virtue of letting "English spirits" like Mill "dominate" for any time would thus lie in this: that travelling *their* over-Europe road would require a set-up for Europe overall that best enables every other to "travel his" own, and hence for each to remain in a condition fit to "to receive the good which the others have offered" without colonising compulsion. Perhaps it could then even cultivate the chance of replacing extreme intolerance, expansionism, and (life-saturating) nationalism with mutual respect, good-neighbourliness, and (more occasional) warm-hearted patriotism.

Nietzsche supposed it undeniable that English-type spirits should dominate in Europe, at least "for a while". However, in the political history of Europe since the Second World War, the period of the unprecedented construction of an over-Europe institutional set-up that specifically aims at putting the mockers on attempts at particular national over-Europe domination, such spirits have actually struggled even to begin doing so. A more exalted desire for attaining "ever closer union" has generally prevailed among those closest to its building(s). In the next part of this chapter, I will track the development of a distinctively English-type vision of European integration after the Second World War, and a growing anxiety among such spirits about more grandiose desires for a European community that is One. Focusing on that "English" vision as it was articulated in post-War British, and especially British Prime Ministerial, political speech-making, and keeping an eye on the ambition to achieve "ever closer union among the peoples of Europe" that has been the watchword of nearly all over-Europe political thinking in that period – British contributions included – we will also make our way into the perhaps not very philosophical opening of "Brexit"; the referendum on the UK's membership of the European Union in 2016, and the majority that was won then for "Leave".

III

The idea of a united Europe found a new lease of life in the immediate aftermath of the Second World War. At that time self-consciously "rational" and "modern" political thinking cleaved to the idea that world peace could be secured only through the institution of a "world government". A major step on the way to such an end was the ambition "to create a kind of United States of Europe", as the rather unlikely figure of the wartime Prime Minister Winston Churchill put it in a speech at Zurich University in 1946 (when he was in fact no longer Prime Minister). This was a "grouping" of nations which, as we shall see, Churchill did not at that time think Britain would be part of.

The nation-state – and the nationalism and xenophobia it cultivated – was increasingly regarded as an inherently pathological and irrational formation, tailor-made for war and international rivalry. A rationally designed federal government in Europe would be able to achieve a more politically advanced and pacific alternative: replacing the particularistic and typically antagonistic politics of national self-interest with a more promisingly peaceful politics formed around the objective interest of the whole. This fusion of national interests into a single European interest would replace national rivalry in Europe once and for all. It is in that context, and in those terms, that the ambition to achieve "ever closer union among the peoples of Europe" most often made its way among those closest to its project. It was the fervent conviction of the founders of "the project" that the aim of cultivating conditions of mutual understanding and respect between the peoples of Europe ultimately required developing the institutional architecture of a European political body with the State-like power of a federal government. And it was the developing design of that institution that was often to the fore in discussing European developments.

While it was not an organisation that served as a building block of the future European Union, Churchill's call for the formation of "a Council of Europe", which was inaugurated in 1949, was one of its spiritual ancestors. The Council of Europe was an initiative that Britain supported and participated in, and the characteristic hope "to achieve a greater unity" among the peoples of Europe was already clear, even if the institutional means to that end remained open:

> Article 1a. The aim of the Council of Europe is to achieve a greater unity between its Members for the purpose of safeguarding and realizing the ideals and principles which are their common heritage and facilitating their economic and social progress. (Statute of the Council of Europe, London, 5th May 1949)

Under the guidance of the French diplomat Jean Monnet, it was, however, the European Coal and Steel Community (ECSC), inaugurated in 1951, and not the Council of Europe that took up the creative effort "to achieve a greater unity" through what was initially expected to be a rapid institutional development towards "a kind of United States of Europe". The preamble of the treaty that forged the ECSC gives clear expression to that effort, and to a distinctively political sense of the unity, it aimed to realise. Britain did not take part in the initiative.

> CONSIDERING that world peace may be safeguarded only by creative efforts equal to the dangers which menace it; CONVINCED that the contribution which an organized and vital Europe can bring to civilization is indispensable to the maintenance of peaceful relations; CONSCIOUS of the fact that Europe can be built only by concrete actions which create a real solidarity and by the establishment of common bases for economic development; DESIROUS of assisting through the expansion of their basic production in raising the standard of living and in furthering the works of peace; RESOLVED to substitute for historic rivalries a fusion of their essential interests; to establish, by creating an economic community, the foundation of a broad and independent community among peoples long divided by bloody conflicts; and to lay the bases of institutions capable of giving direction to their future common destiny. (The Treaty of Paris, 1951)

The "Commission" formed the central institutional expression of the ambitions of this treaty: a supranational authority that would construct an economic union as a transitional phase on the road to a new political union. Indeed, the words of the preamble of the Treaty of Paris show very clearly that the creation of an economic community had always been a stage on the way to substituting government in the national interest with "institutions capable of giving direction" to the European peoples conceived as a community whose interests had fused into one.

The beautiful vague words on "ever closer union" were first introduced in the Treaty of Rome in 1957, officially the Treaty establishing the European Economic Community (EEC), stressing the cosmopolitical objectives of economic integration. The supranational, institutional conditions thought necessary to the attainment of those objectives were understood as likely to develop in a step-by-step "neo-functionalist" way, where integration in specific sectors would lead more or less inevitably to further such developments in other sectors, the historical role of nation-states in those sectors being successively taken up by the supranational body in that process.

An economically flat-lining UK began to turn to Europe at the start of the 1960s, but was twice thwarted in its bid to join by a French veto. President Charles de Gaulle's concern that a Britain too closely aligned to the United States was ill-suited to a pan-European project proved to be the major stumbling block. However, a third application made after his departure from office in 1969 was successful, with Britain officially joining the EEC in 1973, along with Denmark and Ireland. Only two years later the incoming Labour government offered Britain its first-ever referendum on the question of continued membership. The Government's own information pamphlet recommended that voters support "staying in the Community". The pamphlet was explicit that the aims of integration went beyond the promise of national economic advantages, and included the cosmopolitical virtues of a pacific union. The ongoing transfer of competences to the supranational level which those closest to "the project" hoped to see was not, however, on the list of aims (https://digital.library.lse.ac.uk/objects/lse:fug282yox):

> The aims of the Common Market are:
>
> - To bring together the peoples of Europe.
> - To raise living standards and improve working conditions.
> - To promote growth and boost world trade.
> - To help the poorest regions of Europe and the rest of the world.
> - To help maintain peace and freedom.

The "Yes" campaign was supported by Prime Minister Harold Wilson, but without the backing of his own party, which had roundly rejected continuing membership in a special conference vote before the 1975 referendum. It was also supported by the new Conservative leader Margaret Thatcher, and the Liberal leader Jeremey Thorpe. Both the Labour and Conservative parties were already split on the question, the former far more so than the latter at that time. Labour "No" campaigners were largely from the left of the party (represented most notably by Tony Benn), Tory "No" campaigners largely from the right (represented most notably by Enoch Powell). But the majority of the leading figures in both parties supported continuing membership, as did the large-circulation national newspapers and Britain's business leaders. The referendum went decisively in favour of remaining. Britain stayed in, at least for a while.

The first institutions of European union emerged in the wake of two terrible world wars of European origin. It was also, however, the period of European division that marked the Cold War. Sticking as we are to British political voices, it is worth noting that it was the latter that was to the fore in Prime Minister Margaret Thatcher's most strikingly pro-European speech, "The Bruges Speech", delivered in 1988. Anticipating surprise among some of her audience, she insistently affirmed that "our [Britain's] destiny is in Europe, as part of the Community", but she went on even more strongly to recall that still only part of Europe was part of that Community:

> The European Community is one manifestation of that European identity, but it is not the only one. We must never forget that east of the Iron Curtain, people who once enjoyed a full share of European culture, freedom and identity have been cut off from their roots. We shall always look on Warsaw, Prague, Budapest as great European cities. (Thatcher, speech to the College of Europe, "The Bruges Speech", September 20, 1988)

Thatcher, like Churchill in his call for "a kind of United States of Europe" in 1946, emphasised the geopolitical significance of the (by then) European Community (EC), and its role in ensuring "prosperity and security" for Europeans "in a world in which there are many other powerful nations and groups of nations". In the 1980s, however, such a project was more clearly framed by the contemporary circumstances of the Cold War rather than the memory of World Wars. Seventeen years later, Prime Minister Tony Blair, speaking to the European Parliament in 2005, not only distanced himself from Thatcher's "market philosophy", he also framed the historic opportunity for those European countries that had suffered under Soviet domination and totalitarian conditions differently than Thatcher. Like Thatcher, he argued that "enlargement" of the (by then) European Union (EU) to include the (by then) post-communist central and eastern European countries was an issue for the EU's "economy" and "security". However, the political significance of this geopolitical development had shifted again. European integration was no longer a Post-War or Cold War security project, but a politically progressive one: the "extraordinary historic opportunity" offered by enlargement belonged to a politics forged "in the traditions of European idealism", standing squarely against "outdated nationalism and xenophobia" (Blair, speech to the European Parliament, June 23, 2005).

Coming from a country whose semi-detached position seems to have been its only European constant, it is perhaps ironic that leading British politicians of this period – Churchill, Thatcher, Blair – all argued that the major problems facing Europe in their time were not about institutional "principles or conceptions" (Churchill), or questions calling for "arcane institutional debates" (Thatcher), or constitutional "subtleties and complexities" (Blair). In a time of "ruin" and "despair" (Churchill), "a time of change and uncertainty" (Thatcher), a time of "profound upheaval" (Blair), the question of Europe's heading was, they all argued, not only economic or institutional, but first of all political and geopolitical. Moreover, for them, advancing the project of European co-operation was not about making use of difficult political circumstances to announce the necessity of further neo-functionalist developments, but, in the face of such circumstances, to make the case for a moral and political choice in favour of Europe, thus requiring from Europe's national representatives, above all, "moral leadership" (Churchill), "political courage" (Thatcher, twice), "political leadership" (Blair).

In what will never be an affectively forceful expression, Blair emphasised that the decisive political leadership needed in Europe should be from "moderate people". He meant this to contrast with the politics of Nazi, fascist, and socialist totalitarianisms which had cast such a shadow over Europe during the twentieth century. The Europe of nations had created circumstances in which "extremes gain traction". Blair saw the European Union as a union of "values" and "solidarity between nations", a "common political space" and "not just a common market"; a union in which a "social Europe" and an "economic Europe" would mutually sustain each other, and prevent a descent back into political chaos.

It is sometimes suggested that Britain only ever wanted to belong to an economic community, and that perception is not wholly unwarranted. However, with Churchill, Thatcher and Blair, one can also see an underlying commitment to a (variously understood) political and geopolitical project. One could, of course, follow Hitler in thinking that the British approach to Europe is merely a (what might now be called) neoliberal attempt to further "the so-called peaceful conquest of the world by commercial means", an attempt that aims in reality only "at the consolidation of British world hegemony" (MK, p. 500, p. 502). But if Churchill's call in 1946 for a united Europe that could overcome "that series of frightful nationalistic quarrels", if his hope that Europeans "in so many ancient states and nations" might be spared the tragedy of "tearing each other to pieces", if his dream of building a political body in Europe "under which it can dwell in peace", if all that was a call for British world hegemony (or even just "the happiness of England" to use Nietzsche's expression), and not an attempt to rescue Europe from its bloody history, one has to take one's leave of the conversation – even if at times one has to take one's leave from Churchill too. The vision of what Thatcher called the "willing and active cooperation between independent sovereign states" striving "to speak with a single voice", to pool or share sovereignty where things can be done "better together than alone", the vision of what Blair called "a union of values, of solidarity between nations and people", may be typically British, but, is also, I will argue in this chapter, in good part Kantian, and also in main part – good.

This trio of British politicians gives a fair sense of the shifting geopolitical sands across the immediately-post-War, Cold War, and then post-Cold War contexts. However, that simplified timeline overlooks another trio: Prime Minister Harold Wilson, who prepared the ground for joining in the 1960s, Prime Minister Edward Heath who took the UK into the EEC in 1973, and Prime Minister John Major who achieved a hard-won parliamentary majority for the Treaty of Maastricht, which brought the EU into being, in 1992. All three were just as keen as Churchill, Thatcher and Blair to stress the political virtues of European integration, and not just economic benefits. Wilson, speaking to the House of Commons in the run-up to the second (and again rejected) application to join the EEC in 1967, insisted that:

> whatever the economic arguments, the House will realise that, as I have repeatedly made clear, the Government's purpose derives, above all, from our recognition that Europe is now faced with the opportunity of a great move forward in political unity and that we can – and indeed must – play our full part in it. We do not see European unity as something narrow or inward-looking...Together we can ensure that Europe plays in world affairs the part which the Europe of today is not at present playing. (Wilson, House of Commons Speech, 1967).

Heath too saw in the EEC the possibility of "an end to divisions which have stricken Europe for centuries" (Edward Heath, "Brussels Speech", 1972), and still in the time of the Cold War stressed, like Thatcher after him, that this division was not over: "'Europe' is more than Western Europe alone. There lies also to the east another part of our continent: countries whose history has been closely linked with our own". Twenty years later, John Major welcomed the possibility of "embracing the new democracies of the East", emphasising above all that "the most far-reaching, the most profound reason for working together in Europe...is peace" (Major, Conservative Party Conference Speech, 1992). These "joining" efforts were taken on by Wilson, Heath and Major in a British national context that only became more anxious that national political decisions in Westminster would "let Britain's identity be lost in Europe", as Major reported "a lady [in Cornwall]" putting it to him. Speaking to an increasingly Eurosceptical Conservative Party, Major insisted that "being at the heart of Europe" was not about "turning a deaf ear to the heartbeat of Britain" but seeing "our own national interest", what is "right for British industry; right for British jobs; right for British prosperity", as now more than ever inseparably connected to Britain's membership of "the Community" and its flourishing.

There is considerable continuity across these British political speeches on the primarily pacific virtue of European political integration, and of Britain's best future as lying fully in that development. But there is another British continuity that is equally significant, if significantly more problematic, something belonging to the distinctive "Europe of the Atlantic" perspective that Britain has been historically central to. As I have indicated, Churchill did not think Britain would be part of his projection of "a kind of United States of Europe" in 1946. The "coherent natural grouping" of nations from the "mighty continent" would be a partner with what he called another "natural grouping in the Western Hemisphere": "we British have our own Commonwealth of Nations".

(Along with the UK, the members of the Commonwealth at this time were the semi-independent polities that had Dominion status, and in 1946, white governments, within the British Empire. In 1946 these were Canada, the Irish Free State, Newfoundland, and the Union of South Africa.) We have seen that when Germany has been in question for Germany, Europe has always been in view too. As we shall see, when Europe has been in view for Britain, it is the history and memory of Empire that has loomed largest over its horizon.

As the Council of Europe began to take shape, it seems that Churchill began to look more favourably on the idea of Britain joining the European group. Perhaps the "natural grouping" of the Commonwealth started looking considerably less "natural" to him when the organisation of countries that were formerly part of the Empire started to include quite so many countries of the (rapidly diminishing) Empire not ruled by white people. In any case, he was unquestionably in favour of Britain joining the EEC later in his long life, which is no great advert for it. Nevertheless, it is Empire that brings in a further defining aspect of the line of British Prime Ministerial contributions we are considering here – at least until Blair. Successive British politicians still had Empire in view when Europe was in view. In the passage from Wilson's speech cited above I omitted a sentence in which he had underlined the British view of the importance of a Europe to come that was not "narrow or inward-looking" by immediately recalling that, "Britain has her own vital links through the Commonwealth, and in other ways, with other continents. So have other European countries". It was there in Heath's Brussels speech in 1972 when, while claiming not to be thinking of reviving the "Age of Imperialism", he nevertheless stressed "the lasting and creative effects of the spread of language and of culture, of commerce and of administration by people from Europe across land and sea to the other continents of the world". It was even more powerfully present in Thatcher's Bruges speech in 1988 too, where she spoke shamelessly of "how Europeans explored and colonised – and yes, without apology – civilised much of the world". And, in fact, it was still there in Major's conference speech in 1992, when he claimed that, "Britain has always grown and prospered when it has looked outwards – from the time of the First Elizabeth". The post-War British understanding of both itself and of Europe was forged in the history and memory of British and European discovery, colonialism and Empire.

Blair's speech to the European parliament in 2005 was not free of Imperial references, but the attempt was made there to mark a decisive break from the post-War British understanding of both itself and of Europe in that regard. He did not represent the Europe that "had dominated the world, colonised large parts of it, fought wars against each other for world supremacy" as something one might recall without more ado, still less without apology: if there was a time when European leaders had done so, he said, "those days were gone". Moreover, he did not speak up for "the idea of Europe, united and working together", as Churchill had, from the outside, but firmly from the inside, as "a passionate pro-European", confidently affirming his commitment to "Europe as a political project". Not that he advocated ever greater powers for European institutions. Blair gave his speech in the wake of referenda "in two founding member states" in which the EU's attempt to establish a European Constitution had been "comprehensively rejected" by ordinary citizens. He was drily provocative in denying against no one that this was because "people studied the constitution and disagreed with its precise articles". It was perfectly clear that it was a question of perceived EU over-Europe overreach: people were simply opposed to the pretence or aim to establish the EU as a supranational State-like body, a superstate. And Blair agreed with them: "people always see politics more clearly than us. Precisely because they are not daily obsessed with it". In Blair's view, the real challenge for the EU was about the "renewal" and "modernisation" of its "policies" not the statification of its "institutions". Or again, the EU's future depended on the success of its practical efforts to "improve the lives of people", not the promotion of a distant "ideal" that very few Europeans found attractive. It was failing in the former, and Europe was weaker as a result. Thinking in this way was not, he insisted, "anti-Europe" but would help the EU "recover... support amongst the people", without which Europe could find that its citizens and nations had simply "defaulted to Euroscepticism".

Moreover, the whole pacific point of the EU for Blair was to enhance and protect not reduce and replace the power of its Member States. As Blair had put it in a speech two years earlier in Warsaw, "the purpose of the European Union is to give us, the individual nations that form it, greater economic and political strength" (Blair Speech in Warsaw, 2003). An EU which enabled its members "to cooperate in our mutual interest" would ward off Euroscepticism by practically demonstrating that "in collective cooperation they increase individual strength" (Blair, speech to the European Parliament, 2005). His Warsaw speech was explicit about the EU this implied:

> We want a union of nations, not a federal superstate, and that vision is shared by the majority of countries and people in Europe. A European superstate would neither have the efficacy or legitimacy to meet the global challenge... I reject the notion that the "true" Europe is to be found only in the European Commission and European Parliament. The European Union is a balance between the community and the intergovernmental. What we need to do is to strengthen Europe where necessary at every level; but the fount of authority lies in the free will of nations, collectively expressed... [We] need to root the European vision in the identity of the nations that make up Europe. (Blair, speech in Warsaw, 2003)

We will come back to the *prima facie* paradoxical idea of enhancing the strength of individual nations through membership of a political union that limits their sovereignty later in this chapter.

For Blair, the future of the EU lay not in the possibility of a new European federal government, not a new state-like "bureaucracy", but in improved co-ordination on policies that could make the EU the "champion of a global, outward-looking, competitive Europe". The classic "Europe of the Atlantic" figure of Europe is still clearly in view here, but now in the form of what one might call its post-Imperial Europeanisation. It was, I think, a promising development, but in reality, it was only nascently and weakly making its generational way in Britain (see Joseph, 2016). And Blair's pro-European speech to the European Parliament was greeted with jeers – by Britain's own UKIP MEPs. Increasingly hostile to what they saw as centralising forces in the EU overwhelming political freedom in the UK, the right in Britain saw the EU as a regulatory fetter to a self-confident and still globally voyaging Britain. Meanwhile, sections of the left framed the EU as a deregulating neoliberal trap, and part of a neoliberal hegemony increasingly becoming global. For that part of the left, it was better for Britain to escape the EU altogether. Many UK citizens were simply feeling something that the lady from Cornwall was feeling: Britain was losing itself not renewing itself, and not least in Europe. In a desperately ill-conceived bid by Prime Minister David Cameron to quell the divisions over Europe within his own party in a national way, a referendum on Britain's membership of the EU was held in 2016.

Prior to the referendum, Cameron tried to renegotiate a "new settlement" on the UK's membership, and very nearly won what might have been a significant change not just for the UK but for the EU. The draft agreement between Cameron and President of the European Council, Donald Tusk presented on 2nd February 2016 included the following text:

> SECTION C
>
> SOVEREIGNTY
>
> 1. References in the Treaties and their preambles to the process of creating an ever closer union among the peoples of Europe are primarily intended to signal that the Union's aim is to promote trust and understanding among peoples living in open and democratic societies sharing a common heritage of universal values. They are not an equivalent to the objective of political integration. (https://www.consilium.europa.eu/media/21980/decision-new-settlementen16.pdf)

This text did not make it to the final agreement of 19th February 2016, the latter replacing it with the bizarre proposal that EU treaties be amended "so as to make it clear that the references to ever closer union do not apply to the United Kingdom". The draft text of "Section C" may not have anyway given Cameron what he needed to win the referendum, perhaps nothing would have given him that, but its replacement (with its interestingly truncated quotation of the beautiful vague words), the strangest of all UK EU opt-outs, was an unconvincing variation. In the end, the final agreement, with its truncated quotation and its accompanying (very) long explication that "references to ever closer union" in the EU treaties in fact *have no legal significance whatsoever* whether they "apply" to a Member State or not, only served to confirm that the beautiful vague words were also jealously guarded words for those who wanted them, vaguely-if-not-legally, to still "signal" a vision of ("ever closer") political integration, and not on the books, as the draft would have had it, as something definitively and explicitly "not equivalent" to that.

Defending Britain's membership of a Union that few could have thought especially inspiring in its existing condition or trajectory, the campaign for "Remain" was strongest in Scotland, where the leaders of all the major parties at least worked conspicuously together, and (like 1975) effectively marginalised "Leave" voices as retrograde and extremist. Many leading national politicians – perhaps especially the former Prime Ministers John Major, Tony Blair and Gordon Brown, along with the leaders and former leaders of the minority Liberal-Democrat and Green parties – put all their energy behind the pro-European cause. But, with the Conservative Party now divided from top to bottom, and a woefully inadequate present-but-not-participating leader of the Labour Party, a longstanding follower of Tony Benn with a consistently Eurosceptic past who refused point-blank to participate in a cross-party national campaign, the Remain voice in the UK did not compete well against the glittering promise to "take back control" that belonged to Leave supporters; and most of the national newspapers.

Ultimately, however, it is not clear that the result of the referendum was due to the Remain voice being so fragmented, or what beautiful vague words meant, or indeed how much it was specifically or coherently about assessments of the EU's actual role in British political life. Beyond the postures and impostures of political persuasion, the referendum gave an opportunity, a rare opening, for feelings like those of the lady from Cornwall to find public expression. "She didn't tell me her name", Major confessed in his conference speech in 1992, but he was doubtless right to think that there was, articulated in that anonymous voice, "the anxieties of millions".

The referendum was their opportunity, and "Brexit" the all-but-meaningless name of their aggregated preferences. ("Brexit means Brexit" – or "'Brexit' means Brexit" – as Prime Minister Theresa May, who was the first to be tasked with the near-impossible task of picking up the pieces afterwards, came to put it.) While its meaning remains not one, its consequences far-reaching and unpredictable, there was, however, at least one ungainsayable result. As a result of the definitive referendum result, the hope that the UK might find a new post-imperial sense of itself in Europe was, whether temporarily or permanently we do not know, overnight extinguished.

Losing its most effective voice in a world in which it was anyway increasingly marginal, it is also hard to disagree with the English friend of Donald Tusk, who the latter cites as saying, "Brexit is the real end of the British Empire" – and that despite the fact that "Brexit" is itself a symptom of Britain having not got beyond understanding itself through Imperial history. A striking post-referendum period of buyers remorse notwithstanding, the *vox pop* of British citizens remains typically a-typical compared to the rest of Europe. For the first volume of this book I had commissioned Anna Ksiazczakova to gather together the last ten years of Eurobarometer survey responses to the question *Do you see yourself as* [select one of the following]:

European only
European and [NATIONALITY]
[NATIONALITY] and European
[NATIONALITY] only

With the over-Europe German, French and British spirits in view in this volume, Ksiazczakova also supplied, along with the EU average, the country breakdowns in these cases too. Data like this never speaks for itself, but this data still speaks volumes:

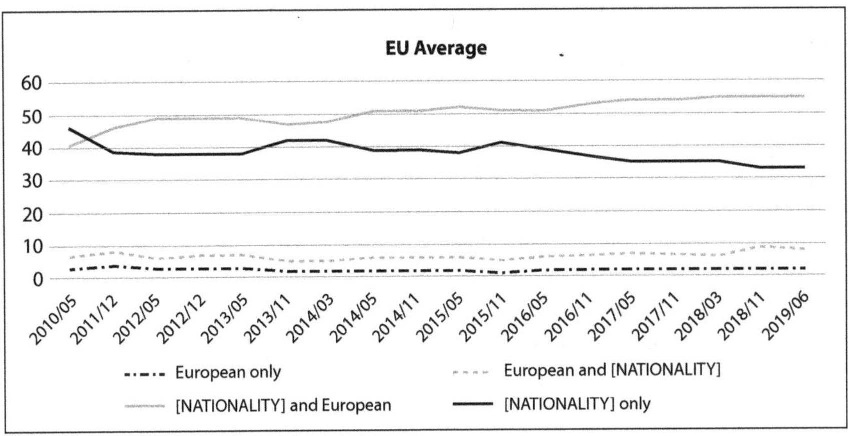

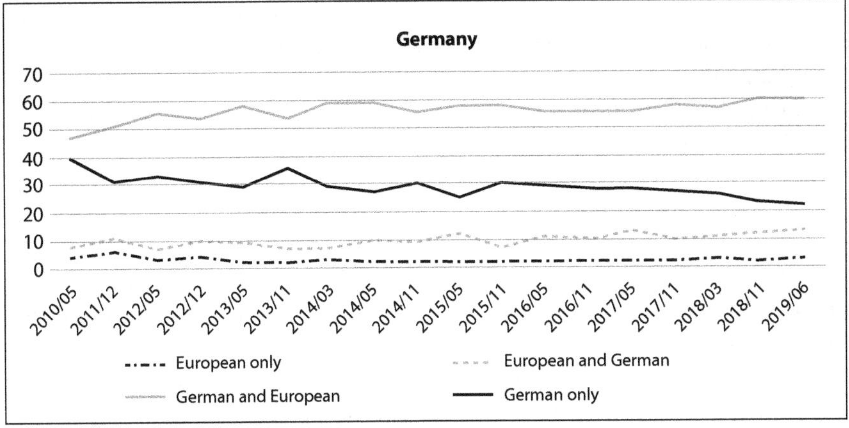

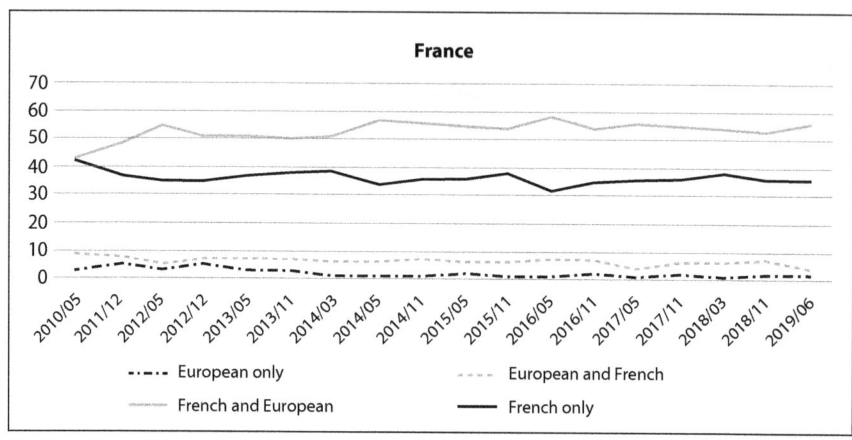

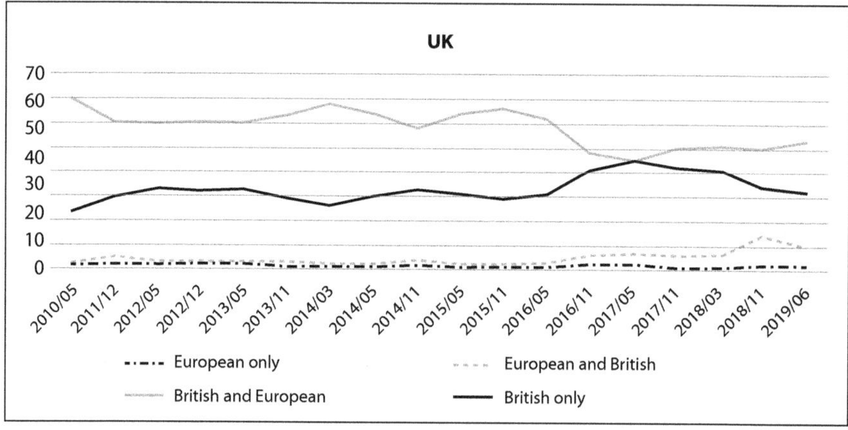

Perhaps paradoxically, British citizens began to see themselves as more European just as the reality of leaving the EU became the un-ending theme of British political news. But perhaps not so paradoxically. Euroscepticism had brought European politics into the heart of British politics as never before, and Europeanised many in Britain as it did so. Brexit was the apotheosis of that. We almost became somewhat more typically European in the process. We did, at least for a while.

IV

Prior to Britain's voice being altogether extinguished in the EU, proposals from pro-EU British politicians over what a British contribution to the EU should look like were fairly diverse, albeit on a familiar political spectrum. In question was typically whether Britain should take the (in Europe not inconsiderable) power of its sovereign voice into the EU project with a more right-wing "free-market" vision, or a more left-wing "social Europe" vision, or with a "third way" vision that embraced something of both. All that is, for now, moot.

On the other hand, those more Eurosceptic perceptions of the EU, right and left, also have some merit, and that was too often ducked by pro-EU voices in Britain. The EU as an institution with power has an undeniable desire to extend its reach and increase its power, and even if its neo-liberalism is, in fact, generally better understood as an ordo-liberal variation, there is no doubt that this holds a majority, and its order currently affects some Member States as adversely as it advantages others. In Europe today, there are powerful forces of centralising harmonisation in that ordo-liberal form, as well as emerging forces of nationalist disintegration in its classical form. Beyond familiar political preferences, beyond the shifting national preferences discovered by regular elections, what is above all side-lined by Britain's leaving is the British vision of Europe that has most continuously presented itself as most promising: the characteristically and consistently mainstream British pro-European preference for "braving the waves" and sailing "on the Rubicon", as the Greek-French and now naturalised British Professor of International Relations at the University of Oxford, Kalypso Nicolaïdis, has put it (EDC, p. 14; see also Nicolaïdis 2018). This "sailing on the Rubicon" preference-for-Europe warns against both crossing it (in harmonising federalism) and halting before it (in isolationist nationalism). That preference, another and philosophically deeper "third way" vision (EDC, p. 1), is as modest as it may seem unstable, but it is, I will argue, still the best one for Europe.

That "third way" vision has not succeeded in dominating, even for a while. In Warsaw, in 2003 Blair was confident that it was not an exclusively British view, and that the pro-European "argument" against a European superstate was "shared by the majority of countries and people in Europe", and "is being won"; he was confident that the historically British-type view, the view of *such spirits*, "can win in Europe". But he was equally sure that Eurosceptic efforts in Britain "designed to spook us" and "whose real purpose is to provide the basis for British withdrawal from Europe" could derail everything. Member States that affirm the long-held British view can win but "we can't do it standing on the touchline". Today, having altogether quit the field, Britain is not even standing on the touchline, at best grandstanding from the stands.

The typically British pro-EU vision of the pacific ambitions of European integration was fundamentally political and geopolitical, but it had little to do with the more exalted post-national hopes of European federalists. Indeed, from the point of view of federalist ambitions to produce a new "fusion of interests", even the pro-EU British voice seemed always only to hold up and interrupt European developments towards "the European ideal". European federalists may be as pleased as the British Eurosceptics to see us gone.

Blair did not think Britain was isolated in its preference; its "third way" vision was not, he thought, reserved for the British mainstream alone, and in the years to come the EU will not need Britain's membership to hear it. But as Britain diminishes its presence in Europe, the force of the argument there is also diminished. Nevertheless, the question concerning the kind of "*kind of*" United States of Europe that might deliver on the cosmopolitan ambitions of "ever closer union among the peoples of Europe" will not go away with Britain's leaving. In this quarrel over the future of European integration and the meaning of beautiful vague words, there is a profound, and I want to say profoundly philosophical divergence that remains at the heart of European politics. Should the efforts to speak (as Margaret Thatcher put it) "with a single voice" lead finally, to the formation of a European government in a Europe where the old nations would have (as Jürgen Habermas puts it) "the function of implementing administrations" where and when decisions are made centrally (LT, p. 14), or, alternatively, should political authority at the European level remain a delegated power where Commission competences are conferred to it by its Member States, its guiding direction and policy-making working to promote their national interests, interests which, of course, includes their (massive) shared interest in maintaining the peace and prosperity of the whole? Nietzsche clearly had a practical hat on (a rather bowler-like homburg apparently) when he noted that the European federation to come would have to serve "the interests of the great cantons" at the same time as it served the interests of "the whole federation" (HH, p. 344). It would be a set-up in which Member States limit but do not annul their own sovereignty in a union that would protect and not dissolve their "separate rights" (HH, p. 344).

This typically "English" project aims to foster the creation of a political body that could both preserve and secure the diversity of Europe's nations and reduce what Mill called their "extreme intolerance of one another". As Edward Heath noted, this was never going to be simple: "imagination will be required to develop institutions which respect the traditions and the individuality of the Member States, but at the same time have the strength to guide the future course of the enlarged Community" (Heath, "Brussels Speech"). The growing worry in Britain, however, was that some of those closest to the project had an altogether different institutional ambition in view: a political body that would aim finally to end the extreme intolerance that had hitherto led to war by effectively eliminating its political source in the conflicts of interest between different national powers. While championing the idea of the "ever closer union between the peoples of Europe", this is a desire finally to overcome the major political expressions of that plurality: the national ones. In what follows, I aim to show that the profoundly modern idea of effecting a movement towards the *ideal telos* of a European political community that really *is* one because it really is *one*, is fatally compromised by the fact that the very *telos* that seems to produce a (supranational) political order that is necessarily *immune* from the destructive threats of war and conflict (because there are no competing national interests to be fought over) is, in fact, and at once, the condition of its own most radical *auto-immune* disorder (spiritual stagnation and even self-destroying conflict). In short, in what follows, I will be speaking up for the more modest but also more imaginatively demanding union that British politicians have most continuously championed.

V

We Europeans are in trouble again now, in our today. Not simply because of some purely external threat from outside us, but from a still too modern spirit within us that is now increasingly desiring for Europe – the unity of a federal State – as its ideal end. This tendency could produce what Mill describes as an odd kind of stationariness for Europe: domination by a mentality or spirit that officially allows change and (oh yes) welcomes pluralism, but just so long as all now change together, and just so long as the pluralism that is affirmed is...the same. ("We [Europeans] should think we had done wonders if we had made ourselves all alike", says Mill.)

The mainstream "English" spirit simply holds fast to Nietzsche's acknowledgement of Europe's possession of "manifold souls". What made us a "we" really worthy of the name – what made it worth speaking about "we, the Europeans" all together as one and all distinctively European – is...our "individuality", the "singularity" of the people and peoples within the diverse nations of Europe, and their "unlikeness" one to another (OL, p. 70). And there, with what Nietzsche called a federation made up of nations "delimited by their proper geographical borders" (even if these borders are "open", i.e. *closeable*) we "English" spirits want to stick. Yet today, Mill says – Mill in his today which is very close to Nietzsche's and also not so very far from our own – this political desire for modest union is outrun by forces, let's say still-too-modern spiritual forces, which imagine it would be strengthened by a more radically assimilating, amalgamating "we": a European community that is One.

Mill did not explore the idea of a federation in Europe, and in his writings on the more demanding idea of federal government, he does not even consider Europe as a possible candidate. Nevertheless, the creation of a European union that wants both to preserve and secure the diversity of Europe's nation-states and to reduce their extreme intolerance of one another is surely something he would have welcomed. And he offers a timely warning for the present generation of European enthusiasts: that its courageous efforts to achieve "ever closer union between the peoples of Europe" carries inside itself the threat of wanting the European plurality that is its singular virtue finally to be eliminated as a politically salient feature of Europe's politics – a final end that would "overcome" what Habermas sees as the debilitating effects of "national particularisms" in European politics (LT, p. 15). That end of Europe would be, I will argue, the end of Europe.

In Mill's view, by contrast, and I think we still need to heed this, the best and most European of Europeans today are those who come to "see that it is good that there should be differences" (OL, p. 68). The alternative is a nightmare of a distinctively modern European form of history-ending "stationariness": the levelling demand for uniformity that, often enough in the form of a profoundly hollowed-out appeal to "democracy" and "community", betrays Europe because it "proscribes singularity" (OL, p. 70). For sure, what many of us singularly will is indeed a united Europe. But this is not a call for a United States of Europe, or only (very) kind of. Rather, it is the call for a transformation of the fractious Nation States of Europe into co-operative Member States of their Union, and a Union institutional body with considerable guiding power but which would not have the ruling power like that of a State.

Nietzsche's synthetic ambition (without its eugenicist attemptations), the becoming "good Europeans" of Europeans, does not have to be sacrificed in this context, nor his stress on the importance to the thinking of unity in Europe on the role of people who are steeped in literature "up to their eyes and ears": "writers and poets" (BGE, p. 170). In the 1920s and 30s, the writer and poet Paul Valéry was among those calling for a new international union of sorts in the context of the development of the League of Nations. In his contributions to this, Valéry invariably insisted that the development of such a body cannot and should not depend only on the work of *minds especially dedicated to government*. It needs, in addition, the co-operation of "*minds especially dedicated to the mind*" (HP, p. 345): not just co-operation between people who work on treaties and constitutions, or policies and priorities, but also among people who work creatively and imaginatively on our self-understanding, our understanding of who "we" are. But the goal here is not the achievement of a Single European Mind that will help draft some future Single European Act. As an artistic experimenter himself, Valéry insisted that the point is precisely *not* "to establish among minds the harmony of uniformity" (HP, p. 348). Far from it:

> That [uniformity] would doubtless be monotonous, and certainly undesirable. It is right that ideas should differ according to men, their ages, conditions, and surroundings, and there is more than one art of thinking. This very variety is a natural and necessary condition of vitality. (HP, p. 348)

Valéry did not think, as a contemporary Eurosceptic might, that such differences create insurmountable "obstacles" to a developing harmony: they do not need to "harden in isolation and become inaccessible to exchange" (HP, p. 348). On the contrary, through the intensification of such exchanges, one can strive to attain a condition of harmony *without* harmonisation. And this is, surely, as close as one could wish to the European cultural ideal of unity in diversity, an ideal that the European project has always officially put at the foreground of its movement towards "ever closer union among the peoples of Europe". As I say, this latter idea should not be understood as a movement towards an increasingly more state-like European federal government, but (more modestly, moderately) in terms of cultivating lasting, stabilisable, supranational institutional conditions of co-operation and mutual respect between Member States of a federation, conditions which make antagonism and war between them increasingly less likely.

And whose idea was this? Who was it who first thought this out with the greatest rigour and future-producing brilliance? The one who was woken from his dogmatic slumber by Hume (a thinker from what Nietzsche called "England",

and Mill perhaps even more oddly called "England (or rather Scotland)"). It was the idea of that great German Scot, Immanuel Kant. Despite the fact that "old Kant" (as Nietzsche often calls him) affirmed that the idea of "a kind of league" of nations, a "pacific federation", is genuinely "practicable" (Kant, p. 104), he was convinced that in a world of linguistic and religious differences – in other words, multiple national cultural differences – a state-like supranational political set-up would be a road to disaster, leading only to a "universal despotism" (Kant, p. 114). His words seem still to fall on deaf ears.

For the rest of this chapter, I will take us back to old Kant to look once more at the Kantian idea of European union, and its future. The basic Kantian idea is quite simple: success in the attempt to realise "the achievement of a just civic constitution" within which "the rights of each [citizen] can be secured" in a *nation*, presupposes the formation of an order "similar to a civil one" at an *international* level, an order "within which the rights of each [*nation*] can be secured" (Kant, p. 102). Like Nietzsche after him, and like many British politicians in our time, Kant will call for the formation of a Federation of Free States, not a Federal State.

VI

In a commentary on Kant's conception of "the pacifying function of law", Habermas notes that when he (Kant) projected the kind of national political constitutions, the "*bürgerliche Verfassung*", that emerged in revolutionary France and America, "onto the global level" he was making the "farsighted conceptual innovation" that brought about "the birth of the idea of the constitutionalization of international law" (BNR, p. 314). As we shall see, Habermas's conception of Kant's extraordinary innovation is profoundly problematic, but the idea of seeing in Kant's political writings on cosmopolitanism and peace from the 1780s and 1790s a projection of something from a national set-up into an international one is absolutely right, and it really is farsighted. It opens the way to the formation of an international order, first in Europe but ultimately on a global scale: a supranational institutional set-up that promises to lead to a level of international security, peace, and cooperation the like of which has never before been seen in the history of the world. It was a set-up, projected over the long term, "a few centuries from now" (Kant, p. 53), which finally began to see the light of day in the formation of the still-faltering project of European union in the second half of the twentieth century.

While it is important to see that Kant's final aim is to achieve "moral" cosmopolitan conditions of "mutual understanding" between human beings – "even with the most distant of their fellows" (Kant, p. 111), his discussion is essentially "political" or cosmopolitical: the internationalisation of the idea of constitutional government, as Habermas aptly puts it. However, as we shall see, this will not conclude with the formation of an international constitutional government. Rather, (and this is the only respect in which it is the same as a civil social contract and a national constitutional government) just as national constitutional government creates conditions in which *the freedom of each [citizen] is made to be consistent with the freedom of every other*, so in the international case, it concerns the creation of institutional conditions in which *the freedom of each [nation] is made to be consistent with the freedom of every other.*

The "social contract" idea – as an idea – relates to the thought of a human collectivity moving from a condition of "lawless freedom" into a life in "civil States" within a framework of law (Kant, p. 98). This is a move from a state of nature which is "a state of war" to the "formal institution" of a state of peace in a "legal civil State" (Kant, p. 98). The claim here is not that this actually happened at some time in history but that the condition we are actually in, can only be coherently *thought* with reference to the "*idea* of an original contract" (Kant, p. 94, p. 100). The actual condition calls for a description which represents the social contract as an attained one: one in which consent has been secured from all citizens to submit to coercive laws (restraints on freedom) that, in each case, restrict (each) my freedom in order, optimally, to maximise the freedom of all. Thought through the idea of an original contract, society can be grasped as one in which peace has become the attained norm not the exception, a society which has become "a community of friends" rather than one in which every neighbour would have to be treated (conceptually) as "an enemy" or at least "a permanent threat to me" (Kant, p. 98).

So, in the formation of a legal civil State, individuals (and their particular wills) can be conceived as having shifted from a barbaric and savage condition to a rational and civilised one where the state is the State. But – and this is Kant's innovation – certain parallel considerations hold for the relations between such States (and their particular wills) and their neighbours (with theirs). And in this case, it will not only be the idea of a contract but a project actually entered into: participants would explicitly agree to submit to coercive laws, legal arrangements, "similar to the civil one", in order to secure the rights of each to govern themselves without fear that their neighbours might be a permanent threat (Kant, p. 102).

For Kant this development also alters the status of individuals *qua* citizens of such States: the ideal attainment of universal equality of liberty for all members of a society as *citizens of a nation-state* leads ultimately to (indeed, ultimately presupposes) an international order in which those citizens are conferred cosmopolitical rights as *citizens of the world*. The political animal "Man" becomes, finally, a cosmopolitical animal. A cosmopolitan existence – the chance of mutual understanding and respect between the most diverse peoples – is to be realised through the institution of a "great political body" capable of securing what is "right" (rather than "wrong") in international relations. As we shall see, however, this body is quite unlike the States whose right they secure. It should not, Kant insists, have the "power like that of a State" (Kant, p. 104). It is, nevertheless a powerful institution; one which can (paradoxically) master the States in order to "preserve and secure" their freedom as States (Kant, p. 104), and "thus" – as the final aim of all this – see to it that "men could live everywhere on earth" (Kant, p. 111) in a set-up that should "lead to mutual understanding and peace" rather than mutual ignorance and war (Kant, p. 114).

VII

In his texts on the idea of universal history from the 1780s and 1790s, Kant asks what "a philosophical mind" might be able to say about history in an *a priori* rather than empirical form. His answer is that a philosophically-informed history of the development of an inherently (divinely created) rational creature should see it as an unfolding movement towards a fully rational form of human life for all humanity: life lived in peace with others, life with a cosmopolitan character. Kant thus attempted to present world history as a movement of moral progress towards a worldwide cosmopolitical condition. In his own time – which was, we should not forget a time of almost continual war and political violence in Europe – Kant thought he could see a nascent movement towards such a condition in the developing international relations among bellicose European nations. It was no more than "a feeling beginning to stir in all its members", but it was, he thought, a feeling, a spectral anticipation, of what was coming nonetheless: as a result of more or less constant wars, attempts at inter-national peace-brokering by European nations affected by but not themselves participating in a war will likely "prepare the way for a great political body of the future, without precedence in the past. Although this political body exists for the present only in the roughest of outlines, it nonetheless seems as if a feeling is beginning to stir in all its members, each of which has an interest in maintaining the whole" (Kant, p. 51).

Kant's prediction of a European union leading to peace belongs to a chain of similar ones – Kant himself cites Abbé St Pierre and Rousseau as the most recent of these, but he ridicules them for thinking "that its realization was so imminent" (Kant, p. 48). Moreover, he does not think that such philosophical announcements are simply outside the developments they describe. The philosopher is inside the event: conceiving history as an intrinsically rational process "it appears that we might by our own rational projects accelerate the coming of this period" (Kant, p. 50). What then does Kant say about this European union he sees coming, and whose arrival his writing wants to accelerate?

I want to approach this question through the interpretations of it offered by Hegel (who really set the tone for later reception of the Kantian idea) and Habermas. As we shall see, Habermas will argue that Kant's vision of the practical ideal of European union falls short of the rational idea of European union that he (Kant) remained theoretically committed to. Hegel, however, thought it was simply a totally fanciful idea and a complete non-starter in the first place. Both, Hegel and Habermas are attentive to Kant. But they really do not hear him, or rather they only want to hear him as belonging to a binary conception of international right that they limit themselves to: the binary we are familiar with today between an international system of sovereign nation-states, on the one hand, or an international system based on a supranational State, on the other. Nevertheless, they both begin with what they think Kant says, and then stake out their own position in relation to that.

Hegel did not dispute the universal significance of philosophical investigations like Kant's into "Man" as such. Indeed, he thought (more or less traditionally) there was no higher contribution one could make as a human being than to achieve a reflective consciousness that *we really are all one*, that each one of us – in the singularity of our own being – really is *one* with every other:

> It is the essence of education and of thought, which is the consciousness of the individual in universal form, that the "I" should be apprehended as a universal person, in whom all are identical. Man must be accounted a universal being, not because he is a Jew, Catholic, Protestant, German, or Italian, but because he is a man. This thinking or reflective consciousness, is of *infinite importance*. It is defective only when it plumes itself upon being cosmopolitan, in opposition to the concrete life of the citizen. (HPR, §209)

So while Hegel would not baulk at the idea (here expressed by Derrida) that "the will to be a philosopher, in principle and in relation to the most firm of traditions, is the will to make a contribution to the universal community" (Derrida, *Le Figaro*, October 16, 1999), he (Hegel) was extremely suspicious of the cosmopolitan conception of that idea, and it was an idea that he saw in full pluming glory in Kant.

Hegel thought that Kant believed this: that global perpetual peace would follow the realisation of a worldwide cosmopolitan existence achieved through the formation of a union of States, a world union or world government capable of uniting the particular wills of nations around the "general will" of all humanity. Hegel thought Kant was fundamentally wrong to believe this:

> Because the relation of states to one another has sovereignty as its principle, they are so far in a condition of nature one to the other. Their rights have reality not in a general will, which is constituted as a superior power, but in their particular wills. Accordingly the fundamental proposition of international law remains a good intention, while in the actual situation the relation established by the treaty is being continually shifted or abrogated. (HPR, §333)
>
> States in their relation to one another are independent and look upon the stipulations which they make with one with another as provisional. (HPR, §330)
>
> There is no judge over states, at most only a referee or mediator, and even the mediatorial function is only an accidental thing, being due to particular wills. Kant's idea was that eternal peace should be secured by a union of states. This union should settle every dispute, make impossible the resort to arms for a decision, and be recognized by every state. This

> idea assumes that states are in accord, an agreement which, strengthened though it might be by moral, religious, and other considerations, nevertheless always rested on the private sovereign will, and was therefore liable to be disturbed by the element of contingency… Therefore, when the particular wills of states can come to no agreement, the controversy can be settled only by war. (HPR §333)

Hegel, then, can be counted as a profound sceptic about international unions. Kant was not opposed to international unions, and so for Hegel, he must be rejected as a fantasist.

Habermas, thinks Kant was not so confused. Indeed, he thinks Kant was basically right. What is it that Kant said that Habermas likes so much and Hegel dislikes so much? What Habermas says about Kant will also give us a clue why both he and Hegel misunderstand him so badly:

> To the very end, [Kant] advocated the idea of a world government, even though he proposed a "surrogate" of a league of nations as a first stage towards realizing such [an end]. This weak conception of a voluntary association of nations which are willing to co-exist peacefully while nevertheless retaining their sovereignty seemed to recommend itself as a transitional stage on the way to a world government. (BNR, p. 314)

It is quite true that Kant thought that we might approximate ever closer to a condition of peaceful co-existence ("cosmopolitan existence"), ever closer to a condition in which war had not only been made less likely but actually abolished, ever closer to the achievement of perpetual peace. But, as we shall see, he never proposed that what he calls his "surrogate" (a voluntary association of nations) would be a "transitional stage" to a world government. Indeed, it was approaching ever closer to this (in principle endlessly perfectible) surrogate, that Kant thought was the best we could hope for. He never thought we could eliminate the chance of war. Making it "less likely" through the formation of the "surrogate" is the best one can hope for. This is the best one can hope for in any world that, like ours, has an international order in which, as Hegel rightly states, following Kant in fact as we shall see, "the relation of nations to one another has sovereignty as its principle".

Although Habermas is wrong to suppose that Kant ever thought that a voluntary association of nations should be conceived as a transitional stage to a world government, Kant does indeed have a transitional stage in view. Not from a World Federation of States to a World State, but from a *European* Federation of States to a *World* Federation of States. Let's look at Kant's extraordinary anticipation of the emergence of the European Union in full:

> The effects which an upheaval in any state [as a result of war with another state] produces upon all the others in our continent, where all are so closely

> linked by trade, are so perceptible that these other states are forced by their own insecurity to offer themselves as arbiters, albeit without legal authority, so that they indirectly prepare the way for a great political body of the future, without precedence in the past. Although this political body exists for the present only in the roughest of outlines, it nonetheless seems as if a feeling is beginning to stir in all its members, each of which has an interest in maintaining the whole. And this encourages the hope that, after many revolutions, the highest purpose of nature, a universal cosmopolitan existence, will at last be realized as the matrix within which all the original capacities of the human race may develop. (Kant, p. 51)

The "great political body of the future" would be the institutional framework through which Europe would transform itself from a condition of war into one of peace – or rather, and putting it negatively, from a condition of war into a condition in which war is increasingly less likely. And in doing so, Kant thought that Europe would be providing an example for the world.

Habermas claims, I think wholly unjustifiably, that Kant conceived the global version of this European Federation to be only "a transitional stage" to a World Government. Moreover, Habermas calls this supposedly transitional stage "weak", "conceptually flawed" and "sterile" (BNR, pp. 314–5). But Kant thinks exactly the opposite is true. Indeed, were the transition (somehow) made to a European (or World) Government, there is no doubt that Kant would see this outcome as a total disaster, leading only to a loss of vitality through what he calls "a soulless despotism" and "the graveyard of freedom" – a condition of spiritual stagnation that can only make conflict and war more not less likely, not at all its perfect eradication in perpetual peace.

I will explain why he thought that at the end of this chapter, which will bring us back to the EU as we see it developing today. However, what perhaps seduces Habermas into thinking that the Kantian idea of a negative substitute (the surrogate federation idea) is a transitional stage of some kind is a remark by Kant where he says that the only rational step to take if we want to achieve perpetual peace would be the formation of an ever-expanding international State:

> There is only one rational way in which [nation] States coexisting with other States can emerge from the lawless condition of pure warfare. Just like individual men, they must renounce their savage and lawless freedom, adapt themselves to public coercive laws, and thus form an international State, which would necessarily grow until it embraced all the peoples of the earth. (Kant, p. 105)

The idea may seem rationally compelling, but far from endorsing this "only one rational way", Kant (the rationalist!) *immediately* dismisses it; and dismisses it completely. *If* we are starting from conditions in which nation-states understand themselves as sovereign powers (which amounts to saying as long as nation-states think of themselves as nation-states, which means – as long as there are nation-states) then the truly rational steps *cannot* be made:

> States, however, in accordance with their understanding of the law of nations, by no means desire this, and the positive idea of a world government cannot be realised. If all is not to be lost, this can at best find a negative substitute in the shape of an enduring and gradually expanding federation of nations likely to prevent war. The latter may check man's inclination to defy the law and antagonise his fellows, although there will always be the risk of it bursting forth anew. (Kant, p. 105)

Do nation-states today have a different understanding of "the law of nations"? That is, do they think that the relations between States no longer has State sovereignty as their principle? Not at all. Indeed, it is just this basic fact about its Member States that constitutes the basic fault of the EU as Habermas sees it today. However, it is also that basic fact that makes his proposal for transferring sovereignty to a supranational European government so absurd. Kant says, nation-states "by no means desire" the formation of an international State. The German is more literally: "it is not the will of the nations". But they don't desire or will this, not because they happen at the moment not to like it. It's not like: maybe next week they will desire it, but right now they don't. No. Kant's point is a logical, not a contingent one: this is not the sort of thing a nation-state, if that is what it is, can possibly desire or will. Self-abolition is not the sort of thing a nation can will. Or again, its interest, which is what this is all about, cannot be conceived in terms of it no longer having any interest in its interest. It cannot be conceived as in the national interest to give up having a national interest: it does not belong in the range of possible things one can possibly conceive of as "in the national interest".

But couldn't it come about? Yes, it could – but not in virtue of a decision that would be "the will of the nations". How then? We must ask: who or what could will it into being? Kant is clear that when he says it is not the will of the nations, it is what we call "nations" that he is talking about, and not some other thing. So, some other thing could will it. There are, I think, three ways it could come about.

First, a people-in-a-nation might elect a government of "rational cosmopolitans" with an interest above all in universal humanity, in which case its will ceases to be "the will of a nation" but of a human collectivity of a completely new sort, no longer understanding its will as the expression of a national interest. That may sound nice, even rationally ideal, but I'll later suggest not, even ideally. It is also hopelessly and piously utopian. Discussing the fact that "nowadays international law is limited by treaties between sovereign states", Derrida cites

Hannah Arendt's reminder ("something the veracity of which still holds today") that not even a "government of the world" would be capable of sorting out human rights abuses that still blight our world:

> Contrary to the best-intentioned humanitarian attempts to obtain new declarations of human rights from international organisations, it should be understood that this idea transcends the present sphere of international law which still operates in terms of reciprocal agreements and treaties between sovereign states; and, for the time being, a sphere that is above the nations does not exist. Furthermore, this dilemma would by no means be eliminated by the establishment of a "world government". (cited, CF, pp. 8–9)

Second, nations-in-ruins could will it. As a last gasp effort, a nation on its knees could give up having an interest in its own interest beyond just surviving somehow-or-other, well short of being a free State with its own rights.

And then third, and at the other end of the scale, another kind of not-simply-a-nation-among-nations could will it too: a nation which is strong enough to regard its own national interest simply to coincide with the interests of the international State, so that, as an implementing authority in this new State, it would be implementing and administering at the national level what it would, in any case, will for itself were it a coiled-up sovereign power. It is a quasi-hegemonic power. A quasi-hegemonic ambition is not in the least ruled out in the formation of a pan-European political space. But establishing itself could no more be an act of international solidarity (as Habermas suggests it would be) than the formation of an international State could be the will of the nations. Solidarity belongs historically to a politics of friendship or "fraternity": of standing shoulder to shoulder with one's "brother" in need. The term is, of course, part of the lexicon of classic socialist calls for collective action too. But it is also used, and politically speaking more broadly used in the international arena where we often see calls for solidarity between States, for example in the aftermath of famine or flood. The act of (supposed) solidarity that would bring about the hegemony of a nation in an international order is radically discontinuous with both of these traditions, however ruined that national order might have become. To use the very words that Kant used when he appealed to the idea of a European Union over two-hundred years ago, the point of an act of solidarity is to help "preserve and secure" the other from disappearance or annihilation – to help them get back to their feet in times of national peril, for example – not to submerge it in a tsunami of political overwhelming.

For Kant, however, all is not lost. Beyond Euro-sceptics and Euro-federalists we can yet hope for an enduring union in Europe likely to prevent war: what Kant calls the formation of a Federation of States, and not a Federal State. And hence Kant reaches a striking conclusion: this negative substitute, while falling short of what seems to be the only fully rational ideal, could not, in fact, be bettered. Sharing or pooling sovereignty in areas where you can enhances the sovereignty you keep by making war less likely. In short, there is a moderate third-way for Europe:

- Not just: the independent nation-states of Europe – the retention of full sovereignty for each State
- Nor yet: a United States of Europe – the transfer of sovereignty to a supranational State
- But instead: a United Europe of States – limited sovereignty all round

On this conception, it is not about shifting the sovereign beast up, but of seeing in limited sovereignty for all a basic condition for optimally maximising freedom for all. Forged in the crucible of war, the nations of Europe find "mutual self-interest" in the formation of their union, and through that a cause of "mutual understanding and peace" (Kant, p. 114). The "social contract", whether at a national or international level is all about optimally maximising – through a "united will" to self-limitation – the freedom of "particular wills", not dissolving them under some fantasy of a "general will".

I said the formation of an international state is something that Kant thought, were it somehow to happen, would, in any case, lead to total disaster. Why did he think it would result in "a soulless despotism…which will lapse into anarchy" (Kant, p. 113)? He gave two basic reasons:

1. "The laws progressively lose their impact as the government increases its range" (Kant, p. 113).
2. Powerful States (indeed this is the secret desire of every State) would like to secure peace by "dominating the whole" (Kant, p. 113).

In a world of super-fast communication, perhaps the first of these reasons is not as powerful as it had seemed to Kant in his time, although a feeling of distance from those who govern us remains a compelling worry in all contemporary politics. However, the second reason seems to me to have lost none of its force, and is perhaps made more likely by developments in communication technology. This hegemonic desire is the truth of even the most radical of "rational cosmopolitans": it is the "characteristic of wanting to direct everything in accordance with his own ideas" (Kant, p. 44). For Kant, this desire for international hegemony is effectively prevented from becoming actual by two types of human differences that, as he puts it, "separate nations and prevent them from amalgamating – *linguistic* and *religious* differences" (Kant, pp. 132–3). Kant thought this separation was the will of "nature", i.e. God's will, and hence nature or God's way of preventing "a soulless despotism" from ruining everything. However, one does not have to subscribe to a providential history to admit that as long as there are such differences, and as long as there are nations who understand themselves according to "the law of nations" – that is, as long as there are nations – the "one rational way" remains not only a fantasy but a dangerous fantasy.

A single government could certainly rule over peoples with such differences. And there is of course a "germ of goodness" in the ambition to end war, which is why the humanitarian ideal and world government can seem so nice. But for Kant world government could only end badly. Instead of a Federation in which peoples might reach various levels of mutual understanding while maintaining the vitality of their differences, Kant considers a single authority always to be the expression of a particular will, never the expression of an abstract general will, and hence will always produce what he calls a "universal despotism which saps all men's energies and ends in the graveyard of freedom" (Kant, p. 114). Ending in the graveyard is not the eternal peace we are looking for. Indeed, as should be clear by now, Kant was not a proponent of a plan for "perpetual peace" at all – but only of cultivating conditions that make lasting peace "more likely". That is the best we can humanly do, getting "ever closer" to such a Federation of States is not something we could better, and it is definitely preferable to the two alternatives: Hegel's world of many States, and Habermas's world of just one.

IX

In 2012, as many citizens and nations in the European Union struggled in conditions of economic insecurity and austerity, the Union itself received a Nobel Peace Prize for a result that at least recognised its past achievements, even if it seemed at odds with its precarious present: awarded for "the successful struggle for peace and reconciliation and for democracy and human rights". And yet, the central institutional expressions of this success – the European Parliament (established in 1979), European Citizenship (established with the Union name in 1993) and a European Single Currency, the Euro, (established in 2002) – are not only experiencing problems today, but belong to a trajectory in which "peace and reconciliation, democracy and human rights" have not been finally won, or even nearly so.

Europe today seems somehow threatened by the very developments which would mark its success. The 2016 referendum in the UK even led some to think that "Brexit" would be the beginning of the end of this short-lived European project: that Europe would fall off a cliff, with other exit-variants to follow. I don't think this is on the cards. The history of the European political institutions is short, but the history of the promise of European unity is long, and much more strong and stable than the current formation of the European Union. There will be, I suspect, no going back to the fraught and hostile environment of a Europe of petty national rivalries. On the other hand, the success of the EU may also require that it breaks entirely from the exalted modern idea of a federalist *telos*. In my view, a united Europe of nations – perhaps still "a *kind* of United States of Europe" – remains the best future and promise for this old place, the homeland of the homelands of "we, the Europeans".

I think anyone thinking about the future of the EU today would do well to read Kant again. Kant warned that a single order of power can only produce the opposite of its rational ideal. In fact, there is a graveyard of freedom at both ends: pure abuse of power in the despotic licence of "lawless freedom", at one end; and pure abuse of power in the despotic licence of a "world government", at the other. There are questions in this area on which old Kant remains telling and compelling. On the other hand, however, there are also new difficulties that Kant did not foresee. Indeed, one of the central distinctions in Kant's description of the "great political body of the future" is likely to strike the contemporary reader as considerably more complex than Kant presents it. Kant says of this great body that it will not aim "to acquire any power like that of a State" (Kant, p. 104). But as we have seen he does not suggest it has no power: it has the power "to preserve and secure the freedom of each State in itself along with that of the other confederated States" (Kant, p. 104). And that's a lot of power. Moreover, since acquiring this power would involve a definite loss of sovereignty for its Member States, the distinction between a "power like that of a State" and a "power to preserve and secure the freedom of each State" can, as Hegel insists, seem empty. State-like or non-state-like-but-with-enormous-power, what, really, is the difference?

Moreover, as a supranational political body with power, it becomes itself a new kind of player in inter-national relations, producing predictable effects, effects which Brexit has made especially visible. On the one hand, there is, as Kant notes, a tendency for "each State to see its own majesty precisely in *not* having to submit to any external legal constraint" (Kant, p. 103), and so "will not let itself become dependent" on other powers, and will resist whatever is perceived as an involuntary diminishing of sovereignty (Kant, p. 117). On the other hand, there is an equally unavoidable tendency, as Kant again recognises, for *every* political body with power to seek "to *extend* its rule" (Kant, p. 117), and to "increase its range" of domination (Kant, p. 113). There are deep instabilities built in to the project to implement the Kantian idea of even a modest European union.

Is it stabilisable? Can one brave the waves and sail on the Rubicon? So long as it is the will of the nations, so long as they see their interest lying in the stability of the whole, yes, why not? Hegel was dismissive of that prospect; Habermas unimpressed by its timidity. But rocky though it is, crooked timber that we are, a Kantian union of States remains its best future. For now, in this extraordinary project, Britain will be taking a back seat – or indeed no seat – in its unpredictable development. But one might still hope that "English spirits", not least in the shape of the old Scot Kant, might yet still "dominate for a while".

X

Such English spirits – in their middle regions they have been, above all, liberal. Indeed, not just English spirits: liberalism is historically, first and foremost, a broadly European tradition, not an exceptionally English one; liberalism the middle of Europe's modern middle ground and mainstream too, as Berlin was always keen to emphasise, and as Hegel regretted. This tradition is also historical in a deeper sense, in a sense that Hegel and Hegelians (both Fukuyama and Marxists, for example) seem less keen to register: it changes. Some of these changes, as we shall see, are likely to have been unthinkable in a pre-Marxist space – without thereby bringing Marxist orthodoxy much closer to the kind of politics that makes most sense to (most of) us. Bringing this long journey of the philosophical history of philosophical history to a close, in the next and final part I want now to turn to our own time, and to push European liberalism, or at least the thought of democracy which has become so deeply intertwined with it, to "think onward, outward, into the dark".

PART IV
In our time

7

A TIME AFTER MARX

Man encounters in himself the unsocial characteristic of wanting to direct everything in accordance with his own ideas

– Immanuel Kant

I

Recall the opening of David Wiggins's reading of how the onto-theological understanding of Man and his teleology stands in our time: "Unless we are Marxists, we are more resistant in the second half of the twentieth century than the eighteenth- or nineteenth-centuries knew how to be against attempts to locate the meaning of human life or human history in mystical or metaphysical conceptions" (TIML, p. 89).

Wiggins was writing in 1976. The collapse of Marxist communism in the Soviet Union and Europe's central and eastern countries just over a decade later seems altogether to have transformed not only the geopolitical but also the geophilosophical horizon. Geopolitically, that collapse promised an end to the Cold War, the end of Europe's internal division, and for many central and eastern European countries it led quickly to EU membership, initiating a period of political-economic transition that seems irreversible, even if uneven – and often unimpressive. Marx and Marxism now have a somewhat puzzling position in the history of modernity that we have been following in the transition from "what it was like to be alive then" to "what it is like to be alive now", a stubborn wrinkle in the history of the process of democratisation in Europe. For it is absolutely clear that Marx stands ambiguously on both sides of the putative distinction between then and now. We can mark the ambiguity by noting, first, that Wiggins's basic way of describing what "we" in our time resist is the "now (I think) almost unattainable conviction that there exists a God whose purpose ordains certain specific duties for all men" (TIML, p. 89). That conviction is, of course, a massive target for Marx, who conceived religious understandings of ourselves and the world as the truth-concealing ideological deformation of our self-understanding *par excellence*, and the greatest barrier to the attainment of full human self-realisation and "real happiness": Marxism is a messianism without religion. So, on that score, Marx stands squarely on the side of "now", and, I think, cannot be lightly dismissed in the history of its coming to be so. As we have seen, however, despite that future-producing participation in the formidable differences between then and now, Wiggins also excludes Marxists from those among us who now resist the general *archeo-teleo-eschatological* shaping of the old default understanding of the world and the significance of our lives (whatever else they resist). That is, on that score, Marx stands squarely on the side of "then". It remains a messianic eschatology.

As a critic of providential history, Marx belongs to our time. But as a messiano-eschatological thinker, he belongs to our past. That's the ambiguity. Should we say that Marx is simply a transitional figure in our history? As a grand design for the political future of a de-alienated humanity, Marxism seems a distinctively nineteenth century phenomenon, belonging firmly to a time when grand designs and great scientific achievements seemed like the sort of thing "we, modern Europeans" did best. So does Marx and Marxism simply drop out at a certain point in the historical shift away not only from conceptions of history that are philosophical and religious, but also in the shift away from a time when what we liked to think of as properly "scientific" ideas (in Marx's case concerning society and its development) were what we liked to think of as our singular excellence? I don't think so. Indeed, I think that Marx's thought is not only internal to the turning from then to now, but leaves its mark on our time more durably and more fundamentally than as an onto-theological leftover still among us. In each of the next three chapters, I will explore still-surviving Marxist legacies in our time.

When we think today about the heading of Europe, about the future of democracy, and the forms of political association that most make sense to us, more often than not we are inclined to think we can do without Marx – unless we are Marxists. I am not a Marxist, and will be most interested in the history of Europe's political mainstream, the developing "liberal experiment" that makes its way there. However, the sense in which our time is a time "since Marx", as well as (say) "since Copernicus" or "since Darwin" or "since Freud", is, I think, underestimated.

There are two aspects to this "since Marx" feature of our time. First, and most obviously, there was the appearance in the twentieth century of socialist societies based on a Marxist orthodoxy, and what that precipitated: a transformation of politics everywhere, evident especially in the history of totalitarianisms (Stalinist and adversarial Nazi, and Fascist developments), and then, "in the end", in "the great clash of ideologies that dominate[d] our world" after the Second World

War (TC, p. 131). However, the virtual disappearance of those societies does not mean that it is all over for Marx or that our time is not still a time "since Marx". There is a second aspect: Marx-survival stories that are visible even where the names of Marx and Marxism have either diminished in their appeal, or altogether disappeared. Something arrived with Marx and Marxism which opened a new chapter in European thought, making Marx's work an inaugural moment for us in that regard.

In this chapter, I want to follow two such spectral Marx-survival stories in European cultural life. First, and most straightforwardly, the case of contemporary leftist thought, something I will explore in relation to Robert Pippin's study of the European intellectual left; second, and more obliquely but in some ways more interestingly, the case of contemporary liberal thought, something I will explore in relation to developments of liberalism in the work of Wiggins and Shklar. I will argue that both of these Marx-survival stories, leftist and liberal, involve developments we should welcome.

In the next chapter, I will explore the survival of Marx in relation to two "theses" one can still find in sociology in its efforts to understand our time and its development: a "post-national" thesis and a "secularization" thesis. These "since Marx" theses are, I will argue, considerably less compelling, and should be given up and replaced. This will lead me to a final "since Marx" consideration in the last chapter. Marxism in the twentieth century not only transformed the geopolitical space; its spectacular failure also profoundly altered its geophilosophical complexion. For some, this situation called for rethinking our condition as a new end of history, one which sees the struggles and strivings that marked life in the epoch of the history of Man culminating in a life without such life-giving features, or, at least, a kind of life in which those life-giving features are significantly diminished. In that view, the history of Man, the history of Europe's modernity, has effectively reached its telic end, and the future beyond that end is not something to look forward to without considerable misgivings, although not entirely without hope. The principle example here is Kojève. For others, however, those same "since Marx" geopolitical events of the twentieth century transform the standing of the old onto-theological conception of Man itself. In the wake of the political and geopolitical tragedies that the spectre of communism gave rise to, that old conception was completely knocked off its pedestal, barely left standing. On this view, our new situation does not herald the attained end of the history of Man but the end, the exhaustion, of the very idea of such a telic history. The principle example here is Derrida. Perhaps surprisingly, both of these readings of our time open on to more or less the same sense of our contemporary condition and its possibilities, its risks and its chances. Following this will take us to the end of the book.

Before all that, however, I will turn to the two Marx-survival stories in the cultural life of our time, leftist and liberal.

II

In *Modernism as a Philosophical Problem*, Robert Pippin presents a view of contemporary academic debates about the "Enlightenment culture" of Europe and the West which illuminates the first of these survival stories: a Marxist spectre alive and well in what Pippin (unsympathetically) calls "the endless struggle of the intellectual Left to find ways to puncture the smugness and blind self-satisfaction of official bourgeois culture" (MPP, p. 8). This is an academic leftist tendency that, as he sees it, reacts "fiercely" against "modern bourgeois culture" (MMP, p. xviii), would like to see a "radical break" (MPP, p. 1) from "bourgeois modernity" (MPP, p. 40), and an "*escape* from bourgeois civilization" (MPP, p. xix).

Pippin's assessment of the current phase of these academic debates is fearful and beleaguered, but he plays with a straight bat and is not unfairly dismissive of work with which he clearly has little sympathy. While it does an obvious injustice to the particular points he is making, the following (rather shredded) citation gives a reasonable summary sense of what is to the fore in his reading of it:

> The emphasis now on new methodologies and research programs ("new historicism", "cultural studies", "post-colonialism") has not altered the nature or the depth of the tone [of]...a great, persistent dissatisfaction... all [expressed] in a still suspicious, wary tone...inspired by political suspicions...;[a] consensus about failure [concerning] the...limitations...of the modernist project..., a very great limitation in [the] received picture. [Given the intensity of the] sceptical attacks [on] modern institutions...it would not be too much of an exaggeration to designate [it as]... a kind of widespread "bourgeois self-hatred", [expressing] dissatisfactions [that] are so powerful and deep...[that] they can be extremely dangerous...
>
> Doubts about the legitimacy and authority of many modern presuppositions, [and about] the possibility of genuine, rational enlightenment... [have] assumed an intensely political, even geopolitical form [in] European philosophy's growing dissatisfaction with...the promises of Enlightenment claims about reason and subjectivity...,[and] the possibility that human beings can regulate and evaluate their beliefs by rational self-reflection.
>
> [Even if] the assumption that the cosmos [is] an ordered and purposive whole...[now] looks like an indefensible anachronism, [on the] question... whether...self-legislation can be said to be rational...the account I present [argues that] Hegel best realizes such a project...[And this] most ambitious and challenging philosophical case [for the modern aspiration for a free existence] ought at least to be on the table...[or] at least be placed back on the agenda. (MPP, pp. xii–15, and p. 76)

Pippin tends to represent the scene as one in which it is those who belong to what he calls the widespread "culture of dissatisfaction" who are the ones that divide it into "a drama of heroes and villains". After all, they are the ones who seek a "great 'confrontation'" with the modern self-understanding (MPP, pp. xv–xv). They have a "crisis mentality" (MPP, p. 29), and "promise" a "*decisive* confrontation with the original aspirations of modern European culture" (MPP, p. xii, emphasis in original). But Pippin's anxieties about the dangers posed by this culture of persistent dissatisfaction suggest that his own effort to defend a distinctively Hegelian position has a "crisis mentality" too, indeed a very classical one. Pippin does not think we have yet reached the "extremely dangerous" situation that he nevertheless fears it might lead to, were that dissatisfaction to become "a mass phenomenon" (MPP, p. xix). However, while he carefully avoids confrontational language himself, he certainly wants to do what he can to limit the threat he sees in the agenda-setting academic leftist radicals, and to help get us back onto a track of "an internally rational view of historical change" (MPP, p. 74), and a "version of teleology" (MPP, p. 75). The quotation of a line from King Lear that provides the epigraph of his book frames it perfectly: "*And worse I may be yet. The worst is not, So long as we can say, 'This is the worst'.*" For Pippin, as for Husserl, the modern self-understanding is not yet dead – but it is in very poor health. In Husserl's time, "the worst" was coming from the "nature cures" of revolutionary nationalists, and of course, they had even come to power in Germany. In our time, Pippin sees at least one example of "the worst" in the work of academic leftist scholar activism, and he writes with the aim of reviving and rejuvenating at least something of the old modern conception of Man in our time.

In his critique of Hegel, Marx described the position taken in his theoretical work as "the resolute opponent of the previous form of...political consciousness" (CHPR, p. 7). Here, theoretical criticism does not "stray...into itself", with one theory opposing another as offering a putatively superior theoretical solution to a problem, "but into problems for which there is only one means of solution – practice" (CHPR, p. 7). In short, philosophical theory – its scholarship – becomes, through and through, critical, activist and political; the task of theory is to become "a material force" (as Marx puts it) of just the kind that Pippin most fears: "as the revolution [of the Reformation] began in the brain of the monk", says Marx, "so now it begins in the brain of the philosopher" (CHPR, 7). "In the struggle against [the existing] state of affairs, criticism is no passion of the head, it is the head of passion. It is not a lancet, it is a weapon. Its object is its enemy, which it wants not to refute but to exterminate" (CHPR, p. 4). In the contemporary phase of leftist philosophical theory, as Pippin sees it, this ambition "has not altered", retaining the basically Marxist hope that intellectual work that develops as "radical critique" could, if it could only connect to and mobilise social movements outside academia, change the world.

By name, Marx is not a significant presence in Pippin's book. In fact, he is mentioned only twice. But the mark of the name is stubbornly imprinted on his text. If you take the "intensely political, even geopolitical" call for a "radical" and "decisive" "escape" or "break" with "bourgeois modernity" as the basic character of the "culture of dissatisfaction" that Pippin finds in "European philosophy" today, then it is, I think, hard not to read it as the persisting expression of a recognisably Marxist spirit, a "since Marx" spectre. In many ways, it is, for Pippin, a (new) Kant/Hegel vs Marx drama. On the (new) Kant/Hegel side that Pippin himself represents there is the effort (despite everything) to revive "a version of teleology" that conceives its task of at least "trying" (MMP, p. 179) to find "convincing 'traces of reason'" in "an assessment of our life-world" (MMP, p. 76); and, on the (new) Marx side, a new leftist effort (despite everything) to contribute to building mass social movements that could bring about a decisive break with the existing social-political-economic order – both sides seeing a road to a more rational and free life for all on the other side of the present "crisis". Pippin feels that the left challengers hold the field – or at least the moral high ground – in academic life today, but he regards his Hegelian alternative as "ambitious and challenging" too. Indeed, he would, I think, feel close to Husserl when Husserl insisted that "I would like to think that I, the supposed reactionary, am far more radical and far more revolutionary than those who in their words proclaim themselves so radical today" (CES, p. 290). So today's stout defender of a new version of teleology makes one more try, in what he perceives as a time of crisis, to save the discourse of Europe's Modernity as the developing movement of an ever-deeper "self-consciousness of reason by itself" (MPP, p. 163); and the leftists make one more try, in what they also perceive as a time of crisis, to form and forge a new world out of the ashes of the old one that is dying. In what follows, I want to explore Pippin's representation of a widespread Europe-crisis scene a little more closely, and to make a start in trying to comprehend it in the terms of the Europe-exhaustion strand that I am (working) in.

III

It is impossible to read very far in Marx without being impressed by his concern with the immiserating conditions produced by a society in which the bourgeoisie and its ever-expanding commercial interests dominate social life. Equally, however, one cannot but be struck by quite how impressed he was by the capacity of the bourgeoisie to create "more massive and more colossal productive forces than have all preceding generations together" (CM p. pp. 7–8). These come together very directly in Marx, since the socialist revolutions he sees coming in "the leading civilized countries" (CM, p. 23) would be, at once, events of both political and economic progress: not only would a transnational proletariat rule by seizing control of the old (nation) state apparatuses, but they would "become masters of the productive forces of society" too (CM, p. 14). The productive forces unleashed by "the giant, Modern Industry" (CM, p. 4) would thus be set to work in a way that would benefit and enrich the lives of all, and "the progress of industry" would be unfettered by intra-bourgeois antagonisms (CM, p. 13). In short, under socialism, the productive forces of Modern Industry would likely become even more massive and colossal. Lenin was particularly drawn to this still very modern promise of increasing productivity, and hence of prosperity for all: "We are entitled to say with the fullest confidence that the expropriation of the capitalists will inevitably result in an enormous development of the productive forces of human society" (SR, p. 101).

The basic character of the classical Marxist relation to European modernity is thus not anti-modern but, as it were, super-modern: the modern promise "for a genuinely new, progressive, fundamentally better epoch" *has yet* to be delivered (MPP, p. 30). For Pippin, this attitude contrasts sharply with the other great revolt against the promise of modernity that he identifies in the descendant of European Romanticism that he calls literary modernism. Modernism as a literary movement was one which, Pippin suggests, is best thought of as seeing the modern promise not as unfulfilled but as "false" (MMP, p. 30), and, without nostalgia for the old order, modernity is simply "condemned as a nightmare" (MMP, p. 31). For these literary modernists, Europe's modernity is not primarily a force for social progress (even nascently), and only gives rise to "sterile, exploitative, commercialised or simply ugly forms of life" (MMP, p. 29). For Marx, by contrast, Europe's modernity remains promising. Just as Hegel had supposed that the form of freedom that belonged to modern European nations under the sway of Kantian liberalism belonged to a history of freedom "still incomplete" (PH, p. 27), so also Marx saw the end of history still lying ahead for humanity, and first of all for "the more advanced conditions of European civilisation" (CM, p. 39), where a proletarian social revolution seemed to him imminent. The leftist progressives that Pippin has in his sights may have lost some of Marx's super-modernist nineteenth century confidence in industry, science and technology, but in the call to escape from bourgeois modernity they carry the Marxist project of creating a new society into our time, seeing our time as a time of crisis for an old world, and wanting not to restore it but to replace it, making their work motivated by what Pippin calls (misleadingly as we shall see) "the promise of a *post*modern epoch" (MPP, p. xii). The Marxist legacy here informs a new politics of hope for a transformation of society that will open onto a time in which, in a crucial sense, politics is over: if it could become a "mass phenomenon" we could begin to forge a society in which those who are present and living would simply no longer have an "enemy…to exterminate". In the terms I have been invoking in this book, we will attain a community that really *is* one by forging a community that finally is *one*.

The "philosophical problem of modernity" is thus represented by Pippin as "an internal European debate" (MPP, p. xi), where the main players are distributed between two rival camps: there is, on the one hand, a cultural self-understanding which is, as he puts it, "founded on the scientific world-view and the political ideals of individual rights protection, a modern civil society, and democratic institutions" (MPP, p. xiii); and then, on the other hand, there are those for whom this self-understanding is "a problem". Note how he summarises this other hand, because it includes quite a variety of positions for which that modern self-understanding might represent a problem: it might be, he says, "a false promise, an ideological distortion, an expression of ontological forgetfulness, the will to power, or ethnocentrism, or a class or gender or race or culture bound strategy, all much more than the expression of a universally compelling, philosophically defensible, human aspiration" (MPP, p. xi).

This line-up in the "diverse spectrum" (MPP, p. xiv) of those so "fiercely" antagonistic to the modern condition is fantastically precise, but also somewhat puzzling:

"A false promise": modernity *did not* deliver on its promise; this is the response to the promise of modernity that Pippin finds in literary modernism.
"An ideological distortion": this is Marx. The last great discourse of modernity: modernity *is yet* to deliver.
"A class or gender or race or culture bound strategy": these are the various "new complex methodologies", critical theory, feminism, postcolonial criticism, etc., whose newness "has not altered" the tone of "great, persistent dissatisfaction" and the call for "a *decisive* confrontation" with bourgeois modernity that belonged to orthodox Marxism.

But there are three other key variations squeezed into Pippin's list:

"Ontological forgetfulness": this is from Heidegger.
"The will to power": this is from Nietzsche.
"Ethnocentrism": this is likely (given his place in Pippin's book) from Derrida.

Here, the unnamed trio Heidegger, Nietzsche and Derrida, are corralled into the problem field that Pippin represents as the "crisis mentality" that he takes to be so characteristic of our time. Indeed, they are, he supposes, the central figures for the contemporary "culture of dissatisfaction" that announces "the promise of a *post*modern epoch" (MPP, p. xii) in the sense of a society that will have made a "radical break" with modernity (MPP, p. 1).

All three of these figures regard their work as contributing, in some way, to a movement that forges "a passage beyond" the Greco-Biblical (onto-theological) self-understanding that has called itself (to be) European. However, I do not mean only to be quibbling with a name (which they don't in any case use) when I say that, with respect to their thought, if there is anything that might deserve the name, and indeed has been conferred the name, of a postmodern epoch (or condition), then we are already in it. They are readers of a condition not of a Europe-crisis or world-crisis but a time (marked no doubt by heterogeneous in-the-world crises) of the exhaustion of the great *archeo-teleo-eschatological* discourses of Europe's modernity, including within that its "Europe-crisis" or "world-crisis" concepts – and hence also its old projects of restoration or replacement. As such, all three are better thought not as representing a "crisis mentality" but, as Derrida puts it, as philosophers who try to "'think' this beyond-of-crisis", of "crisis" as a concept "no longer able to measure what is happening"

(WS, p. 63). For this exhausted-Europe strand that I introduced in Chapter 2, and to which each of these figures belongs, it is not that we already have another more adequate discourse that would displace the old onto-theological understanding, but – and hence the call for thinking – that we do not. As Derrida puts it, "perhaps we no longer have at our disposal a…discourse" through which to answer such a question about "what is happening" in our "world":

> We are speechless at this point, at this, the most acute moment of the *paroxysm*, the point at which this crisis recalls no earlier crisis. At least this is what we think we sense. There is no lack of interpretations – we have too many of them. They are pertinent but insufficient. In particular, they do not lend themselves to being *joined*: no unique or dominant discourse, no system, no arbitrating tribunal to decide on the unity or the unicity of the said crisis…This, then, is the most abyssal "crisis", the crisis of crisis… There would thus be no more "world", much less "present world", whose common horizon would be able to delimit a *determinable* experience [of what is happening] and, as a result, an assured competence (philosophical, scientific, economic-political) [in its description]. The anticipation of this unity, even its language, seems to us to be withheld…In its turn in crisis, the concept of crisis would be the signature of a last symptom, the convulsive effort to save a "world" that we no longer inhabit: no more *oikos*, economy, ecology, liveable site in which we are "at home". One more try, the word *crisis* says to us (which is indeed one of our homemade words), one more try to save the discourse of a "world" that we no longer speak, or that we still speak, sometimes all the more garrulously, as in an emigrant colony. (EC, p. 70)

The Europe-crisis strand would want to articulate an all-linked-up sense of the history and future direction of the world-as-a-whole (and what is a "world" if not such a whole?). The great difference between the two strands comes at that point. The second (exhausted-Europe) strand regards that effort as slated to disappointment: the very language of its language, including the language of "world crisis", is itself in crisis, less than ever the homeland of our lives – indeed a homeland of our lives (a "world") seems increasingly lacking. We lack any way of speaking of the unity of our world, we lack the kind of single and all-joined-up unitary discourse that would be a discourse of the world and its history. Hence our perplexity. We are living, as Heidegger suggested, more and more in a world that is no world.

For the first strand, we live in a time of "world crisis" which can only be overcome through an effort of either restoration or replacement – in either case advancing an historicism of development that would attest to the history of the unfolding of reason and freedom in time. For the second strand this configuration of our time and history is itself in crisis, this conception of progress or emancipation itself in question: "as soon as one questions or exceeds this axiomatic configuration, then the most disturbing aspect of the Thing no longer appears on *a stage of crisis*" (EC, p. 73).

Pippin's corralled three are not the only thinkers of our time who might be better thought as thinkers of an exhausted-Europe condition rather than a Europe-crisis condition. We have already seen Wiggins's summary of that. Here is Bernard Williams with a similar avowal:

> We know that the world was not made for us, or we for the world, that our history tells us no purposive story, and that there is no position outside the world or outside history from which we might hope to authenticate our activities. We have to acknowledge the hideous costs of many human achievements that we value, including this reflective sense itself, and recognize that there is no redemptive Hegelian history or universal Leibnizian cost-benefit analysis to show that it will come out well enough in the end. (SN, p. 166)

This condition, as Williams also remarks, has lost the convictions of Christian hope, and hence also the hopes of Kantian and Hegelian theodical history, that belong to an earlier time in our history. It is, he says, already "beyond" those legacies (SN, p. 166) in the sense that we cannot go back to their theodical terms to come to terms with the condition we find ourselves in; a condition in which, as Williams puts it, basically citing Lyotard, there is, precisely, widespread "scepticism" about "*les grands récits*" through which, in that earlier time, we had made sense of our lives (IBWD, p. 47). As I will continue to try to relate this to ourselves, this is not about an epochal world crisis but epochal world exhaustion – and (almost everything) in the old Marxist spirit that haunts Pippin is as much part of that epoch as the older Kantian and Hegelian visions of the end of Man.

For his own part, on his side of things, Pippin is fairly dismissive of this sort of thought, mentioning it just once and merely recording "sighs about philosophical exhaustion" (MPP, p. 63). However, perhaps I sigh only because I take more seriously than he seems willing his recognition that "the assumption that the cosmos [is] an ordered and purposive whole…[now] looks like an indefensible anachronism within the modern non-teleological view of nature", and the implications this has even for his supposedly "weaker version of teleology" (MPP, p. 75), a version which seems to me still too strongly impressed by what he regards as the "very difficult to reject" conception of history as "internally rational" (MPP, p. 74). I am not averse to having this idea on the table. Indeed, I would be happy to have it nailed there, as something we still need to study and think through. Nevertheless, the idea of an internally rational history of the world and its crises really does not, to use a Wittgensteinian expression, "stand fast" for me, and I don't think I am alone in that. I know too that this idea belongs internally to the history of the European world as it has actually unfolded. Indeed, it is not only an "idea", but has been history-producing, producing a missionary history – colonial, for example – which has been inseparable from the metaphysics of Greco-Biblical *archeo-teleologism*, and its conception of the future attainment of a condition in which the capacities of Man may finally flourish.

We today are the inheritors of the "modern" European understanding of the world and the significance of our lives that belongs to this epoch of *archeo-teleological* reason, and its inseparable anthropocentrism, androcentrism, ethno-centrism and Eurocentrism. We live in a time of its epochal exhaustion and unravelling. And in this space, the contrast Pippin draws, between those for whom the modern self-understanding is experienced as a problem and those for whom it is not, is not so sharp. The "all are free" claims of the modern self-understanding frees up the movement of democratisation, and the voices Pippin finds so troubling are part of this just as much as those who cleave to modern "democratic institutions". Indeed, you shouldn't be surprised if participants in the process of democratisation find "a class or gender or race or culture bound strategy" still at work in those institutions; no surprise that they experience them as falling short of "the expression of a universally compelling, philosophically defensible, human aspiration". Insofar as these participants call for a de-limitation or escalation of the universality expressed by the affirmation that "all are free", they too are defenders not opponents of the modern self-understanding.

IV

The grievances that occupy Pippin's leftist challengers make good sense within the movement of democratisation that drives resistance to the old default. On the other hand, just that point might make one wonder whether they, like Marx, are really so foreign to modernity. First of all, they are marked by a distinctively modern stress on and confidence in political agency: they offer themselves to us as presenting unprejudiced reflections that might build a mass social movement that could fix a time that is "out of joint". They do not see themselves as belonging inside the same ideological space occupied by their opponents, for sure. They are outsiders to global capitalism, unseduced by corporate media, critics of the pantomime of parliamentarism, and so on. Nevertheless, I do not think we should see the professoriate that Pippin identifies (and who he finds so eager to demolish most of what he cherishes) as a set of people who see problems and inadequacies with modernity where others see none. On the contrary, we should see the whole "internal European debate" that Pippin highlights as internal to modern Europe in a strong sense: internal to the "democratic era" (BGE, p. 107) of Europe's modernity – including in that, as Nietzsche stressed, "the lands where Europe's influence predominates" (BGE, p. 106), and especially America ("All the countries of Europe and likewise in America" (BGE, p. 53)). The European world of the "democratic enlightenment" (BGE, p. 14), opens the space to ongoing expressions of dissatisfaction with what we have hitherto forged as democratic institutions. This is not best understood in terms of a legitimacy problem with modernity felt only by some, but a still-modern condition felt by all. At issue here are relatively new political spaces in which social differences of power and possibility have generally come to be regarded as legitimate only in so far as those differences are up for discussion and deliberation by everyone, or at least by democratically elected representatives of everyone.

Differences of political experience and standing emerge in this space in connection with what one might call *places of speech*, the places from which the speech of a speaker "well[s] up" (DPC, p. 269). Such places are at once both singular, "mine", and relationally situated in a "public" way, marked by the historically differentiated placement of people and groups of people in the space of "public discussion" and its medium. If not altogether or no longer entirely excluded from the most central places, economically disadvantaged people, women, people of colour, disabled people, lesbian, gay, and transgender people, remain groups of subjects speaking from places of speech which are typically nowhere near the centre of public discussion. There is no reason why Pippin could not agree that it is especially incumbent on "democratic institutions" to put their convening power to work to respond to the infinite demand that "all are heard".

Calls for democratic progress of this kind are themselves vulnerable to not being heard. They make their way with whatever force they can muster. In those efforts, they do not all make the same type of appeal. Following Judith Shklar, herself following Emerson, I want to distinguish two broad types according to the temporal leaning, what one might call the characteristic messianicity of their appeals to justice and injustice (see LF, p. 26). Some political speech is primarily *future projecting*. It articulates the hope that we can build a society that can effectively realise justice. Shklar calls this a "utopian" sensibility, a politics of hope. Some political speech is, in contrast, primarily *past correcting*. It articulates the hope that past and existing injustices will not be repeated. Shklar calls this a "never again" sensibility, a politics of memory. The first has an ideal of justice in view. The second, past and existing injustice in view. Both, however, have existing political institutions in view, and those as an ongoing source of problems.

Where effective political intervention is in question we are either dealing with everyday democratic politics and policy to reform conditions, or with a call for some more ambitious effort to transform the state of the central place of politics, the State – perhaps even with calls to abolish and replace it. Keeping in view the contrast between a politics of hope and a politics of memory, the contrast between a focus on realising justice and eliminating injustice, the contrast between attaining conditions of ideal adequacy and attaining conditions that overcome existing inadequacy, we should note, however, that both sides of Pippin's modernity problem, both the Kant/Hegel side and the Marx side, are, in fact, on the same side. To be sure, Marxist messianism is to be distinguished from its predecessors insofar as it articulates a messianism without religion, but it remains "future projecting", as do the leftist voices that carry it into our time. In this context, one might see the chance for an effective radicalisation of the Marxist legacy that would go beyond Pippin's "problem of modernity" and the two sides of its "crisis mentality": it articulates a messianism without messianism; it becomes a resolutely non-utopian politics of memory.

Pippin's leftist challengers are alive to injustices that existing democratic institutions of State politics (including its media medium, the "free press" that it grants) remain a major source of. And I think their memory of those injustices is inseparable from their own characteristically "since Marx" struggles to un-bound such class-bound, race-bound, and gender-bound set-ups. Those struggles should be affirmed. But we should affirm them only with great caution: they should be affirmed without giving in to the old modern politics of hope. Inspired by these memories, democratising movements in our time have the chance of giving strength and speed to the kind of messianicity without messianism that, I believe, we really must seek today: opening the space to the democratised perfectionism of the pluralist ideal. However, I am equally sure that the politics of hope that still runs through the "since Marx" formation of contemporary leftist radicalism, its desire for a community that really *is* one because it is a community that finally is *one*, has no hope of giving force or form to that possibility in our time. That, at any rate, is my claim, and I will continue to do what I can to make good on it as I push on now from considerations of "since Marx" leftism to "since Marx" liberalism.

V

In order to get started on the theme of "since Marx" liberalism, I want to focus first on the aspect that presents itself when the existence of State politics is, itself, perceived as the ongoing source of injustice. This can, I think, helpfully be thought through in terms of the structure of sovereignty in the State – in terms, that is, of the power to make political decisions without having to ask for permission first. Such a decision may be the conclusion of wide public discussion, deliberation and participation, or it may be the conclusion of a much smaller body of "decision makers" (representatives and other emissaries of the State, along with other voices with the most central places of speech). In either (indeed in any) case of such a set-up, the capacity to bring the discussion to an end somewhere (at some point in time), and then to decide without having to seek permission to do so from some further body or bodies (who might object) is the condition of any political action whatsoever. But the very same condition also installs the possibility of abuses of that sovereign power. Indeed, "abuse of power", as a possibility, is, as Derrida puts it, "constitutive of sovereignty" (R, p. 102). Or again "every sovereign State is in fact virtually and *a priori* able, that is, in a state [*en état*], to abuse its power… The use of State power is originally excessive and abusive" (R, p. 156). The point here is that such abuses are not just occasional eventualities, something evil or wrong that happens every now and again, often, or even all the time. The claim is not that excess and abuse is always actual (even if it sometimes is), but, rather, that it is something which, in the nature of the thing, *always can happen* – and that is what makes it a sovereign State in the first place. The politics of hope holds out for a State that never would abuse its power (a regime without evil, as it were), or for a state of finally doing without a State altogether which would thus overcome the potential for such abuses (anarchism, Marxism-Leninism). The politics of memory aims only at damage limitation: eliminating injustices that belong to abuses of power and make them more likely.

This is very clearly the case in Shklar's own reformulation of liberal politics as a politics of memory, "the liberalism of fear", which emphasises "damage control": calling for the formation of institutions (especially democratic institutions, representative government, regular elections, separation of powers, the rule of law, etc.) that can effectively limit or even abolish specific abuses. In general, this approach aims to reduce the fear and cruelty that devolves from the existence of State sovereignty, especially for those groups that are (at any time) radically disadvantaged with respect to what one may fear from the State and other actors. It might still be called "hopeful" regarding such developments – whether through the reform or the transformation of whatever holds the field in a given place or time. It is (still) hopeful because, as Bernard Williams notes, it "is conscious that nothing is safe, that the task is never-ending" (IBWD, p. 61) and "it asks how secure what has been secured is" (IBWD, p. 61). Hence it can *only hope* that its work will succeed.

For example, in the messianic spirit of the promissory "never again" of the politics of memory one might do what one can here and now to abolish slavery. And one might do a lot that one might reasonably hope will make the future better in so doing. For example, one might be part of a movement that brings about an enforceable law that abolishes slavery. But that achievement – if one is not to sink into pessimism or cynicism – can retain a hopeful countenance only because one cannot be unaware that it might come back, or remain in other forms, or get outsourced somewhere else. What the politics of memory does not promise is the attainment of a New Civilisation or Future World where it is renounced in a manner that can do without further appeal to the (past-correcting) promise. Renouncing is (if it is anything more than gassing) promising not deliverance – "the task is never ending". The kind of messianic thinking that thinks otherwise belongs to the utopian politics of hope in this picture.

Proponents of the politics of hope might think that a politics of memory like the liberalism of fear, or, indeed like the "politics of memory" that Derrida explicitly affirms in *Specters of Marx*, to which we will also return (SM, p. xviii), has little chance of making real progress on its own ambitions. For example, Simon Critchley has suggested that resolutely eschewing the messianism of a utopian political project leaves one's politics with a problematic "motivational deficit": the weakness of liberalism, for example, lies in "its inability to translate [its universalism and rationality] into something embedded and lived" (PL). Populism, libertarianism, anarchism, fascism and Marxist socialism (all forms of the politics of hope), by contrast, hold out the promise of radical social transformation into what amounts to a new world of the future: a radically new and better embedded and lived condition for us, either communally or individually, or both, in which injustices like slavery will have been abolished in an (apparently) stronger sense. It will have become the past of that new world order. Non-utopian thinkers cannot deny this limitation in their thinking. As Isaiah Berlin stressed in his "Message to the 21st Century" (1994), when he was very old and everyone seemed to him very young, thinking which eschews the idea that there is a political "solution to human problems" that lies in a vision and conception of "an ideal society", has to accept that it does not offer "a flag under which idealistic and enthusiastic young men and women may wish to march – it seems too tame, too reasonable, too bourgeois, it does not engage the generous emotions" (MC). I'm not so sure that the politics of memory fails to engage generous emotions: "never again" has fire as well as resolve. But a past correcting promise really doesn't have the same motivational allure as a future projecting one. And that's all one can say about that.

However, one can give coherent answers of another kind to ameliorate that structural motivational deficit. Shklar, for example, highlights with some considerable understatement that the "historical record" on the results of "longings" for "either more communal or more expansively individualistic" futures is "not encouraging" (LF, pp. 35–6). In the other direction, T.S Eliot stresses that "we cannot imagine what it would feel like to live in that new civilisation" anyway (TDC, p. 18); the embedded and lived phenomenology of a Future World is as fundamentally inscrutable to us as it is, in reality ("believe me", says Berlin), unplannable. I would add, for my own part, a worry about those "longings" for a new embedded and lived condition that I think of as Kantian: namely, the suspicion that the imaginary future of utopian thinking is imagined as the becoming-universal of the political activist's own political sensibility. So, on the one hand, the proposed innovations only recommend themselves to us by "the specious glitter of unmeaning promises" about the future (TDC, p. 18), and, on the other hand, they are really only recommendations that everyone become more like (some) *me*.

As Kant emphasised in the context of a consideration of utopian hopes for a direct democracy of the masses – and the idea that in such a world we would finally be free of tyrannical rulers and abuses of power – such hopes belong to the projects of people who are ardent about their own ideals of communal life, and so, again, what their hopes really hope for is for a world in which, as it were, everything has changed except themselves; the arc of history has bent (or has somehow been bent) their way, and hence each one of these supposed democrats (more or less secretly) "wants to be a ruler" (Kant, p. 101). The non-utopian thinker, by contrast, wants every other (equally) to be able to (in Wiggins's unusually passionate phrase) "rejoice in the freedom" of not having to believe what anyone else supposes they should. There is an anthropological claim here: we are "crooked timber". We are not rational cosmopolitans, and if an ethnologist from Mars looked over Earth they would not count us among the gentle creatures either.

No doubt all of this only serves to reinforce Critchley's sense of liberalism's weakness. Indeed, it is not just liberalism. Every "messianism without messianism", whether it calls itself liberal or not, seems distinctively detached from the future-glitter that stirs our souls, and hence "in this respect", as Critchley notes, "the force" of more viscerally attuned transformation projects "will always win". Thankfully, given its track record, although it may indeed always win in the game of affective forcefulness, it does not always win.

Of course, none of this is intended to minimise the force or the urgency of struggles against the class- or gender- or race-bound character of societies (anywhere). Indeed, in the next section, I will argue that the call for an un-bound politics belongs to a profound shift in the character of European liberalism at the other end of the dissolution of the old default understanding of Man and his history. Although, characteristically, it is not politically Marxist, this shift too has some justification for being considered a Marxist legacy. Here we will move from the Marx-survival story in "the endless struggle of the intellectual Left to find ways to puncture the smugness and blind self-satisfaction of official bourgeois culture" (MPP, p. 8), to a rather different and rather more spectral kind of Marx-survival in the development of political liberalism as it shows itself in the work of two followers of Berlin: Wiggins and Shklar.

VI

The Marxist legacy I will try to identify can be brought out by considering a complication to the passage in Wiggins's text where Marx appears to be dismissed from the field of most thinking today: "Unless we are Marxists, we are more resistant in the second half of the twentieth century than the eighteenth- or nineteenth centuries knew how to be against attempts to locate the meaning of human life or human history in mystical or metaphysical conceptions" (TIML, p. 91). What is so striking is that Wiggins immediately qualifies his affirmation of our now-more-freely-than-ever resisting such attempts by stressing that this resistance does *not* mean that "we have lost interest in emancipation or progress themselves" (TIML, p. 91). My question is whether the way that interest makes sense to us makes much sense "unless [in some sense] we *are* [still] Marxists". When Wiggins excludes Marxists he means to exclude those among us who still cleave to "mystical or metaphysical conceptions" of the meaning of human history, and orthodox Marxists certainly do cleave to quite a lot in all that. But there is a complication in the legacy of Marx which makes Wiggins's exclusion less simple and straightforward than perhaps he would like it to be, a complication to every discourse that would claim that our sense of the importance of emancipation or progress could, today, be radically non-Marxist – even if we affirm clearheadedly that we are not Marxist.

This point can be clarified by considering two dimensions of Marxist thought that we have already touched on: its teleologism and its messianism. The former marks the thought of Marx as belonging to something we, today, resist: an *archeo-teleological* conception of Man unfolding towards his proper self-realising, de-alienated end. The latter, by contrast, is an orientation of thinking that inflects or shapes the significance we attach to what we do "here and now" by forging an internal relation to a future to come. The two are tangled together in Marxism as a politics of hope: the *telos* of developments taking place here and now is the arrival of a quite specific future, one with an identifiable content (communist society). Nevertheless, the messianic shaping of the significance of what we do that belongs to Marx's thought has a distinctive form that can be specified independently of its politics of hope. Derrida calls this its "absolute singularity", a first-time-in-history within the history of humanity that transforms our history. He calls it a "messianic promise":

> A messianic promise, even if it was not fulfilled, at least in the form in which it was uttered, even if it rushed headlong toward an ontological content, will have imprinted an inaugural and unique mark in history. And whether we like it or not, whatever consciousness we have of it, we cannot not be its heirs. (SM, p. 91)

What was so world-changing? What did Marx bequeath to our time other than the burden of millions of ghosts, terrifying failure and totalitarian horror? Derrida's claim is that alongside, or, rather, inside everything that belongs with the "Marxist dogmatics", and in particular "its metaphysics", inside everything that rocket-fuelled its disastrous legacy, something happens there that we can and should remain faithful to and take responsibility for just as much as (indeed internal to) the Marxist spirit of self-critique we have already discussed. And Derrida stresses that this is a responsibility that is incumbent especially on "those who… managed to resist" Marxist theoretical dogmatics and metaphysics (SM, p. 90), and "never gave in to Marxist intimidation" (OH. p. 57). Within a project whose form was no longer providential, no longer national or religious or mystical, there is an emancipatory promise in Marxism that "one can try to liberate from any dogmatics, and even from any metaphysico-religious determination, from any *messianism*" (SM, p. 89); independently, then, of its politics of hope. Something happens in and through Marx's work that can and should be saved or rescued from its miserable history, and which can and should be dissociated from those other spirits of Marx that we should not inherit – and the latter includes, as we have seen, "*almost everything*" (SM, p. 89, emphasis in original).

At issue is a distinctively *universal* (non-national, non-religious) promise or pledge internal to the significance we attach to what we do here and now. It belongs, that is to say, to a wholly new experience of politics in an age when it can no longer pretend to be, as Valéry put it, "localized". We will follow this development concretely in the next chapter, when we discuss the future of national party politics in our national political lives – and the distinction of Marx's conception of a party as a communist party making its way in those places. However, my interest at this point is the idea that – dissociated from the Marxist teleology of a politically de-differentiated humanity at the end of history, and from the Marxist "International" that would lead the way to that end – there is an opening in Marx, and since Marx, for the possibility of new international ethical-political constituencies that attest to a messianic promise of emancipation or progress beyond (and without essential reference to) national, religious or linguistic communities. Wherever there is this simultaneous movement of: (i) abandoning "the/idea that the importance of emancipation or progress" is tied to an onto-theological or metaphysico-religious understanding of Man and history, while (ii) maintaining an interest in "emancipation or progress themselves" *for all* without national, religious or linguistic reference, there, I want to say, is a spectre of Marx; and that is so even if, as Derrida puts it, this universal promise is "put to work otherwise" than in Marx, in a politics of memory rather than a politics of hope (SM, p. 90).

I will return to this idea of "new international" constituencies again in, the next chapter, in relation to practical suggestions from both Williams and Derrida to extend and diversify international law, but it is, I think, anything but fortuitous that we can find the general shaping of our interest in emancipation or progress that I am concerned with here silently but visibly at work in Wiggins's own discussion of our contemporary condition. Most of that discussion is concerned with an effort to reconstruct a form of anti-cognitivism about life's meaning beyond both the naïve cognitivism of the modern default and the equally naïve anti-cognitivism that has characterised much of the recoil against it in both "its Anglo-Saxon and Continental variants", expressivism and existentialism respectively (TIML, p. 95). However, at various points, Wiggins also engages with more concrete questions, most notably in relation to, and against, ways of thinking about life's meaning which affirm what he considers a "too easy a distinction between human welfare on the one side and the environment on the other" (TIML, pp. 103–4, fn. 15). Central to Wiggins's opposition to such ways of thinking is that they inure us to the ongoing human subjection of animal life (for example, in modern industrial, factory farming) and environmental destruction (for example, in deforestation, mineral extraction and fossil fuel exploitation) taking place in our time on a scale never seen before in the history of the world. This is a case that Derrida too explicitly identified as among the most serious in our time, or rather, as having "always been a serious one", but which he thinks is becoming "massively unavoidable" today (SM, p. 85). Reflecting on a documentary film he had seen about creatures eating one another at the bottom of the ocean, Wiggins concludes his discussion as follows:

> If we can project upon a form of life nothing but the pursuit of life itself, if we find there no non-instrumental concerns and no interest in the world considered as lasting longer than the animal in question will need the world to last in order to sustain the animal's own life; then the form of life must be to some considerable extent alien to us. (TIML, p. 103)

He continues this thought with a worry in a footnote:

> Here, I think, or in this neighbourhood, lies the explanation of the profound unease that some people feel at the systematic and unrelenting exploitation of nature and animals which is represented by factory farming, by intensive stock rearing, or the mindless spoliation of non-renewable resources. This condemnation of evil will never be understood till it is distinguished by its detractors from its frequent, natural but only contingent concomitant – the absolute prohibition of all killing not done in self-defence. (TIML, pp. 103–4, fn. 15)

What Wiggins is saying is that the "profound unease that some people feel" in the face of an increasingly global political economy which plays out a distinction between human welfare on the one hand (economic growth and prosperity) and the natural world on the other (who cares) is due to such people seeing humanity having become like those ocean-bottom-feeders, with "no interest in the world considered as lasting longer than the animal in question will need the world to last in order to sustain the animal's own life". The evils of factory farming, the whole business of the mechanised food industry, and the spoliation of non-renewables are not to be understood as such because, say, they involve us killing animals and destroying natural environments – but because it shows us as a creature without interest in the future of life on Earth (human or not) beyond the presence of those who are currently present and living there. Our modern lives are no sort of contribution, contain no kind of promise, to all those unknown others who are not here and are yet to come. Uncannily, we would in this condition have become akin to a form of life that we cannot but think of as "to some considerable extent alien to us". Issues of alienation and de-alienation remain live in this "unease", and open onto calls to resist the "too easy" distinction between human welfare and the environment, and the practices and policies that its too easy acceptance informs. I will come back to this is the final chapter, where Covid-19 type events swing into view too.

We should be very clear about what this resistance movement involves. Two things should be emphasised. First, doing what they can to resist such practices and policies is nothing over and above participants doing (individually and collectively) what, by their lights, is a good thing to do "here and now" for "us" – but this "us" has an implicitly de-limited or *un-bound* sense: beyond the "us" of those who are now present and living, it includes those who are not here and are yet to come. It is in this sense that it is the bearer of what can be called a messianic promise. It is, however, a messianic promise that is entirely *without messianism*. For it precisely leaves open "what it is like to be alive" in the future; wanting *only* that participants (today) will have contributed to there being *something* that it is like to live then which will enable those new and unknown participants (tomorrow) to want the same: that they too will belong to this history of the promise. This is not only a pledge for survival (though it certainly is that), but also the survival of the promise *as* promise – without end. What is central to Wiggins's thought of this maintained interest in "emancipation or progress itself" is thus the idea, first of all, that we comprehend "our existence" in this temporally un-bound way, and hence with a sense of responsibility beyond the living present before those who are not yet born – and no doubt before those already dead ones who understood their lives as participants whose sense of what is "a good thing to do for us" bore on the future beyond their own living presence in a promissory way too.

There is, however, a second distinctive feature of Wiggins's example that is equally important. The concerns that are pressing in his case exceed those that might belong simply or exclusively to the life of a society or political community with a history that forms a constituency of persons who have lived and continue to live, as Bernard Williams puts it, "contiguously with each other" (IBWD, p. 50): beyond the idea of an immemorial national community and its interest of the kind so powerfully described by Edmund Burke. It is not just experienced as a responsibility before those who are not yet born in "our nation" (though it may well also be that, and may also, contingently, be sometimes best thought practically through that), but a responsibility that can belong to anyone before *all* those who are not yet born, and born anywhere. Here, what one does "for us" amounts in some way and to some extent to a contribution to the universal community: it is de-limited or un-bound not only in worldly time (as it is in Burke), but also in worldly space.

The point here is not that, today, it is a feature or fact about the contemporary world that it has a global dimension. What is so novel is rather our coming to regard ourselves as belonging to new ethical-political constituencies – constituencies with a universal vocation – that can be scattered across the globe and linked perhaps only by experiences, fears, suffering, and so on, without any essential reference to national, religious or linguistic communitarian bonds. Coming to see ourselves in this way, this form of "international" alliance with a universal "messianic promise" belongs, I want to suggest, to a time "since Marx" (SM, p. 19), just as the old default belongs to a time, as Wiggins suggests, "before...Darwin" (TIML, p. 90) – whether we know it or not, whatever consciousness we have of it. As I say, the possibility that such "unities of ethical experience" that "cross [state] boundaries" (IBWD, p. 50) could find practical expression will be taken up again in the next chapter in the context of the idea of a "new international" beyond Marx.

The example I have just run through illustrates how a continuing interest in emancipation or progress is taking place today in ways that are, at least arguably, unthinkable in a pre-Marxist space. But it doesn't stop there. We can imagine variations on the theme of Wiggins's ocean-bottom-feeding-unease which generates examples that are equally telling of a similar "space-opening" legacy of Marx. These are cases where the primary agencies of supposedly modern democratic political power (nation-states, their political unions and their alliances) sustain conditions of security and co-operation of the sort that are necessary for the exercise of personal freedom only for a minority within them; cases where the "us" who can expect to be able to make effective decisions about how her or his life is lived falls a long way short of the "all" promised by that set-up. This would be anything but the de-limited or un-bound "we" which would be genuinely expressive of what Marx called an historical "movement of the immense majority, in the interest of the immense majority" (CM, p. 14).

This is an especially sharp problem within modern societies; societies where the State political set-up explicitly claims to recognise and realise both "the principle of *freedom* for *all* members of society" and "the principle of legal *equality* for *everyone*" (Kant, p. 99). If such modern States effectively promote and sustain a form of individual and social life that displays little or no interest in what is going on anywhere unless it impacts on what a powerful minority within it will need the world to be like in order to sustain its own freedom, we do not only have a time-bound interest but in addition a (for example) class-bound, gender-bound, or race-bound interest. In other words, just the kinds of bound interest that Pippin's leftist radicals have in view, and which is the focus of the politics of hope today. Moreover, it seems undeniable that a great many of "us" (construed in an un-bound way) have lived and continue to live in conditions that not only inhibit freedom, but subject many to an acute fear of becoming victims of State violence or abuses of power: people who have been or still are, as Derrida puts it, "victims of wars, political or other kinds of violence, nationalist, racist, colonialist, sexist, or other kinds of exterminations, victims of the oppressions of capitalist imperialism or any of the forms of totalitarianism" (SM, p. xix).

The cases here involve a sort of reversal of the unpromising failure identified in the environmental example: it is not only that our form of life literally cannot, unless something quite radical is done about it, sustainably go on like this, but that, unless something quite radical is done about it, it *can* (as long as the environment can sustain it). As Judith Shklar puts it, "the assumption, amply justified by every page of political history, is that some agents of government will behave lawlessly and brutally in small or big ways most of the time unless they are prevented from doing so" (LF, p. 28). And it is not only totalitarian regimes that concern us here. In the movement of democratisation, the modern liberal State has its modern distinction in being a political set-up whose massively asymmetrical power can be legitimately sustained only if, in general, it backs off from putting pressure on anyone to think or believe anything in particular, or telling them what should please them, and in this way secures the political conditions necessary for the exercise of some measure of personal freedom (a measure of "negative" liberty) for all. But, as Bernard Williams puts it, when its "unsuccess" in this is due to "misuses of its *own* powers or its failure to curb people's use of their powers to subordinate others", it does not just fail to forward aims of the sort we might expect from it in policy terms (to reduce unemployment and eliminate child-poverty, for example) but fails directly to be what makes it a "modern" and not "despotic" State in the first place (IBWD, p. 61).

VII

The appeal to an un-bound extension of the "us" is one dimension of a "since Marx" condition. But there is another dimension to how we respond to the unpromising failures of modern societies today that suggests another oblique spectre of Marx continuing more or less unaltered into our time, and one that I think is particularly visible in the elaboration of a new liberalism, the liberalism of fear, in the work of Judith Shklar. As Shklar notes, the idea of a liberalism of this kind is concerned above all with differences of power, and especially between "the weak and the powerful", and this means that it differs "sharply" from earlier types of liberalism (LF, p. 26). Shklar mentions, in particular, its difference from the classical "liberalism of natural rights", which, as we have seen, envisages a "society of rights claiming citizens", a "society composed of politically sturdy citizens, each able to and willing to stand up for himself and others" (LF, pp. 26–27). The liberalism of fear has no such expectations; indeed, appealing to what we can see on "every page of political history", it expects the opposite and its relation to the future, its messianism, becomes explicitly promissory: "never again" (LF, p. 27). The liberalism of fear is concerned above all to respond to this memory of political violence and brutality – the memory especially of abuses of State power – a fear-inspiring violence that falls disproportionately on the poor and those who are not powerful (Shklar, p. 28). And as I mentioned earlier its ambitions are, as a result, "more a recipe for survival", more about "damage control", than utopian hopes (LF, p. 27). Nevertheless, it is not, as I have indicated, merely about survival: its messianic promise ("never again") is never over, and in every here and now remains internal to our future projecting sense of what we do here and now – even if this messianism is entirely without messianic content.

In making this turn, liberalism is quite transformed. Completely untied, as the liberalism of fear is, from classical liberal ideas of a proper order of "the lives of individual citizens", an order "pre-established" by "nature or God" (LF, p. 26); completely untied from any given political regime, and regarding "abuses of public powers in all regimes with equal trepidation" (LF, p. 28); completely untied from any essential reference to nation, religion or language – and tied only to the "undeniable actualities" (LF, p. 27) of something that comes as near as one could want to something simply humanly universal, indeed something that is "common to animals as well as to human beings" (LF, p. 29) – "the fear of systematic cruelty" – when one's politics "makes a universal and especially a cosmopolitan claim" (LF, p. 29) with the universal vocation for "building a political order" (wherever we are) that can, as far as possible limit (though never finally overcome) the fear and cruelty produced by abuses of State power and other powerful agencies (LF, p. 32), and thus "would benefit the vast majority of human beings" (LF, p. 30) – with this we are, once again, I think, in the wake of Marx, even if we are resolutely non-utopian adherents to a politics of memory.

The "political order" that Shklar regards as best fit to these ends is one in which a measure of "negative" liberty has been effectively institutionalised. These are democratic institutions. The existence of democratic institutions cannot, however, eliminate the possibility of abuses of power. Nevertheless, I would think there has been considerable progress in "damage control" over the last two hundred years wherever representative government and electoral democracy has become the norm. On the other hand, there are some outstanding examples of continuing problems even in places where it has become the norm. Nowhere is this more visible today than in the kinds of concerns that are voiced by Pippin's leftist radicals. At issue is the fact that those who have most power within such States, hence those whose decisions have the greatest chance of contributing positively (or not) to our lives, those who occupy the most central places of speech – elected representatives and the governments they form, and along with them the media, business leaders, cultural figures, religious authorities, and so on – are increasingly felt *un*representative. T.S Eliot, writing in 1948, called this group an "élite", and he was especially conscious that the generational succession of such an élite has been tied historically to familial and social continuities in "the dominant class" (TDC, p. 42). Whatever Eliot thinks about that tie (he liked it) is of less significance than his clear sense of the way thinking is shifting on this question in the development of democratic societies in our time: namely, the increasing resistance to the idea that the kind of "qualitative differences among individuals" that makes some and not others "apt" to belong to an élite (those who are "best fitted to exercise the functions of the positions") should be tied to a blood principle. Eliot cites Karl Mannheim asserting that "it is the most important contribution of modern democracy...that the achievement principle increasingly tends to become the criterion of social success" (TDC, p. 39), and hence an unbinding of power from hereditary structures, and hence equally, an unbinding of a restriction to the élites of the kind of un-bound temporal bond (such as a blood bond) which, as we have seen, belongs centrally to our own neo-Burkean sense of a promising humanity today: "a piety towards the dead, however obscure, and a solicitude for the unborn, however remote" (TDC, p. 44).

Bernard Williams stresses that the legitimacy of the modern State (as a coercive power) rests on "its capacity to offer a justification of its power *to each subject*" (IBWD, p. 4). But there is a new qualitative inflexion of this that belongs to European societies in our time that Williams does not see, but one whose importance Berlin had acknowledged in his discussion of the struggle for recognition; an inflexion which comes into view when we take account of the fact that when each subject *looks back* to the representatives, the officials of the State and others whose status depends on the acceptability of that justification, *too many* among the present and living today will want to say *I don't see me in you*. Williams considers a case of "a group of subjects of the state – within its borders, required to obey officials, and so forth – who are radically disadvantaged relative to others [in regard to what one can fear]" (IBWD, p. 5). One thing you can be sure about that group: they won't be, in the respects that makes them a group, *like* the officials they are required to obey. There is, of course, no guarantee that a group of officials who were in the relevant respects sufficiently "like me" would eradicate the disadvantage. But for each subject to regard themselves as such today (to regard themselves as belonging to the "us" of a political community or communities); it is no longer so acceptable, or acceptable at all, for the coercive power of the State to be qualitatively representative, so massively and conspicuously, of only one "group of subjects of the state": mostly a lot of wealthy white men.

And the same would be true of all other cultural élites: in the media, in business, in academia, in publishing, in religious hierarchies, and so on and on and on. Those who see "a class or gender or race or culture bound strategy", see and hear, first of all, a bound "us" when they see and hear élites say that *their* efforts are intended to contribute positively to *our* lives. They see and hear, the voice of those who occupy central places of speech as having little or no interest in what is going on anywhere unless it impacts on what those who occupy such places will need the world to be like in order to sustain their own personal freedom and well-being. We have come to regard a situation where the group of subjects of the State who are "the decision makers" do not represent the diversity of social identities and groups in society as a fundamental concern of and for democratic politics. There has been progress in many emancipatory battles, but change is often glacially slow.

VIII

The legitimacy problem for Pippin was almost entirely theoretical: the task is to provide an account of why we should affirm the scientific world-view and the political ideals of individual rights protection, a modern civil society, and democratic institutions. Or again: the problem was to show that the confidence placed in the modern worldview that has dominated the European West since the Enlightenment is well-founded, justified – and is not, as sceptics might suspect, the rule by force of an arbitrary or illegitimate authority. What he hardly mentions in any of this – surprisingly for an Hegelian of sorts – is the modern State. If modernity is characterised intellectually by a shift from the authority of the Church to the authority of Science, it is characterised politically by a shift from the divine right of Kings to the sovereignty of the people in a nation-state. Indeed, the modern political ideals and institutions he mentions are inseparable from the nation's modern State form. With this in view, I think we should see that the question of legitimacy is, first of all, a question of legitimate State power: the legitimacy or otherwise of the State as a coercive power. I know no better account of this issue than that given by Williams, who connects it to what he calls the "first" (national) political question:

> I identify the "first" political question in Hobbesian terms as the securing of order, protection, safety, trust, and the conditions of cooperation. It is "first" because solving it is the condition of solving, indeed posing, any others. It is not (unhappily) first in the sense that once solved, it never has

> to be solved again. This is particularly important because, a solution to the first question being required *all the time*, it is affected by historical circumstances; it is not a matter of arriving at a solution to the first question at the level of state-of-nature theory and then going on to the rest of the agenda.
>
> It is a necessary condition of legitimacy that the state solve the first question, but it does not follow that it is a sufficient condition. …[One may well think] that more than one set of political arrangements, even in given historical circumstances, may solve the first question [and] it is entirely reasonable to think that only some of such arrangements are such that the state will be legitimate. (IBWD, p.3)

The "opposition" to modernity that Pippin had in view included those who do not think the existing arrangements meet the conditions of legitimacy. It may also include those who do not think any State arrangement do (classical anarchists). But they can raise their concerns in the way they do because *the demand for legitimacy now belongs to the idea of the State thus defined*: the State should not be or become part of the problem the existence of the State should remove. Looked at in this way, the legitimacy question is not answered by a self-grounding theory of modern legitimacy but by practical success or unsuccess in eradicating legitimate grievances (grievances arising from the State becoming part of the problem). "Nothing succeeds like success", Williams notes, following that with the famous line from Goethe's *Faust* that Wittgenstein appropriated: "in the beginning was the deed" (IBWD, p. 14). And, with respect to the still "bound" character of the élites in our time, the ongoing legitimacy of democratic institutions which answer the first question demands that, in our time, some deed or deeds must be done to "un-bound" it.

The problem of justification of power is only one side of a problem facing nation-states today. Indeed, if the *beginning* was the deed, the threat of an *end* comes when suspicions arise that the nation-state is simply incapable of being a sustainable or stabilisable means of solving the "first" political question in the first place. Williams does not spend much time with this worry, but he is alive to it, and alive to it in a way that connects with the way I have wanted to frame Europe's modernity problem more generally:

> [There is a particular worry] that technical or commercial considerations often have more determinative power than the policies of states…[and] a more general tendency to distrust the capacity of states to bring about ethical transformations of society… Scepticism about the practical and ethical consequences of *les grands récits* that have been enacted in the past century here meets the sense of the declining effectiveness of the nation-state. (IBWD, p. 47)

How should we understand this weakening of the nation-state as the place for politics? In the next chapter, I want to take up this question by way of two further "since Marx" legacies, this time from sociology. These are, first, a "post-national" thesis (the withering of the nation-state), and second a related "secularization thesis" (the withering of religion). As I hope to show, neither of these theses is in good shape, and both articulate a Marxist legacy in our thinking about our contemporary condition that we would do better to leave behind. On the other hand, working through both will take us towards a better understanding of something implicit in Williams's sense of the meeting of scepticism about grand narratives and the weakening of the nation-state in an era of technological and commercial globalisation, something we have been tracking throughout this book: How goes the world? – It wears, sir, as it grows.

8
STATE AND RELIGION BEYOND MODERNITY

Everyone is similar by dint of being incomparable

– Pierre Rosanvallon

In an era dominated by processes of globalisation, one might assign to sociology, at least now and then, two distinctive "since Marx" characterisations of our time. Here is a faithfully and fully Marxist summary of the two, from the website of "Strategy for Revolution in the 21st Century" (http://sfr-21.org/lenin-religion.html):

> Marx…believed that religion was an historical phenomenon, tied to the oppressive structures of human history such as feudalism and capitalism. Just as [he] believed that the State, as we know it today, would no longer be needed and would "wither away" after the world had turned completely to socialism, so too [he] believed that religion would wither away when there was no longer a need for it.

Alive to the fact that "national mystique" has always been inseparable from religion, Marx would have seen these two withering processes, the withering away of the State and of religion, as intertwined, bound together as among the most striking developments of an epic process of the social transformation underway in the shape and shaping of our lives. In this chapter, I will treat them separately. However, I do not want to dispute the sense of their interconnection. The historical emergence of the "secular" nation-state in Europe in the wake of the Treaty of Westphalia of 1648 was, at the same time, a process of their "confessionalization": to each realm, its religion. While obviously not arising together, national and religious differences were in lock-step together in the process of nation-state formation – and a Marxist might well expect them to altogether wither together too "after the world had turned completely to socialism". Nevertheless, since what I take to be withering in our time is, above all, the kind of epic messianic eschatology that Marxism represents (Feudalism-Capitalism...Communism), I am content to take the transformations we are witnessing in these domains in our time one after the other, taking the withering of the nation-state first, and then religion. Considerations, *pace* Marx, concerning the ongoing significance of the nation-state will open out onto a question concerning the fate of the humanitarian ideal of a united humanity at the end of history, and a discussion of that theme will be spliced between our two putative witherers.

THE STATE OF THE NATION

I

In the wake of Marx, we find the weakening of the nation-state as an effective site for political deliberation and decision over *res publica* conceived through the lens of a "post-national" thesis: this weakening, it is sometimes thought, belongs to an historical movement that is set to continue such that the nation-state will, one fine day, likely wither away altogether. Modernity has "stripped" people "of every trace of national character" (CM, p. 14), and "national differences and antagonisms between peoples are daily more and more vanishing" (CM, p. 23). Perhaps this can be affirmed (when it is affirmed) with a sense of regret, but in the main, it is conceived as progress beyond an irrational and fundamentally pathological configuration of human lives; the post-national future promises a united humanity living without the national distinctions which have hitherto parted and divided it. Call this the hope of the humanitarian ideal.

Not all sociologists are so lost to feelings of national involvement and belonging. Benedict Anderson, for example, conceives the formation of national identities as an integrative-imaginative process that has allowed people to feel solidarity for contiguous strangers, and urges us to acknowledge that "in an age when it is so common for progressive, cosmopolitan intellectuals (particularly in Europe?) to insist on the near-pathological character of nationalism, its roots in fear and hatred of the Other, and its affinities with racism, it is useful to remind ourselves that nations inspire love, and often profoundly self-sacrificing love" (IC, p. 229). Such an affective bond to a nation has not gone away, and is no longer always (or at least less frequently) lived with the kind of nationalism one might reasonably think near-pathological, although that kind of nationalism has certainly not gone away either – and anti-cosmopolitan thinking is thriving (particularly in Europe?). Nevertheless, like religion, which, as we shall see later in this chapter, is not withering according to plan either, nationality remains a powerful marker of cultural identities, perhaps the most powerful. The national "imagined community" is a constituency of "embedded and lived" involvements: something that is, for the great majority, beyond gainsaying, not "merely" imagined even if the society of strangers that constitutes it is manifestly "phenomenal" or virtual.

Kant had supposed that the main differentiating markers of what became national identities – linguistic and religious differences – were permanently hardwired into nature for nature's own ends; they could not be stripped away. But one does not have to give them that kind of status to acknowledge their abiding existential significance. Our lived involvements with others, with the mutuality but also (perhaps especially) the frustrations attached to them, are the primary facts of our social lives, and national belonging remains part of that even in conditions of the weakening of the nation-state. Speaking as a French citizen, Derrida will be specialising in the sense of the universal when he attests that "it is a fact that I feel, in this order, more obligations towards those who closely share my life, my people, my family, the French, the Europeans, those who speak my language or share my culture, etc." (BS, p. 109). Such step-by-step involvements are a social fact about us. That fact will never found ethics (we will come back to that), but if we keep it steadily in view, the post-national withering thesis can look like hopelessly wishful thinking by men of modern ideas.

The weakening of the nation-state as an effective political force is, as Williams insists, a reality in "the politics of now" (IBWD, p. 57). But that should not be taken to imply that nation-state politics is no longer important. On the contrary, it remains, Williams insists, "*primarily* important" (IBWD, p. 46). This primacy has been strikingly visible throughout some recent upheavals in Europe: during the migration crisis since 2015, the Brexit events since 2016, and the Covid-19 lockdowns and aftermath since 2020. National government still really matters, even if nationally localised politics is increasingly impossible. On the other hand, it is not only the declining effectiveness of that space that is a political reality in conditions of globalisation. The modern *topos* of democratic politics is the nation-state. But for a long stretch of modern Europe's history democracy has been elaborated – when it has been elaborated at all – through a politics of "the community of friends" in which the paradigm "friend" relation was conceived through ideas of the filial relation of "brothers"; a community of "natural" friends represented as rooted in the "native soil" of a "fatherland". Right across Europe, this was a basic feature of *les grands récits* through which the newly forming nations understood themselves as such. This kind of blood and soil conception of a political community of friends, ideas of peoples and fatherlands, is weakening too; now far more likely to be part of the language of racist extremists rather than mainstream democrats. In conditions where neither the hope for a nation as a localisable space for effective politics nor belief that certain people are its "natural" inhabitants stands so fast for us, one might think that the nation-state is on its way to losing its status as something "*primarily* important".

For those for whom nativism and "fatherlandishness" still does stand fast these two developments (globalisation, on the one hand, and scepticism about the naturalness of national communities, on the other) might be thought to be connected in this kind of way: the strong sense of a nation as a people and a land has been denuded by developments in global mobility and migration. As a result of globalisation, European societies are far more "multi-cultural" than they once were, and that cultural diversity makes appeals to a national community of blood brothers (regretfully) increasingly difficult to sustain. However, not only was that kind of "syngenealogy" of a nation always a fantasy, not merely an imagined but "a *dreamt* condition" (PF, p. 92), but the explanation just given puts the cart before the horse anyway: within the movement of Europe's democratisation, the forces of xenophobic exclusion were already weakening. Atavistic nativism and ethno-naturalism could not remain altogether untouched by the processes which dissociate the universality of the "all are free" of Europe's modern metanarrative from any supposedly homogeneous "we" of a "natural" national community. Of course, one can re-naturalise everything internationally, for example, in ideas of a European community of race, or (dreaming bigger) in ideas of a universal brotherhood, the brotherhood of Man. But, in Europe, in a Europe today which will not have broken with ethno-nationalism or nativism by any stretch of the imagined community, democratising mutations are underway which invite us to think and live a democratic ethos that breaks, or at least has the chance of breaking, with naturalness and homogeneity. As Derrida puts it,

> a self-deconstructive force in the very motif of democracy, the possibility and the duty for democracy to de-limit itself...through the abstract and potentially indifferent thought of number and equality...can impose homogenizing calculability while exalting land and blood, and the risk is as terrifying as it is inevitable – it is the risk today, more than ever. But it perhaps also keeps the power of universalizing, beyond the State and the nation, the account taken of anonymous and irreducible singularities, infinitely different and thereby indifferent to particular difference. (PF, pp. 105–6)

Derrida's affirmation of democracy as holding within itself "the power of universalizing, beyond the State and the nation", returns us to the thought of the humanitarian ideal, and we will come back to that in the context of considering his appeal to "irreducible singularities" in the middle phase of this chapter. However, while the democratic movement is in the process of emancipating Europeans from dependence on "any *definite* milieu" (BGE, p. 153), and thus opens the space for a politics without "land and blood" exaltation, we must not forget that these developments still unfold, and cannot not unfold, within a space marked by what I am calling the step-by-step social fact of our involvements: the reality of feelings for ("imagined", virtual and symbolic) constituencies of involvement – with people, places, linguistic and religious cultures – that are existentially primary for us. Nietzsche kept this in view too when considering the formation of the "good Europeans", acknowledging that national belonging will *not* have been "done with" in the life of the new nomadic type of Europeanised Europeans of the future (BGE, p. 152), and in his integrated Europe the "great cantons" – Europe's nations – preserve their rights. The feelings associated with those who are closest to us, including a "warm-hearted patriotism", are not something one can expect human beings to slough off.

It would be a fantasy every bit as dreamt as the syngenealogist's to suppose that people might attain a way of being that is no longer shaped by the fact of differential involvements. We are not rational cosmopolitans. However, if the nation-state is weakening as a site for effective deliberations and decisions on matters of public concern in conditions of globalisation, and if democratisation itself gives rise to "scepticism" about a naturalistically construed national community that had been internal to "*les grands récits* that have been enacted in the past century" (IBWD, p. 47), national politics may seem beyond saving. Such "*grands récits*" made sense of our lives as national citizens but were freighted by "historical memories" of natural rootedness. If processes of democratisation underway in those national places itself "deconstructs" the racinating function of those grand narratives, if "exalting land and blood" becomes an increasingly unacceptable way of rooting national citizenship, one can only wonder whether national politics can retain its primary importance. It wears, sir, as it grows.

Given the fact of our involvements can there be a democratic solution to this double-whammy to the nation-state? One possibility would be to look to strengthen (specifically) nationally configured democratic resources that are already up-and-running; resources that can do national political service without recourse to syngenealogical dreams. The obvious candidate, and one I will want to endorse in its spirit if not its letter, is the democratic potential that resides in *national party politics*. The thought here is that one might seek to acknowledge and respect feelings of belonging to a national "whole" by reviving its expression in a fundamentally ideational rather than a spuriously natural form. This is something I will enthusiastically affirm. The specific proposal is that the most appropriate ideational candidate can be found in the machinery that is already most closely associated with, and gives content to, concerns for "the good of the whole": the political party form. This is something I will entirely reject.

The possibility of reviving the virtues of national party politics is something one finds clearly if somewhat uneasily articulated in the work of Jonathan White and Lea Ypi in their book *The Meaning of Partisanship*. The opening chapter is about the history of political parties. That history is far shorter than one might suppose, and was intimately connected to the development of nation-states in the passage from the sovereignty and divine right of Kings to the sovereignty and political freedom of the people in the eighteenth and nineteenth centuries; it belongs to "the institutionalisation of popular sovereignty and liberty" (MP, p. 16). This party-state nation-state set-up is fundamental to the understanding of the partisan claim as White and Ypi present it as coming down to us from Edmund Burke: the partisan claim is not to represent and pursue the interests of just one section of society but, rather and precisely, "the good of the whole" (MP, p. 17). It is this idea, it might be thought, that we need to recover and reconstitute beyond old ideas of a "natural" national community: strengthening the national political whole by strengthening opportunities for the politically partisan expressions of its good.

White and Ypi speak of the whole, and the good of the whole. Burke was in fact more immediately specific: the claim of the party, the partisan claim, is to implement principles and policies in "the national interest". White and Ypi's less specific identification belongs to an analysis that is alive to the abstract and indifferent thought of democracy: they abstract the partisan claim from any particular whole. On the other hand, they acknowledge (if only in parentheses) that the historically understood "whole" at issue in the formation of political parties in Europe in the eighteenth and nineteenth centuries was, as they put it "state, society, and the 'fatherland'" (MP, p. 17). It was and has hitherto only been in the context of peoples and fatherlands that the party-state form of the nation-state made its way.

White and Ypi leave it open that a partisan claim may find a "whole" of some kind beyond the nation-state, and in the final chapter of their book explore the possibility of supranational political parties. But that projection is cautious and uncertain – and, in fact, it only becomes an issue at all for the reasons that motivate talk of national party-political revitalisation in the first place; reasons that concern, above all, the contemporary condition of the whole which had marked its birth, the contemporary condition of the party-state nation-state set-up as a site for deliberation and decision over matters of public concern: a much weaker condition. Thinking about the possibility for a party renaissance gets its purchase precisely from a sense of that weakened reality.

One might think that strengthening the normative ideal of partisan speaking for the good of the whole might itself assist in strengthening the whole. On the other hand, that White and Ypi themselves effectively resist speaking of the whole as *primarily* a national whole reflects some considerable unease on their part that such a whole can, in our time, be unproblematically invoked. Indeed, it reflects their own (characteristically academic) unease in even wanting to. Although they do not get very far invoking any other whole, both a clear sense of the weakening of the party-state form of the nation-state and a lurking political resistance on their part to the idea of speaking for the national whole anyway makes their plea for a revival of the normative ideal unconvincing: a last gasp effort to speak the old language of Europe's modern political language, but without its old primarily national framing. The fact of national involvements is not really something they want to have much to do with. This too may be regarded as a "post-national" Marxist legacy, and Marx's work informs much of theirs. His own treatment of partisanship is worth exploring as we attempt to come to terms with the condition of the party-state nation-state in our time.

II

Marx more than most saw this weakening of the party-state coming – and he thought its coming demise would belong to the end of the nation-state too. He conceived the party-state form as increasingly belonging to the past, and his vision of a communist party and its fundamentally international character as belonging to the future. The idea of a party as a specifically communist party is also (and in fact for the same reason) a *prima facie* exception to the Burkean understanding of the partisan claim. As White and Ypi note, such a party is, in a straightforward way, quite unlike the bourgeois national parties it would displace: it openly concerns itself only with the interest of a "whole", that is, in fact, only one sectional part of any national whole, the proletariat. As Marx puts it in the *Manifesto*:

> The Communists...have no interests separate and apart from those of the proletariat as a whole...The Communists are distinguished from the other working-class parties by this only: 1. In the national struggles of the proletarians of the different countries, they point out and bring to the front the common interests of the entire proletariat, independently of all nationality. 2. In the various stages of development which the struggle of the working class against the bourgeoisie has to pass through, they always and everywhere represent the interests of the movement as a whole. (CM, p. 21)

The "whole" here is not the nation as a whole but exclusively the whole (and hence international) proletarian movement in politics – the political becomes immediately geopolitical. However, as White and Ypi are keen to stress, the idea of a communist party does not break entirely with the old Burkean understanding of the partisan claim. On the contrary, "the point was exactly that the greater good of society as a whole, properly understood, was aligned with the interests of the working class" (MP, 19). The "properly understood" qualification is ugly and condescending, and the specification of "society as a whole" indeterminate, but the point will be familiar: the interest of the proletariat as a *particular* class can be aligned in this way to the whole because it already is, in essence, a *universal* class, with nothing other than their own labour as their own, their own interest is simply human interest as such. The communist party is still concerned with "the good of the whole" because it is primarily concerned with the good of all.

But the transformation of the space of the party political that Marxism announces for the first time – its becoming international and geopolitical – was not something the communist party would or could simply bring about by itself. According to Marx, it belonged to a form of "withering" of the nation-state already underway. Moreover, this was not due to the successful world-wide-isation of bourgeois *political* culture – national party politics, parliamentarism and electoral representation as it then existed – but the unrelenting globalisation of bourgeois *economy*. Again from the *Manifesto*:

> The bourgeoisie has through its exploitation of the world market given a cosmopolitan character to production and consumption in every country. To the great chagrin of Reactionists, it has drawn from under the feet of industry the national ground on which it stood. All old-established national industries have been destroyed or are daily being destroyed... In place of the

> old local and national seclusion and self-sufficiency, we have intercourse in every direction, universal inter-dependence of nations. And as in material, so also in intellectual production. The intellectual creations of individual nations become common property. National one-sidedness and narrow-mindedness become more and more impossible, and from the numerous national and local literatures, there arises a world literature. (CM, p. 8)

Marx will take the fact of involvements onboard only by acknowledging that communist struggles will perforce be, in the first instance, national struggles, or struggles at the existing national level. But the "post-national" condition is "more and more" a coming reality. And for Marx, this meant that the national shaping of the fact of differential involvements will increasingly cease to be actual. The party-state nation-state has had its day.

What should we make of that idea? Marx saw the party-state shaping of our political lives giving way to a new and newly international configuration, with the communist party at the head of a world-wide international proletarian movement. Under the conditions of market globalisation, and the binary class struggle those conditions threw up, the motif of democracy was itself breaking from all natural nationalism, every politics of blood and soil. From now on, interest in the greater good of society as a whole is, when "properly understood", no longer about the politics of the national interest, it is the end of interest in the national interest. Many social facts change, so why not this one too?

I think this confuses what I am calling the step-by-step fact of involvements with social facts like levels of unemployment, which can be subject to fairly radical and rapid ("more and more") alterations. The fact I am concerned with, our step-by-step involvements, is different. There is contingency here too, and mutability, for sure. One only has to think of the newly imagined (virtual and symbolic) communities that are made possible by social technologies to see this. But even here there are the "close" and the "far" – the space and time of those distances have been transformed but are still in step with step-by-step involvements. This social fact is (to use Wittgenstein's metaphor) the "riverbed" of our social lives, not the stream that runs over it. We will have to rethink both the national and the international if we are to avoid the specious glitter of unmeaning promises about the future of our affective connections and step-by-step involvements. In what follows, I aim to show that, in our time, this will call for us to conceive not a "post-national" thesis but a "post-party" thesis, and this at both the still primarily important national level and the newly emerging international level.

III

As we have seen, Paul Valéry was also witness to the national and international transformations underway. In conditions in which there was not a rock without a flag, a globalised "*age of the finite world*" had begun, an age which was simultaneously the end of an age in which politics could be "localized" – that is to say, merely national. Localised nation-state politics, always only ever relative given the interminability of wars, was becoming increasingly impossible effectively to conduct even in times of peace. This new condition for national politics has only accelerated since the First World War. White and Ypi are well attuned to the disadjustments of national party politics in our time, but the conditions for politics since the Great War are so transformed today that in a sense (though not his sense) Marx was right: the space and time of national party politics, the time of the party-state nation-state may well be over. These conditions are, as Marx also emphasised, economic conditions of market globalisation. But they are not only that. They are also profoundly technological. Gone are the days when the political and public space was structured by the time it took to take "news" from one part of a national space to another by cart, road or rail. This transformation of public space is described by Derrida in *Specters of Marx* in a way that brings us up to our time, where the medium of public space – the media – has itself been utterly transformed by tele-technology:

> Let us recall the technical, scientific, and economic transformations that, in Europe, after the First World War, already upset the topological structure of the *res publica*, of public space, and of public opinion. They affected not only this topological structure, they also began to make problematic the very presumption of the topographical, the presumption that there was a place, and thus an identifiable and stabilizable body for public speech, the public thing, or the public cause, throwing liberal, parliamentary, and capitalist democracy into crisis... These transformations are being amplified beyond all measure today. This process, moreover, no longer corresponds to an amplification, if one understands by this word homogeneous and continuous growth. What can no longer be measured is the leap that already distances us from those powers of the media that, in the 1920s, were profoundly transforming the public space, dangerously weakening the authority and the representativity of elected officials and reducing the field of parliamentary discussions, deliberations, and decisions. One could even say that they were already putting in question electoral democracy and political representation *such at least as we have known them up until now.* If there is a tendency in all Western democracies no longer to respect the professional politician...it is because politicians become more and more, or even solely characters in the media's representation... However competent they may personally be, professional politicians who conform to the old model tend today to become structurally incompetent...: on the one hand, [this transformation of political space] takes away from them the legitimate power they held in the former political space (national parties, parliament, and so forth), but, on the other hand, it obliges them to become mere silhouettes, if not marionettes, on the stage of televisual rhetoric. They were thought to be actors of politics, they now often risk, as everyone knows, being no more than TV actors. (SM, pp. 79–80)

Derrida wonders whether we can still speak confidently today about "the virtues" of what we call "parliamentary democracy" – a term with which, as we have seen, he "designate[s] not parliamentarism and political representation *in general*, but the *present*, which is to say in fact, *past* forms of the electoral and parliamentary apparatus." Those forms have always and only been party-state forms, whether the pluralist parties-state form of liberal democracy or the party-state monopolies of totalitarianism. It is in the context of this unprecedented role of modern media technology that we should understand Derrida's reservations about effective parliamentary democracy in our time, and his call for "the end of the party":

> Here is perhaps one of the strange motifs we should talk about: What tends perhaps to disappear in the political world that is shaping up, and perhaps in a new age of democracy, is the domination of this form of organization called the party, the party-state relation, which finally will have lasted, strictly speaking, only two centuries, barely longer than that, a period to which belongs as well certain determined types of parliamentary and liberal democracy, constitutional monarchies, Nazi, fascist, or Soviet totalitarianisms. Not one of these regimes was possible without what could be called the axiomatics of the party. Now, as one can see foreshadowed, it seems, everywhere in the world today, the structure of the party is becoming not only more and more suspect (and for reasons that are no longer always, necessarily, "reactionary", those of the classical individualist reaction) but also radically unadapted to the new tele-techno-media-conditions of public space, of political life, of democracy, and of the new modes of representation (both parliamentary and non-parliamentary) that they call up. [We need to engage in] a reflection on the finitude of a certain concept or of a certain reality of the party. And, of course, of its state correlative. A movement is underway that we would be tempted to describe as a deconstruction of the traditional concepts of state and party [in a manner that does] not signify the withering away of the state in the Marxist sense. (SM, p. 102)

It is not over for parliamentarism and political representation. But something is happening, Derrida suggests, "a movement is underway" even if it is still only in its early stages, that spells the end of the party-state form of that nation-state set-up, doubtless transforming the state of the "state correlative" as well. For Derrida, the party form, as Simon Critchley puts it, "cannot adapt to the exigencies of the contemporary public space with its domination by the media and tele-technology" (HCMP, p. 107). Critchley is not so sure of this himself, and cites the success of Sergio Berlusconi's made-in-heaven marriage of media and politics with *Forza Italia* founded in 1993. Critchley says it has "a fairly classical party structure", and thus calls into question Derrida's sense of the current situation (HCMP, p. 107). But the idea that *Forza Italia* has a fairly classical party structure is not obviously true: it has, as Hopkin and Paolucci have argued, the typical structure of a firm, not a party; it is "a lightweight organisation", and its sole purpose is to mobilise "support at election time" (BFM, p. 35). Indeed, its own self-understanding was as a "light party" (*partito leggero*), precisely without the encumbrances of the classical party structure. Far from speaking against Derrida's hypothesis, it belongs strikingly to the "movement underway". The old party form is unadapted to the new media conditions. *Forza Italia* is an example of an adaptation, and one made possible because its leader was already the owner of four of the main private television stations in Italy. Here the adaptation goes (frighteningly transparently) in the direction of a "media-party-state", but the important point is that the party has become a machine for fighting elections in conditions of modern media technology, formed for that purpose, and alive for just as long as it can survive in that business. The French "party" created by Emmanuel Macron in 2016, *En Marche!*, (EM's party) is similarly "light" and firm-like. Macron was already an "independent", and his "party" explicitly seeks to be "transpartisan". "Change UK" (CHUK, perhaps first programmed to be Chuka Umunna's party) and the "Brexit Party" (essentially Nigel Farage's party) are other recent (and short-lived) examples in Britain. The success of Donald Trump, who hardly drew on the party structure of the Republican Party in the United States, might be another. Short-shelf-life "media-party-state" parties led by charismatic and telegenic individuals clearly belong more to "the political world shaping up" than the old parties and their ideational partisan claims. It is not to defend these developments but to open our eyes to them and reflect on what is happening that Derrida opens a new call for the end of the party:

> There was a moment, in the history of European (and, of course, American) politics, when it was a reactionary gesture to call for the end of the party... Let us put forward here...the hypothesis that this is no longer the case... This mutation has already begun; it is irreversible. (SM, p. 103)

In an interview on his Marx book, Derrida reaffirms his thought that "the party form is no doubt disappearing from political life in general" but he accepts too that it may be "a '*survivance*' that...turn[s] out to have a long life." The party-state configuration of a nation-state may last for ages, doubtless with light-parties built for media messaging to becoming increasingly common. And I think White and Ypi's efforts to restore trust in the old "normative ideal" of the partisan claim is an anxious reaction against these new conditions of political life, conditions which are transforming everything. Their admirable conviction in "the political ideal that lay at the heart of the partisan claim" – namely, the always contestable claim to speak for "the greater good of society as a whole" – faces the greatest challenge when the mediatic *medium* of the "whole" (its space and time) not only has the potential to overflow all national territorial borders, the old *topos* that would delimit the whole spatially, but operates in a manner that demands "rolling" news that is relentlessly *immediate* and *continuous*, so that its time has changed just as much as its space. Partisan speaking in these new conditions reduces politicians to mouth-organs: not ideational advocates for competing visions of the greater good of the whole but script-readers for today's tele-friendly soundbite – an immediate political response that seeks equally immediate public approval (a "like").

The old individualist reaction to party-state politics was that no-one can speak their mind if they are speaking always from a party perspective; it was not so much a reaction to cultish "group-think" as to collective thinking itself, hostile to the very idea of like-minded people coming together to formulate a manifesto for government. The complaint was that the party form discouraged people from thinking for themselves, it discouraged people from speaking their own mind concerning the good of the whole. This is not simply reaffirmed when we acknowledge that, today, in politics no one can speak their mind (still less change it). What was once just a reactionary complaint or the complaint of individualists now belongs to anyone looking at or engaging with "party politics". The good partisan today, more than ever, is the one whose speech (as Nietzsche put it) "admits no pro and con, of weighing and discarding" (HH, p. 146). In these conditions, questioning, even (perhaps especially) self-questioning through which one's own political thinking concerning the good of the whole makes its way, becomes strictly intolerable, and makes every politician "structurally incompetent".

If we want a future for ideational politics in the old nation-state space that remains *primarily* important, if we want to cherish the virtues of the partisan claim to speak in the interest of the national (and not sectional) interest, if we want to find in ideational politics a democratic alternative to ethno-nationalism and nativism, it will require forms of nationally localised parliamentarism and political representation beyond the present (which is to say past) forms of national politics, beyond party politics. What this might or should look like…I frankly do not know. At the close of this book, I will outline what one can reasonably hope for from political speech-making addressed to the public at large, whether by elected representatives or not. But we should get thinking about forms of parliamentarism and political representation that can save the virtue of the partisan claim – speaking your mind on questions concerning the good of the whole – without the party.

IV

The party-state form in the tele-techno-media-conditions of today's public space is not the only feature of the contemporary condition of politics that weakens the nation-state as a site for effective deliberations and decisions over matters of public concern. With multi-national corporations exercising enormous power in economic decision-making and multi-national news media corporations increasingly making the message in politics, the field of authority and effectivity of the party-state nation-state is immeasurably weaker anyway. On the other hand, these same forces – forces which "upset the topological structure of the *res publica*" that were localised in party-state nation-states – also produces new non-national "constituencies" which go beyond national borders. At this point, one might want to follow Marx once more, and to affirm the necessity of international party set-ups. But if the party-state form of the nation-state is losing its way in the new commercial and media conditions of our time, it is hard to imagine – given the step-by-step fact of our involvements – that it might be better suited to this new international dimension. I would suggest that Williams sees this more clearly: the new non-national constituencies do not call for political parties beyond the nation-state, but for strengthening and institutionalising something rather "thinner" and more procedural beyond the nation-state: international law. This is the kind of "public morality" that – given the step-by-step fact – can get a purchase beyond national boundaries; one where decisions "may have to be argued about and justified", as Williams puts it, "in more abstract, procedural terms, with a 'thinner' ethical content" (IBWD, p. 49) – deliberations of a type that can be conducted *without* presupposing the kind of patriotic allegiances and "thick" ethical content one can rely on in the imagined community of a national setting – allegiances of the kind that people like Jürgen Habermas have long- (and I think hopelessly-) hoped could be transferred from national to supra-national bodies in Europe.

With the emergence of constituencies that comprise "groups that cross [the nation-state's] boundaries", and hence without the "thick" ethical resources of national, religious and linguistic traditions, "thinner" – legal and regulatory – notions of the good and right "would", Williams suggests, "be more appropriate" (IBWD, pp. 50–1). Moreover, they have the chance of providing the kind of bulwark against international agencies, whether in business or the media, which (most) nation-states alone now simply lack. The European Union is one such opportunity for this, and sometimes proves its worth in that respect. But its regionality does not capture a condition that is today entirely global. Indeed, if it really believes in its project "on our continent", perhaps it should put its money where its Kantian mouth is, to work to help other regions do the same.

Williams acknowledges that re-thinking political institutions in an age of the declining power of the nation-state has only just begun, and regards his own thinking on this as "only a gesture to the direction in which one might think" (IBWD, p. 51). But I think Williams is right to see international law as the place to start at the international level, and it has an interesting parallel in Derrida's equally speculative thoughts on the idea of a "New International" which gave the subtitle to his book *Specters of Marx*. Derrida's thought on this begins with an acknowledgement that the concept of human rights has slowly become a successful lever for social progress within democratic political communities in sovereign nation-states. We now need, he suggests, a similar development in international law. In the Marx book, he specifies this development more fully:

> The "New International" refers to a profound transformation, projected over a long term, of international law, of its concepts, and its field of

> intervention. Just as the concept of human rights has slowly been determined over the course of centuries through many socio-political upheavals (whether it be a matter of the right to work or economic rights, of the rights of women and children, and so forth), likewise international law should extend and diversify its field to include, if at least it is to be consistent with the idea of democracy and of human rights it proclaims, the worldwide economic and social field, beyond the sovereignty of States. (SM, p. 105)

And he further identifies the kind of "alliance" involved in this development:

> The "New International" is not only that which is seeking a new [extension and diversification of] international law. It is a link of affinity, suffering, and hope, a still discreet, almost secret link, as it was around 1848, but more and more visible. We have more than one sign of it. It is an untimely link, without status, without title, and without name, barely public even if it is not clandestine, without contract, without coordination, without party, without country, without national community (international before, across, and beyond any national determination), without co-citizenship, without common belonging to a class. The name of "New International" is given here to what calls to the friendship of an alliance without institution among those who, even if they no longer believe or never believed in the socialist-Marxist International, in the dictatorship of the proletariat, in the messiano-eschatological role of the universal union of the proletarians of all lands, continue to be inspired by at least one of the spirits of Marx or of Marxism (they now know that there is more than one) and in order to ally themselves, in a new, concrete, and real way, even if this alliance no longer takes the form of a party or of a workers' international, but rather of a kind of counter-conjuration, in the (theoretical and practical) critique of the state of international law, the concepts of State and nation, and so forth: in order to renew this critique, and especially to radicalize it. (SM, p. 107)

I will come back to the sense of a "radicalization" of Marxism that Derrida has in view here, which is closely connected to our no longer believing in the kind of messianic eschatology that it still carries. In any case, Derrida emphasises that the "New International" whose spectre he wants to provoke onto the geopolitical stage is "different from what in the Marxist tradition was called the 'International'" (DN p. 12), and the crucial practical difference concerns the stress Derrida (like Williams) gives to the role and rule of international law ("which is a good thing"). Having marked this point, Derrida makes two qualifications about presently attained conditions in this area. First, that today this is a law that is still closely tied to classical concepts of internationality as inter-state relations: it articulates a form of "associating citizens belonging to given nation-states" (DN, p. 13). That conception is very clear and decisive in Kant, and informs his treatment of cosmopolitan right – which is always a right of citizens in a nation-state-differentiated cosmo-political totality. Derrida's thought, which seems to me close to Williams's, is that certain realities (Derrida speaks primarily about people all over the world who are simply "aligned in their suffering") produce what Williams calls "constituencies" beyond the "contiguity" of persons in a nation-state, and in forms no longer even mediated by such States and their inter-nation-state relations. Second, Derrida notes that existing global institutions such as the UN are also hugely dependent (especially financially) on especially powerful nation-states, in particular the United States. He accepts that this too is "sometimes a good thing", but he also raises it as a worry, as a problematic hegemony, which needs to be addressed. Neither Derrida nor Williams present more than speculative gestures regarding this new international projection and the new ethical constituencies that belong to it, but both see the "thinner" character of international law as most fitting to its future, and not at the expense of nation-states either, but for their ethically "thicker" political future too, even if that too must cultivate possibilities of deliberation and decision making in new forms of localised electoral democracy and representativity. In both cases, however, national and international, without the party.

Party-state – or "parties-state". The latter have been the practical reality and focus of most liberal political thinking: equality in liberty for all, including political liberty, was to be established first in a national political context; localised spaces for public speech – nation-states – were the place of politics, and the plurality of partisan claims was its life-blood. During the nineteenth century, these developments were becoming established, where they were in any sense becoming established, only in Europe. As Shklar notes, "in the world beyond Europe [the idea of equality in liberty for all] was not heard at all. It was powerful in the United States only if black people are not counted as members of its society" (LF, p. 22). With respect to such counting and not-counting, one could develop related accounts in the history of the slow and in many parts of the world still far from over struggles for universal suffrage. One should not be too sanguine about the electoral conditions attained today even in countries where liberalism has been most successful, and the representativity of elected officials is also, as we have seen, a pressing question: whether citizens can look back at such officials and say *I see myself in you*, something more-than-amplified by modern media conditions. On the other hand, even the conditions of equality in liberty unevenly attained in Europe remain wholly unattained in many countries which have hardly been touched by it, and liberal politics, even while it was nationally configured, was never indifferent to that. As Shklar goes on to stress, it is a "mark of liberalism" as a political tradition "that it was cosmopolitan and that an insult to the life and liberty of a member of any race or group in any part of the world was of genuine concern" (LF, 36), or again, "the liberalism of fear makes a universal and especially a cosmopolitan claim, as [liberalism] historically always has done" (LF, p. 29).

The trajectory for this contemporary liberalism remains universal. But its "since Marx" concern for developments that "would benefit the vast majority of human beings" (LF, p. 30) does not untie it from that which it has contingently been tied, from localised nation-state democracy. This marriage is not over, even if it faces severe strains in our time. For participants, the step-by-step social fact of their involvements means that the nation-state remains, and in some (small s) state of the nation or other, likely to remain, "*primarily* important", even if not in a party-state form. But with the step-by-step fact in view, what chance does universalism have in such a world of ongoing political parting and division?

A NEW UNIVERSALISM

V

The most exalted form of thinking *against* the fact of involvement with a nation has been, as we have seen, "post-national": it projects a humanity to come that has been effectively de-differentiated in this regard, a humanity where the religious, linguistic and national differences that have divided the world are no longer politically salient. This ideal – the humanitarian ideal – may seem not only rationally compelling on its own moral merit, but in contemporary globalised conditions historically timely, especially once it is acknowledged that "incredulity towards metanarratives" is so closely tied to the weakening of nation-states as sites in which politics can be meaningful. However, as I argued in Chapter 6, what seems, from the outside, rationally compelling may not be best; and what is rationally ideal will be the worst if it does not respect the fact of our involved lives.

The committed humanitarian might respond to this, more or less patiently, by saying that it is early days but the humanitarian ideal is still what we should aim for, or, more urgently, that it is high time for change, and we should move as rapidly as possible towards world government without nations and borders – or indeed a world of no governments anywhere at all. What should we make of this apparently congenial humanitarian "alter globalization" politics?

As we have seen, the humanitarian ideal of a politically de-differentiated world has to look beyond the differences between human ways of being – beyond everything Kant summarised under the big cultural markers of "linguistic and religious differences" (Kant, pp. 113–4). However, such thinking must still see in that cultural subtraction a sufficiently common human way to be in terms of which a politically de-differentiated humanity can live in harmony: a kind of human and humane minimum. It would be a life where *all*, as Lenin put it, have become habituated to "the *necessity* of observing the simple, fundamental rules of human intercourse" that will enable us to get along in peace (SR, p. 108, emphasis in original). Kant had something of the luxury of being able to suppose that linguistic and religious differences permanently stand in the way of that happy outcome (Kant, p. 113). But one does not need to appeal to anything so fixed and immutable to object to the apparently nice idea that there are such "simple, fundamental rules of human intercourse" that could be universalised for all humanity.

One objection to that nice idea – the quick way – would be to look to the history of humanity and remind oneself that what we have most "in common" is that we are an unbelievably and consistently dangerous animal. One has to wonder what sort of fantasy it is to think that we might say "Never again" to all that, or to suppose we can take ourselves somewhere without that dangerous animal coming with us. A related and more interesting objection would be to argue that the very idea of taking ourselves to such a place is an example of that dangerous animal taking charge. This objection begins by asking why the humanitarian ideal presents itself as an ideal. The typical kind of answer is that there is something (sufficiently) common to all human beings that is far more fundamental than even the big historical markers of human differences that have been the cause of so much bloody conflict. We have much more in common than those (ultimately superficial and, *pace* Kant, historically labile) differences might suggest, it might be claimed. As I have just noted, what we have in common could be something terrible, so it had better be something both universal and worthy of the humanitarian hope.

Since any realistic hope has to accept that some human differences in all populations – inequalities in fact – might well be thought inevitable, differences of individual ability and need for example, what has to be found is a human way to be that is maximally tolerant of such differences. That idea is central to what Lenin thought so significant in the Marxist formula for communist society: "From each according to his ability, to each according to his needs" (SR, p. 101). Here human differences that are empirically unavoidable or simply should not be avoided are taken into account in a maximally just way. So it is a formula for social peace. It is also, in fact, a secular variant of the one affirmed by "the multitude", who, after Christ's crucifixion and resurrection, decided to hold all that they had in "common" in order to support the Apostles (who had more important tasks to get on with) "according as he had need":

> 32 And the multitude of them that believed were of one heart and of one soul: neither said any of them that ought of the things which he possessed/was his own; but they had all things common. 33 And with great power gave the apostles witness of the resurrection of the Lord Jesus: and great grace was upon them all. 34 Neither was there any among them that lacked: for as many as were possessors of lands or houses sold them, and brought the prices of the things that were sold, 35 And laid them down at the apostles' feet: and distribution was made unto every man according as he had need. (Acts 4:32–35)

This communalism may seem ideal, but since long-term harmony in this (small s) state of human universality depends completely on its members adhering to the "universal" way to be, there will be, as Lenin puts it, "no way of getting away", "'nowhere to go'" (SR, p. 107), for those who might prefer not to, or who find it less than ideal. All social set-ups may be thought to have some level of fear attached to them, what Lyotard rather dramatically calls "a level of terror" devolving from the injunction to "be operational (that is commensurable) or disappear" (PC, p. xxiv). However, the level of fear or terror attached to a society in which a humanitarian ideal holds sway is staggeringly high. Lenin admits this with chilling calmness when he notes that, for "*all* citizens" (SR, p. 106, emphasis in original), attempts at "escape" from the "universal" habits of communist society will not be tolerated. Indeed, they will be met, he says, by "swift and severe punishment (for the armed workers are practical men and not sentimental intellectuals, and they will scarcely allow anyone to trifle with them)" (SR, p. 107). Be operational comrade, or disappear. Look who came too.

Is there any reason to think that such brutality would not accompany us, for this sort of reason, whatever noble vision of a regime without evil you manage to conjure up as the single, universally "human" way for all to be? You always have to ask yourself if what you are really imagining is: a world where everyone has finally come round to thinking...like you. (As Nietzsche said of Hegel: "... for Hegel the climax and terminus of the world-process coincided with his own existence in Berlin" (UM, p. 104).

VI

Are there, or better, do we have, any other routes or resources available to think about human universality – something that might be more in keeping with the fact of involvements, and the particularities that will, for that reason, always, in fact, be inscribed in our identities? A risk-free approach to thinking through the question of our common humanity would be to identify it not with a universal and common way to be but with something in everyone that is both completely independent of all contingencies of human differences and also worthy of respect. As Bernard Williams notes, in Europe this thought has been most rigorously and influentially developed by Kant: in Kant's idea that "the respect owed equally to each person...is not owed to that person in respect of *any* empirical characteristics, but solely in respect of the transcendental characteristic of being a free and rational will" (IBWD, p. 102). Williams is right, I think, to find Kant's recourse to such a metaphysically demanding conception unappealing, and he thinks it anyway simply "a secular analogue of the Christian conception of the respect owed to everybody as equally children ["sons" in fact SG] of God", a (barely) secularised version of the Christian conception that also supposes there is nothing "empirical about people that constitutes the ground of equal respect" (IBWD, p. 102). So if not something too empirically demanding or something too metaphysically demanding, is there anything else we can look to in order to sustain *some* kind of humanitarian ideal?

Staying close to Kant's sense that shared empirical characteristics will not do the job, but wanting too to do without Kant's still-too-theological metaphysical concepts, Williams attempts to find another way of sustaining our inherited ideas of all people's equality by distinguishing between, on the one hand, the interest we can take in some way of living a life (which can be assessed in all sorts of ways and may be marked by all sorts of different empirical characteristics and titles) and, on the other hand, regarding that way of living a life "from a point of view which is concerned primarily with what it is *for that person* to live that life" (IBWD, p. 103). From this point of view what is of interest is something which is precisely *not* common, or rather what is common is the fact that every human existence has, as Heidegger puts it, "*in each case mineness* [*Jemeinigkeit*]" (BT, p. 68).

This focus is intended to capture a relation of identity with every other which is not bound up with any particular human way to be or anything shared in common. Instead, there is the idea of an interest in the *singular individual* (irreplaceable, unsubstitutable) who actually lives any such life. Wittgenstein famously describes this kind of attentiveness as "*eine Einstellung zur Seele*" – "an attitude towards a soul" – and suggests that is most visible in the relation to what we call a "friend" (PI, p. 178). Wittgenstein's drawing in the word "soul" here speaks to the ancientness of this theme. But in its newly new experience it is not, or is no longer, the religious idea (or secular variant of the religious idea) that we attend to something that is (even notionally) separable from the life lived by a human being. Retrieving the great word "soul" from that religious and metaphysical context, Wittgenstein uses it here to specify the focus of an attitude towards *an altogether other "me"* – a relation of identity with the other who I am *not* – a relation to the singular, unique, irreplaceable, unsubstitutable, incomparable "*mineness*" of another life, the mineness of a life that is, in each other case, *not* mine.

The limitation of such a relation to another human being may not (and in fact need not as we shall see) be felt so sharply necessary on this construal: there are singularities in the lives of non-human animals too. But with respect to the humanitarian ideal, the important point is that this relation might be capable of something always in view in the literature on Wittgenstein's example: its universal generalisability beyond personal friendship. Derrida will call it "a universalizable culture of singularities" (FK, p. 18).

In view with this suggestion is a universalism of the singularly different not of the common. Like classical liberalism, and quite unlike Leninism, it too calls for a discourse on "tolerance" – but not, this time, tolerance by the majority towards some social (for example, religious) minority but a detheologised tolerance drawn from the point of view that "respects the distance of infinite alterity as singularity" (FK, p. 22), and hence (now with respect to *every* other) one that depends on "a capacity to see how things look to *them*" (IBWD, p. 138). In its universalisation, it recognises that "*everyone* is owed the effort of understanding" that belongs to "*eine Einstellung zur Seele*" (IBWD, p. 104), even if that is an infinite (and hence strictly impossible) demand.

When Williams considers this infinite demand, he is clear that it cannot entail making it so that everyone will, even ideally, be equally afforded the effort, or even that it should be "in the case of everyone the same" (IBWD, p. 104). And this incalculability (*who* to give *what* effort to, and *how much*?) is, one might say, the beginning of politics and law as a way of organising a response to the impossibility of doing justice to the infinitely demanding effort that is nevertheless owed to every other. Whether this newly "tolerant" politics is elaborated in national spaces, with their linguistic and religious traditions, or international spaces – which must also respect the singularity of these national-cultural differences by remaining "thinner" – this infinite demand can nevertheless follow it there, and can be appealed to in criticism too. This is the aporetic character of this new politics of friendship: a universalisable politics not founded on but not simply divorced from the fact of step-by-step involvements. Call it embedded cosmopolitanism.

As Williams notes, we should not move too fast from "the mere idea of regarding people" in this friend-like way to any determinate politics, and stresses that on its own it "has nothing especially to do with political equality" either (IBWD, p. 104). Nevertheless, "hazy" and "general" though it is (IBWD, p. 105), unsatisfactorily expressed in Kant's "noumenal" self beyond the world of appearances or older ideas of an immortal soul though it is, the idea of an injunction to attend to others in ways that "should be abstracted from certain conspicuous structures" of their lives (not only their titles, but also their national, religious or linguistic identities), does, if one's own politics is not to be wholly contemptuous about the fate of every other, provide "some of the grounds of the ideal of political equality" (IBWD, p. 105). By articulating an approach to our common humanity which is unburdened by the requirement to find it in anything common or universal as a way to be – without assigning *identity in sameness* – this idea points towards a democratic cosmo-politics of friendship conceived in terms of a "universalizable culture of singularities" rather than of the "universal community of the common".

However it has been heard hitherto, I believe we are beginning to hear and recall in the founding thought of political liberalism, "equality of liberty", the political expression of the relation to the other that is visible most perspicuously in the relation to a friend; demanding a politics whose point consists in recognition that "everyone is owed the effort of understanding" – even if that is not in the case of everyone the same.

Such a democratic politics of friendship thus still makes a universal and cosmopolitan claim, just as it had in Kant. And like Kantian state-differentiated cosmopolitics, it wants to take account of the step-by-step fact of involvements too. It is thus not simply a reformulation of the humanitarian ideal. No doubt there are issues to be thought through here that Kant's cosmopolitics takes for granted, perhaps especially its unthematised restriction to "citizens" as such, which is still a way of apprehending the other under a title that not everyone has, and thus raises the question who counts, and the not-unproblematic history of that issue. On the other hand, as Derrida has noted, the "citizen" title *also* belongs to a way of apprehending "the universality of the singular" – *as* a countable singularity – without which all politics would be "doomed to the incalculable" (PF, 104), i.e. simply doomed. Moreover, one might add, anything less formal and *more* friend-like in its focus on the singularity of the other would risk a limitless extension of the political to the whole of life – totalitarianism – which is certainly *less* friend-like to the friend. Whether we are concerned with national contexts (ranging over citizens of a nation) or international contexts (ranging over nations and their citizens), democracy, as a political response to the imperative to take account of the singularity of every other – where each one counts one irrespective of all identities – thus opens a "wound" that cannot be sutured: in order to respect singularity, we *must* also count each as the same. That is its threat – and its life, its chance.

VII

The grand narratives of the nineteenth century will have typically been articulated in terms of "progress" for a people in a land. However, for the nation-states of Europe, this will never have been a merely national affair. Every European nation will, in its own way, each conceive itself, as Prime Minister Margaret Thatcher put it for Britain, as much an "heir to the legacy of European culture as any other [European] nation" (Bruges Speech). Bernard Williams speaks of "*les grands récits* that have been enacted in the past century" (IBWD, p. 47), and these were enacted in national contexts. But we should remember that Lyotard's original list ranged further than that in time, covering the whole modern period, and included everything, especially, that goes by the title "philosophy of history" (PMC, p. xxiii). The discourses of every European nation's modernity in the last one hundred years have always also been caught up in older not-simply-national figures of Europe and its "exemplary" modernity.

Recalling Europe's old modern Europe-of-the-Atlantic sense of itself (the sense, as Derrida, describes it, of Europe as "the advanced point…the point of departure for discovery, invention, and colonization" (OH, p. 19)), Thatcher, happily (unhappily) claimed, "without apology" Europe to have "civilised much of the world" (Bruges Speech). However, she was also well aware that prosperity in a European nation-state today could no longer be a localised achievement, well aware that, in Europe, and for Europe today, national politics and a national economy was no longer sufficient to "ensur[ing] the future prosperity and security of its people in a world in which there are many other powerful nations and groups of nations" (Bruges Speech). No grand-narrative of an exclusively localised kind could be remotely convincing in this new globalised condition. And this is Williams's point too: this developing incredulity toward the old grand-narratives takes place in the context of both the growing interdependence of nations in a global *political* system with some very powerful nation-states, and the development of a global *economic* system which gives rise to "agencies, such as multi-national corporations, [which] have greater international power, in certain fields, than *any* nation-state has" (IBWD, p. 47. See virtually the same point made by Lyotard at PMC, p. 5). In view, then is, on the one hand, the world-wide-isation of the European political world and of tele-techno-scientific international capitalist decision-making power (marking the end of an epoch in which either politics or economics could be localised), and, on the other hand, the simultaneous exhaustion of Europe's old modern *grands récits* through which the becoming-hegemonic of that very world made sense to Europeans. Exhaustion and world-wide-isation of the European world (wearing and growing) – these belong together, one inside the other.

"The seeds" of this development were, Lyotard stresses "*inherent* in the grand narratives of the nineteenth century", especially with their emphasis on freedom for all as a political concept (PMC, p. 38, my emphasis). Europe's modernity gave rise to a resistance movement that has freed itself from faith in the old Greco-Biblical *archeo-teleo-eschatological* understanding of world history and Europe's centrality. The wearing and growing world of that faith is no longer one that we can entirely inhabit – but we do not have a new one. We drift towards life lived out in little more than an optimally functioning economic system. None of this is separable from what we have explored under the title of the death of God. Indeed, this *is* Europe wearing and growing in the first shadows of the belief in the Christian God becoming unbelievable. Here is Heidegger, reflecting on "the word of Nietzsche" with which we began this volume:

> Into the position of the vanished authority of God and of the teaching office of the Church, steps the authority of conscience, obtrudes the authority of reason. Against these the social instinct rises up. The flight from the world into the suprasensory is replaced by historical progress. The otherworldly goal of everlasting bliss is transformed into the earthly happiness of the greatest number. [New ideals are set up: specifically doctrines regarding world happiness through socialism.] The careful maintenance of the cult of religion is relaxed through enthusiasm for the creating of a culture or spreading of civilization. Creativity, previously the unique property of the biblical god, becomes the distinctive mark of human activity. Human creativity finally passes over into business enterprise. (NW, p. 64)

Lyotard seems to me very close to this understanding in his bleak picture of the occupation of the space left vacant by the inner dissolution of the classic metanarratives of the emancipation or progress of Man by a life-system whose only *raison d'être* and only criterion of progress is economic-technocratic: the continuing effort at optimising its own efficiency, performativity and functioning (PMC, p. xxiv). In this new world order, the old modern political set-up in Europe (democratically elected representatives and party-based governments) becomes increasingly life-lacking too, with all sorts of denuding processes (for example, overall declines in party membership) and reversals (for example, the Party of Order can readily become a Party of Modernisation, and the Party of Progress can become a Party of Nostalgia), and we see, again and again, last-gasp-efforts to mobilise mass popular support behind emancipatory discourses, national or international, deploying messiano-eschatological road-signs from another age. It is not all over for national or international politics. But it all seems in our time in a newly fragile condition.

People often talk today of the hegemony of "neoliberalism" in an age of globalisation – and tend to mark its practical emergence with the regimes of Reagan and Thatcher in the 1980s. But what people are seeing emerge at that time was already well underway, and belongs inside a much longer sequence of Europe's history: the epoch of the death of God, and the end of the old discourse of the *archeo-teleo-eschatological* history of Man.

In the holding sway of a world made with Men in mind, with God and God's plan for Man as the horizon-fixing ground of our spiritual centrality to world history, the lives of modern Europeans made sense, and the plurality of events in the empirical flow were all tied together. And now they are all being untied together in a world that is no longer a world:

> What has happened, at bottom? The feeling of valuelessness was reached with the realization that the overall character of existence may not be interpreted by means of the concept of "aim", the concept of "unity", or the concept of "truth". Existence has no goal or end; any comprehensive unity in the plurality of events is lacking. (WTP, p. 13)

Again, here is Nietzsche thinking about what would give existence a meaningful character:

> This meaning could have been: the "fulfillment" of some highest ethical canon in all events, the moral world order; or the growth of love and harmony in the intercourse of beings; or the gradual approximation of a state of universal happiness; or even the development toward a state of universal annihilation – any goal at least constitutes some meaning. What all these notions have in common is that something is to be achieved through the process – and now one realizes that becoming aims at nothing and achieves nothing. (WTP, p. 12)

Hence *der tolle Mensch* concluded: "Are we not straying, as though through an infinite nothing?… God is dead. God remains dead. And we have killed him".

We have been exploring a thesis in sociology that some "since Marx" have found compelling: the post-national thesis. What we are preserving from this is a post-party thesis. However, there is a second and perhaps equally important thesis one might assign to sociology in its "since Marx" formation, one which might be thought of as its way of reading the death of God event. In its discipline-defining texts, sociology has had its say on this too. From the weakening of ecclesiastical power in the Middle Ages through to the falling away of religious theism in Europe since the Enlightenment, scientists of society after Marx (Weber and Durkheim most famously) had predicted that European culture will become only more and more "secular", and that, perhaps along with national differences, religious ideas will probably wither away altogether too. Today this is called the secularisation thesis. It is not in good shape either. As we make our way towards the final chapter and its closing questions, it will prove helpful to see why.

THE FATE OF RELIGION

VIII

The first step in the historical story is perhaps uncontroversial: the breakup of Christendom in the Reformation led to a massive diminution in the power of the Roman Catholic Church. The Thirty Years War, which began as a war between Catholic and Protestant powers, culminated in the Treaty of Westphalia in 1648, which introduced a confessional nation-state system governed by the principle of the Peace of Augsberg of 1555: *Cuius regio, eius religio* ("Whose realm, his religion", meaning that the religion of the ruler was to dictate the religion of the nation). But Europe's emerging nation-states, once they had broken with older forms of centralised ecclesiastical authority, also began to produce a new relation of the political to the religious during the course of what is sometimes called the "long 18th century" (1685–1815), the time of the Enlightenment. Here is Derrida:

> The experience Europe inaugurated at the time of the Enlightenment (*Lumières, Aufklärung, Illuminisimo*) in the relationship between the political and the theological, or, rather, the religious, though still uneven, unfulfilled, relative, and complex, will have left in European political space absolutely original marks with regard to religious doctrine… Such marks can be found neither in the Arab world, nor in the Muslim world, nor in the Far East, nor even, and here's the most sensitive point, in American democracy, in what in fact governs not the principles but the predominant reality of American political culture. (PTT, p. 116–7)

How should we understand this singularly European relationship between the political and the religious that has so marked its modern condition? The secularisation thesis gave us a compelling answer to this. One might call it the modern interpretation of Europe's modernity, and for some time now it has been matter of course for many Europeans. It is a story about the decline of religious theism, and the rise of an increasingly secular public sphere and an increasingly atheist population. The public sphere is becoming increasingly secular because we are becoming, by dint of scientific advances in our understanding of nature and ourselves as natural creatures, increasingly non-religious. With the proper understanding, we see believers as reasoning wrongly, as under a delusion or illusion or confusion about the world and the significance of our lives. There has been, that is to say, a massive weakening not only of supernatural explanations in natural history, but also of providential conceptions in human history. On this view, religion is likely – some rear-guard actions notwithstanding – to wither away, and our lives (and the way we understand our lives) will become increasingly secular and non-religious.

In the following passage, the British philosopher Michael Rosen outlines the kind of philosophical (hi)story of European history that informs the secularisation thesis:

> Once upon a time, so the story goes, human beings (or European ones at least) lived in a world in which morality was seen to be embedded in nature. Nature was an expression of the will of a benevolent creator-God, who had revealed his purposes in it, and morality and science went hand in hand. Each was out there to be discovered objectively. Yet the rise of modern science put an end to that. Various rear-guard actions notwithstanding, the mechanistic, physicalistic, nomological – in short, disenchanted – view of the universe has triumphed and the natural world has become one of (as William James put it) "aimless weather". (Rosen, p. 152)

Rosen's story relates the modern narrative of our modernity as the story of a radical break from forms of society dominated by magic, myth and supernatural superstition, of a society *en route* to a rational, scientific, and perhaps ultimately Godless future. In our time it is thus commonplace to suppose that the understanding of the world and the significance of our lives that has been spreading out across the globe for at least the last three hundred years has become increasingly "disenchanted", religious ideas will probably wither away and we will all become modern rational and scientific atheists.

The problems for the secularisation thesis all begin with another unavoidable fact about our involvements: despite the world-wide spreading-out of the European world, religion, religiosity, "enchanted belief" simply has not gone away, and has even revived. If someone said today that they wanted to think or study "religion" – who would be surprised at that? No one. But for many, it is a real surprise that, today, religion could be the thing that comes to mind. Writing about this situation, Derrida noted that it is more astonishing for some than for others, and is especially so for those who thought it was all over for religion. Those who, he says, "believed naively that an alternative opposed religion", and that what opposed it was nearly everything characteristically modern: "reason, Enlightenment, science, criticism (Marxist criticism, Nietzschean genealogy, Freudian psychoanalysis)" (FK, p. 5). We have not only come to believe that one was opposed to the other, but that one side of all this (the modern side) "could not but put an end to the other" (FK, p.5). In thrall to modern scientific conceptions of ourselves, we come to see religion as an enemy of truth and justice – an ideological yoke, illusion or delusion that stands in the way of true happiness in this world.

Derrida completely rejects the idea that the picture of modern atheism putting an end to archaic theism is sufficient to making any sense of religion's ongoing significance in our time, and especially to making sense of the fundamentalisms that he (like Fukuyama too) suggests, "are at work in all religions" today (FK, p. 5): "an entirely different schema" will be required. As we shall see, the schema that emerges in Derrida's work on this theme opposes the *secularisation* thesis, a picture of the ongoing world-wide-isation of a modern atheist world, with a *globalatinization* thesis, a picture of the ongoing world-wide-isation of the Christian world. Developing this new schema, Derrida focuses first on rethinking the singular relationship between politics and religion forged in Europe's Enlightenment. Let's follow this.

IX

Speaking to a group of European philosophers, and having marked the Christian roots of their "hermeneutic" method, he risked speaking in the first person plural: "We also share, it seems to me, something else – let us designate it cautiously – an unreserved taste, if not an unconditional preference, for what in politics, is called republican democracy as a universalizable model" (FK, p. 8).

This unreserved taste or preference is, he says, inseparable from a commitment to maintaining the tie between philosophy, and especially "the lights of the Enlightenment", to "the *res publica*", to properly public things, and hence a commitment to what he calls "the enlightened virtue of public space" as a thoroughly secular space (FK, p. 8). This concerns the uniquely European achievement we began with in the last section. It is an achievement which consists in "emancipating [public space] from all external power (non-lay, non-secular) for example from religious dogmatism, orthodoxy or authority" (FK, p. 8); an achievement which seems inseparable too from thinking religion without religion, without recourse to religious revelation and religious doctrine or dogma: thinking religion, as Kant would put it, "within the limits of reason alone".

This commitment to the secularity of public affairs, this commitment to Enlightenment virtues of secular morality and secular (non-confessional) understandings of religion, might suggest that the atheist's ambition to put an end to religion was already inside Europe's unfolding political form: internal to the development of republican democracy itself. With Derrida's assistance, I want to reject the premise that the development of political secularity belongs to the movement of the end of religion.

Derrida offers a powerful argument to do so. He argues for seeing how the taste or preference for republican democracy and its political secularity is essentially connected to the way morality and religion came to be conceived in the Enlightenment, most conspicuously in Kant's thought. There is, he argues, a thesis in Kant on the connection between what it means to conduct oneself morally as a human being and what it means to be faithfully religious that will make this European public space at once *both* increasingly secular *and* still Christian.

It is a thesis in Kant that Derrida will also regard as a crucial interpretive key to understanding the rise of radicalised fundamentalisms which he saw developing in the geopolitical relations between, especially, Christianity and the two other great monotheisms, Judaism and Islam. The Kantian thesis could not be more simple, but Derrida asks us to "measure without flinching" its implications (FK, p. 10). If we follow Kant we will have to accept that "Christian revelation teaches us something essential about the very idea of morality": namely, that "in order to conduct oneself in a moral manner, one must act as though God did not exist or no longer concerned himself with our salvation" (FK, p. 11). The relevant Kantian point here is the claim that decisions on right conduct have to be made exclusively with the resources of our (inherent) rationality, without claiming to know that we are doing God's will: it is thus opposed to what Kant calls "dogmatic faith" insofar as the latter claims to know what God requires of us.

The "reflective faith" of Christianity makes the faithful Christian someone who, as Derrida puts it, "no longer turns towards God at the moment of acting in good faith" (FK, p. 11). Derrida asks regarding Kant's thesis "is it not also, at the core of its content, Nietzsche's thesis?" (FK, p. 11). The core content here is the idea that Christians must suffer the absence or death of God when they are called to deliberate and decide over questions of right conduct. Derrida does not understate it: this thesis tells us "something about the history of the world – nothing less":

> Is this not another way of saying that Christianity can only answer to its moral calling and morality, to its Christian calling, if it endures in this world, in phenomenal history, the death of God, well beyond the figures of the Passion? That Christianity is the death of God thus announced and recalled by Kant to the modernity of the Enlightenment? Judaism and Islam would thus be perhaps the last two monotheisms to revolt against everything that, in the Christianising of our world, signifies the death of God, two non-pagan monotheisms that do not accept death any more than multiplicity in God (the Passion, the Trinity etc) two monotheism still alien enough at the heart of Graeco-Christian, Pagano-Christian Europe that signifies the death of God, by recalling at all costs that "monotheism" signifies no less faith in the One, and in the living One, than belief in a single God. (FK, p. 12)

And what is the effect of this logic of the monotheisms? With the effective Christianising of the world – secular political and economic globalisation as essentially a "*globalatinization*" – we see, Derrida suggests, nothing less than "an infinite spiral of outbidding, a maddening instability" in the dimension of revolt and mutual strangeness between these religions of the book (FK, p. 13). Each, in some part of itself, and often against itself (as we see, for example, in the rise of Islamism within Islam), striving to become more insistent, more fundamentalist, less tolerant, than the other. And they do so at the very time when the world-wide-isation of the European (Christian-secular) world is both hegemonic, ultra-powerful, and, Derrida thinks, "running out of breath", seriously and perhaps catastrophically exhausted (FK, p. 30).

It might be tempting to conceive this simultaneous exhaustion and globalisation of the European world as part of an overwhelming and spreading "spiritual" decay that modern secularisation brings about: seeing in the replacement of rich theological concepts and conceptions by merely secular ones the erosion of communitarian bonds, leaving a void at the heart of modern life, the emptiness of secular liberalism. That would be the pessimistic modern reading of modernity, still opposing political secularity and religion. But it entirely misses the thought that a purely secular morality – which is, I think, the sense of what is proper to public deliberations and decisions that makes most sense to us today – is still "a sort of Christian domesticity", it is "distinctively Christian" (FK, p. 22). If one sticks to the old idea that secular modernity and religion are opposed to each other, as if one has come to replace the other, "if one continues to oppose so naively Reason and Religion, Critique or Science and Religion, techno-scientific Modernity and Religion" (FK, p. 28), one will understand nothing of the history of the world and the revival of religion today, nothing of the wave or surge of Islamist fundamentalism in particular. We should not say that secularisation is a process that replaces old theological concepts and conceptions with modern secular ones. Rather, what we should wake up to is that the ongoing withdrawal of non-lay, non-secular Christian authority from the major political, economic, legal, and coercive powers of society follows a strictly Christian imperative, not a modern atheist one.

Political secularity belongs most clearly to the governance of modern European nations, where there is a constitutional separation of Church and State. Derrida talks about republican democracies, but it is not only self-declared republics that conform to the democratic and secular form of political organisation at issue here. Nevertheless, recourse to this old title of "the republican model" is helpful: it highlights that to affirm a preference for this form is to be willing to bind one's own thinking and acting to a vision of public affairs where deliberations and decisions regarding such *res publica* are emancipated from domination by religious powers and religious authority. However, this preference takes shape within and not against a Christian culture, within and not against a Greco-Biblical culture, a European culture. It is there that the space is opened up for the idea that deliberations and decisions on right conduct must be freed "from all religious dogmatism, orthodoxy or authority, from the rule of any religious *doxa* or religious belief". To affirm an unreserved taste for a more or less republican democracy as a universalisable form of political governance is thus to stake oneself to the cause of a political community that can deliberate and decide with regard to properly public affairs without first having to seek permission or approval or direction from any religious authority first. This is Kant's thesis. And it would be a profoundly Christian inheritance.

This point is not lost to all Christian thinkers. As Rowan Williams, a former Archbishop of Canterbury, argues for example, that we need to distinguish between "programmatic secularism" and "procedural secularism" (RL). He criticises the first as envisaging an "empty public square", where deliberations are conducted and decisions made with the aim merely to optimise the efficient administration of things – the pessimist's nightmare, the atheist's dream – but the second he regards positively, as allowing "maximal private licence, and a crowded and argumentative public square which acknowledges the authority of a legal mediator or broker whose job it is to balance and manage real difference" (RL). This is a set-up he wants strongly to defend, insisting that such secularism "alone guarantees the kind of political freedom I am concerned to define and to secure" (RL). Rowan Williams was also keen quietly to stress that this secularism is "the outgrowth of a specific religious position" (RL). Right.

Christianity is not forced to submit to this development of democratic political freedom as an externally imposed demand. On the contrary, it calls for it itself, and hence calls itself to withdraw, called to endure the death of God in the world – daily, serially, eternally. However, in so doing it also frees up the very freedom which rejoices in not having to believe the old authorities at all (what Nietzsche called its "misarchism"). This is Greco-Biblical Europe taking itself – through its own processes of democratisation – into the first shadows of a condition in which the belief in the Christian God becomes unbelievable. And in that new space, modern atheism makes its way.

X

Looking out over the ramparts of contemporary Europe, Nietzsche asked himself in his today, which is not so very far from our today, "*Why atheism today?*" (BGE, p. 53). If one is looking for a defence of or recommendation for accepting atheism today in Nietzsche one will likely be thoroughly baffled by his answer:

> *Why atheism today?* – "the father" in God is thoroughly refuted; likewise "the judge", "the rewarder". Likewise his "free will": he does not hear – and if he heard he would still not know how to help. The worst thing is: he seems incapable of making himself understood: is he himself vague about what he means? – These are what, in the course of many conversations, asking and listening, I found to be the causes of the decline in European theism; it seems to me that the religious instinct is indeed in vigorous growth – but that it rejects the theistic answer with profound mistrust.

This is anything but a defence of taking an atheist position. It is more like a "*vox pop*" of Europeans on their views on the decline of religious theism. And what Nietzsche supposes himself to have heard here is the vigorous growth of what he called misarchism: hatred of authority (the father figure "thoroughly refuted", as if one could refute such a thing). Moreover, he did not see this as the end of our religious instinct for a community bound together by profound trust. But the profound trust in the Christian God was giving way to (an equally religious, equally binding) profound mistrust.

And yet even the terms of that profound mistrust are still Christian. To illustrate this I want to cite from a "Thought for the Day" on the *Today* programme on BBC Radio 4 in February 2012. The day's "Thought for the Day" was given by the Christian author Anne Atkins, and her theme was ways of knowing others that are made possible with words, through the use of language. Atkins began by talking about modern technologies of communication, which open channels to people well out of earshot. She spoke next about the idea of communication with non-humans (dogs, specifically), where there is some communication but where expression in language gets us only so far. Finally, she considered the question of communicating with God, and invited listeners to imagine a curious scenario in which a channel for communication could be opened in this case too:

> Now suppose for a moment God could communicate with us. We can't see Him, touch Him, or smell Him. But imagine how it would revolutionize the human condition if we could hear His voice; we would be able to know his will, understand his character, and follow his ideas. If he could speak to us, we would be able to know him, as a friend.

For the Christian, the human condition in the world is experienced as one in which, first of all, God is self-evidently *absent*, it is a condition in which we cannot know his will, and so cannot be sure of his ideas. We cannot know God even as we might know our dog. He is incapable of making himself understood. In short, everything that might be regarded as *causes* of the decline of European theism *belongs* precisely to the understanding of the human condition in the world that characterises a religiously construed life for Christians.

Of course, Anne Atkins did not leave it there. On the contrary, for her, the "theistic answer" remains alive and available. Immediately following her acknowledgement of everything that might be cited as a reason for the decline in European theism, she breaks into a different mode altogether: "'In the beginning was the word'. He came to earth, not just God as man, but his very thoughts expressed in language we can understand." The possibility of a relation to God is embraced here despite the Christian acknowledging that the idea of a revealed text takes us beyond anything that belongs to empirical knowledge. In other words, the most radical objection to faith, the objection of the modern atheist ("We can't see Him, touch Him, smell Him"), belongs to the Christian experience of faith. Our being alone, the non-presence of God in the experienced world and phenomenal history, is acknowledged here as, precisely, *undeniable*, and hence as something with which Christian believers must grapple in order to make their way – and make their way through seeking God, not to attain knowledge of God but the profound trust of faith. Modern atheists, by contrast, take the non-presence of God in the world ("We can't see Him, touch Him, or smell Him") as a reason to reject any theistic answers whatsoever. What Atkins's expression of faith suggests, however, is that modern atheists in Europe today are, fundamentally, a ground-floor moment of Christian experience itself.

Atheism is certainly a salient feature of contemporary Europe's cultural landscape. But is it a point of view which should, narratively speaking, dominate, as it does in the modern interpretation of our modernity? As should be clear, there is good reason to think that it should not, and that the dominant culture of this modern European culture has remained remarkably Christian. No more than political freedom and secular society, modern atheism is not a radical break with that Christian heritage. One way in which this is visible is in the persistence of a specifically Christian understanding of ourselves: namely, as *totally alone*, of existing in a world where God is absent. One can call this the culture of the death of God in the world. This Christian point of departure for religious faith has become the norm for contemporary experience without it.

The death of God: this is a Christian event. In this event a simple opposition between atheism and religion begins to seem compelling, the modern idea that religion is the archaic enemy to be eliminated can seem unavoidable.

As we saw in Chapter 2, modern atheists, the atheists of the marketplace, cannot make sense of the death of God event except in terms of an epistemological break from a culture dominated by an illusory ontological commitment, and they cannot understand their own relation to religious beliefs except in terms of a conflict over the shape of a well-formed, not-mad, human life. In the marketplace – that space of exchange where everything has its value, that place, call it Europe today – there are, so the modern atheist thinks, the views of the religious theist believer and, apparently, alongside them, diametrically opposite them, contradicting them, the views of the modern atheist disbeliever. So the modern atheist thinks: "There is no God, but this other person reasons wrongly, and he believes there is. I believe the opposite of him. I contradict him". It is to this characteristic conviction of the modern atheist that I will turn to next.

XI

Not everyone who is not religious endorses the kind of marketplace atheism represented in Nietzsche's Madman story. Ludwig Wittgenstein was not able to believe in God, but he knew that when it came to his relations with people who cleave to religious creeds he was not – at least not always and at every moment – in a marketplace of contradicting beliefs. For example, regarding his relation to someone who believes in the Last Judgment, and by this, he meant someone whose life was run through with this belief so that "whenever he does anything, this is before his mind", Wittgenstein (LC, p. 53) says this:

> If someone said: "Wittgenstein do you believe in this? I'd say "No." "Do you contradict this man?" I'd say: "No."... If he said "there is a German aeroplane overhead," and I said "Possibly. I'm not so sure," you'd say we were fairly near. [But with religious belief] it isn't a question of my being

> anywhere near him, but on an entirely different plane... If you ask me whether or not I believe in a Judgment Day in the sense in which religious people have belief in it, I wouldn't say "No. I don't believe there will be such a thing." It would seem to me utterly crazy to say this.

As a non-believer in God, Wittgenstein accepts that you can say of him that he "believes the opposite" of the religious believer, but it is, he insists, "entirely different from what we would ordinarily call believing the opposite". It is not about having the opposite thoughts, but of having different sorts of thoughts altogether and of typically *having no thoughts at all* concerning what is to the fore in the believer's life.

Wittgenstein does not give up on the idea that some people are convinced by "superstitions". At issue here are cases where (among other things) someone draws conclusions on the basis of *extremely weak* reasons or on the basis of *faulty* reasoning. It is in such cases where, opposing that evidence or correcting their reasoning, we really do contradict them. And Wittgenstein also insists that if a religious believer were to think that he holds his beliefs in the kind of "rational" manner characterising our scientific beliefs then we should certainly say at this point: "here is a man who is cheating himself". But this is not the point of view that interests Wittgenstein. What we might call the "authentic" religious believer – a believer who is not "cheating himself" – is not someone who, as the modern atheist supposes, "reasons wrongly" on some point. The religious believer's beliefs (articles of faith) are of a very distinctive sort, quite different from typical scientific beliefs (bodies of knowledge). The modern atheist supposes that there are two beliefs in view here – the believer's and the non-believer's – that really do contradict each other, and oppose each other. Suppose you think there will not be an eclipse tomorrow and you find someone else saying the opposite. You might say: "there won't be an eclipse tomorrow, but another person says there will". In the latter case, the two market sellers do contradict each other. However, to think the same about a believer and someone who does not have religious beliefs – and this is the interpretation of the modern atheist – is, Wittgenstein thinks, crazy. He would never say such a thing, he would think it obscene to say such a thing. Wittgenstein said of himself that he is "not a religious man" (Rhees, p. 94), but it is quite wrong to confuse him with the modern atheist of the marketplace. Beyond the modern way of opposing atheism and theism, he was, I believe, bearing witness to the condition of a non-believer in God in a newly new way. And Wittgenstein was making propaganda for a new way of thinking about this condition, beyond the modern atheist's picture. I will call this an a-theist variation.

The feature of modern atheist disbelief that encourages the idea that it does straightforwardly contradict religious belief is that it construes the believer in God as "reasoning wrongly" about the world and our lives. The mark of an a-theist variation will be some kind of resistance to this way of construing religious points of view. We might think of this variation not in terms of an intermediate position in a spectrum between theism and atheism but in terms of two related spectrums: the first one concerning one's distance from the beliefs of the religious theist (nowhere near them), and the second concerning the degree of tolerance to making the reasonableness of every point of view, including every religious point of view, a question of science (not tolerant at all).

Whether they found themselves already in this condition or shifted into it later in life, the defining characteristic of what I am calling a-theists is that (unlike religious theists) their everyday understanding of the world and the significance of our lives is not articulated by religious beliefs. The non-believer is on an entirely different existential plane to the believer in this respect. However, (unlike modern atheists) they do not experience this as the achievement of a rationally superior position but merely (whether temporarily or permanently they do not know) as the facticity of their current condition. The idea that a large segment of the population (the largest segment in fact) does not find either religious theism or modern atheism compelling should not be so rapidly interpreted as evidence that they just do not care one way or the other, or that they are indifferent to questions about religion, but as evidence that, while nowhere near the believer, they also find the rationalism of the modern atheist "utterly crazy". In this scene it is the self-assured modern atheist, the one in thrall to reason and science, that looks like the real madman. Indeed, as efforts to cultivate a distinctive culture of a-theism grow, as we begin to see that faith and knowledge are not opposed to each other, that the believer and non-believer are not rivals opposite each other in a marketplace of beliefs, perhaps it is not religion but modern atheism that will...wither away: "nothing seems more uncertain, more difficult to sustain, nothing seems more imprudent than a self-assured discourse on the age of disenchantment, the era of secularization, the time of laicization" (FK, 65).

XII

If we want to jettison the two "since Marx" conceptions of a world that is withering, how then should we understand the development of European culture into our time? And what sense, if any, can we make of its future? If our old worn-out world is to carry a future at all, we need to attain a better conception of what we have already attained, and greater clarity about our contemporary unclarity. We need to make what we can with the resources granted our time to see what (if anything) heralds itself there as remaining to come for us. In the next chapter, the last, I will attempt to sketch such a conception – and if not a newly epic grand narrative, perhaps a new "epic gesture" for our time.

9

OUR CONCLUSIVE TRANSITORINESS

The earlier culture will become a heap of rubble and finally a heap of ashes, but spirits will hover over the ashes

– Ludwig Wittgenstein

I

The self-consciously modern European affirmation that "all are free" opened the space for Europeans to, as David Wiggins puts it, "rejoice in our freedom to disbelieve in that which provided the contingent foundation of the specificity and certainty" of their sense of the meaning of life and history – of history as the emancipation or progress of Man with Europe at the head. That "freedom to disbelieve" has seen the weakening of the very world that made it possible: the weakening of theocratic authority in European politics, the weakening of theodicy in European history, and the weakening of theology in European science. The modern European understanding of the world and of Europe's centrality to world history presupposed a conception of Man; of Man understood as the centre of creation in a universe made with Man in mind. But this conception could not survive the movement of its own unfolding, becoming increasingly unbelievable.

Freud offers a compelling image of this Man-decentring movement as it unfolded in European science, describing a sequence of events that he conceived as especially significant in the passage of the history of the world into our time. His little story, which he told more than once, and which we have already touched on in this book, relates together three extraordinary scientific achievements that inflict increasingly severe "blows" (*Kränkung*, insults, injuries) to what he un-self-consciously calls "*human* self-love". They are, in fact, decentring blows to the *European* self-understanding: blows to the conception of what "we, the Europeans" mean and understand by "Man". The blows are the "cosmological blow" from Copernicus (1843), which demands that we accept that our planetary home is not the centre of the universe, but just a planet among planets; the "biological blow" from Darwin (1859), which demands that we accept that we are not the centre of creation, but an animal among animals, with an animal descent; and finally the "psychological blow" from Freud himself (1900), which demands that we accept that we are not even "master in our own house", that conscious motives are just one motivation among others, and that our lives are, in fact, largely dominated by unconscious motives and drives. Freud's comparative history tracks a decentring sequence that takes place inside the unfolding world that was dominated by European humanity's sense of itself as existing within a world supposedly designed with Man in mind. These scientific developments, Man's greatest rational achievements, serve only to de-centre that self-centred understanding. Man – and especially European Man – is knocked off his pedestal.

It is with this sequence in view that a further and ultimately most dramatic "since Marx" legacy suggests itself. As we have seen, in a short passage of *Specters of Marx* in which he briefly returns to Freud's comparative history, Derrida wonders whether, today, we should acknowledge something like a fourth blow: the "Marxist blow". Coming, in fact, after Freud's blow, the Marxist blow amounts to the whole history of European politics, and ultimately planetary and global politics, in the twentieth century, delivering a *Kränkung* even more terrible than the other three because it gathers them and brings them all together with it in one massively magnified traumatic storm on the old European self-understanding:

> There is the temptation to add here an aporetic postscript to Freud's remark that linked in the same comparative history three of the traumas inflicted on human narcissism when it is thus decentred... Our aporia would here stem from the fact that there is no longer any name or teleology for determining the Marxist *coup* and its subject....The Marxist blow is as much the projected unity of a thought and of a labor movement, sometimes in a messianic or eschatological form, as it is the history of the totalitarian world (including Nazism and fascism, which are the inseparable adversaries of Stalinism). This is perhaps the deepest wound for mankind, in the body of its history and in the history of its concept, still more traumatizing than the "psychological" lesion (*Kränkung*) produced by the blow of psychoanalysis, the third and most serious in Freud's view. For we know that the blow struck enigmatically in the name of Marx also accumulates and gathers together the other three. It thus presupposes them today, even if such was not the case in the [nineteenth] century. It carries beyond them by carrying them out, just as it bears the name of Marx by exceeding it infinitely. The century of "Marxism" will have been that of the techno-scientific and effective decentring of the earth, of geopolitics, of the *anthropos* in its onto-theological identity or its genetic properties, of the *ego cogito* – and of the very concept of narcissism whose aporias are, let us say in order to go too quickly and save ourselves a lot of references, the explicit theme of deconstruction. (SM, pp. 97–8)

We can summarise Derrida's claim about the aporetic character of the Marxist blow like this. In the case of the three previous blows, there was a ready answer to the question of determining the subject of the blow: it is "Man" (what we mean and understand by our own being) that suffers the insult. And it does so as a result of a new notation in some domain which displaces an older and more "Man"-centred notation. Derrida calls the fourth blow aporetic in comparison. The aporia of the fourth blow would result from the fact that it is no longer clear who or what suffers it. Although it must be Man, it cannot simply be Man, since the long-cherished self-understanding of "Man" is itself what is at stake here. Moreover, it is so not because of the arrival of a new notation on our being that replaces or displaces it: the blow is not the upshot of a new extraordinary scientific achievement, even if it all began a century earlier with Marx's first-time-in-the-history-of-the-world history of the world in philosophical and scientific form. No, it is the upshot of an extraordinary political failure. As Levinas puts it, "the end of socialism in the horror of Stalinism, is the greatest spiritual crisis in modern Europe...The noble hope [of Marxism] consisted in healing everything, in installing, beyond the chance of individual charity, a regime without evil. And the regime of charity becomes Stalinism and [complicitous] Hitlerian horror" (RB, pp, 80–81).

The Marxist blow belongs to the twentieth century, the century of Marxism, which saw European politics becoming, in the wake of the spectre of communism, geopolitics, and the "noble hope" of Marxism to create a regime without evil giving rise to its opposite, three totalitarianisms (Stalinist, Nazi and Fascist). In this event, Derrida is suggesting, the force of the first three blows coalesce in one decisive decentring blow to the European understanding of "Man". The old notation of "Man" ceases to be a living or vital discourse on the meaning of our being; it loses its credibility as a discourse through which "we, the Europeans" can understand the world and the significance of our lives. The old modern philosophical (hi)story of the History of Man and his teleology, with Europe at the head, that sense of ourselves and of our history, is finally blown apart.

Freud tells his story in terms of advances in science. But the fourth blow belongs to that comparative history only in terms of its decentring power. Ultimately, it belongs to a history of Europe's modernity that shatters the most fundamental postulates of that modern condition and its promise. The European world that promised a "history of peace, freedom and well-being" and which did so "on the basis of a light that a universal knowledge [of Man] projected onto the world", that world is, in our time, in ruins: "a worn-out Europe!" (AT, p. 132, see also HH, p. 148). As a result, we can seem lost today in a way that exceeds any thought of "crisis", beyond any discourse of anticipated revival or replacement. For us today – "we, the Europeans" – "the future tolerates neither foresight nor providence" (FK, p. 46).

Is this "post-Historical condition" of an exhausted Europe literally hopeless? Because the fourth blow is not struck by an extraordinary scientific achievement that replaces the old notation with Man at the centre with a new notation, because it does not come about from the force of a new perspective releasing us from the grip of the old one in a new affirmation, we seem to be left floundering, even while the European world is increasingly spreading out on a world-wide scale. Without a new understanding of the meaning of our being, the European self-understanding is running out of self-esteem. Worn-out Europe. Exhausted Europe. Is it all over for the culture of the Bible and the Greeks?

II

One might think that those who have claimed to see an "end of history" in the "universal and homogenous state" are altogether spared such anxious concerns about our contemporary cultural condition, altogether undisturbed by "sighs about philosophical exhaustion" (MPP, p. 63). However, both Fukuyama and (even more so) his philosophical master Kojève have some considerable disquiet about life in our time too; life after the end is not obviously something to look forward to at all. As Allan Bloom puts it in relation to Kojève's sense of this – but one finds this gesture in Fukuyama too, indeed, in the very title of his book – one is left wondering "whether the citizen of the universal homogeneous state is not identical to Nietzsche's Last Man" (IRH, p. xii); the European "ideal" man, the one who has become the weakened herd-animal that is tired of life, takes no risks, and seeks only comfort, security and prosperity.

This kind of anxiety was, as Derrida notes, rapidly swept away by those (unlike Fukuyama himself) who tried to cleanse Kojève's thought (and indeed Fukuyama's) of such after-the-end-thoughts, and "wasted no time translating it and putting it on display as a weapon of philosophical propaganda or an object of prime-time media consumption" (SM, p. 74). In fact, Kojève's reading of the one kind of life proper to "the post-Historical period" following the attained end of what he called the "Hegelian-Marxist teleology", namely, "'the American way of life'", conceived it as nothing short of a "return to animality" (IRH, p. 161). Hardly the ideal end celebrated by those who preach "the vulgate of the capitalist paradise as end of history" (SM, p. 74). And here is the striking thing. Whether one is thinking of our time as the time of the end of history or as the time of the exhaustion of every philosophical (hi)story of Man and his teleology which might announce such an end, our condition seems to leave us with nowhere to go but more of the same, with technical optimisation of the economic system – economic "neoliberalism" as we call it today – as the only "progress" game in town, and "operational" citizens who look forward to no more than the new iPhone and voting…in the next series of the X-Factor. As Fukuyama notes, no one today can avoid the question "of whether the post-historical house which they have built for themselves…is one that they will be content to live in over the long term" (EH, pp. 283–4). The Last Men, on the other hand, are not only good avoiders of this question but want nothing more than the same from here to eternity. Fukuyama cites Nietzsche on the "ideal" life of these happy *isothymotic* herd-animals: "No shepherd and one herd! Everybody wants the same, everybody is the same: whoever feels different goes voluntarily into a madhouse" (EH, p. 305).

In *Specters of Marx*, Derrida reflects further on Kojève's own discussion of what's left for "post-Historical Man". While Derrida will want to subject Kojève's account to critical questioning (concerning, especially, its highly idiosyncratic reading of "the American way of life" as the fulfilment of a specifically Hegelian-Marxist teleology) and deconstructive questioning (concerning, especially, its onto-theological and *teleo-eschatological* presuppositions), he urges against reducing it to a celebration of unending economic neoliberalism. Moreover, while Kojève does not recant his extravagant claim to see "Man's return to animality as a present certainty" in America (IRH, p. 161), Derrida insists that one take account of the "Postscript" to the *Introduction to the Reading of Hegel* in which Kojève states that he had "radically changed his opinion" about the singular finality of the American end that he had presented in the original text (IRH, p. 161). In the "Postscript", Kojève has in view what he came to regard as an altogether different and, if one can say this, even more, final finality for Man, one attained already in Japanese culture during the last three hundred years; an end of history he conceived as still to come for the West and Russia as globalisation becomes "'Japanization'" (IRH, p. 162, "a process now well underway" (EH, p. 320), says Fukuyama only half playfully, and not at all in Kojève's sense). Derrida takes as seriously as he can the "nutty" projection of what Kojève describes as Japanese "snobbery" going worldwide (a projection "which is his genius but which is also his entire responsibility") (SM, p. 71). In particular, Derrida invites us to focus on the "last and also most enigmatic sentence" of Kojève's "Postscript" on the Japanese end of history – where we all become snobs – which, Derrida suggests, seems never to have been read (SM, pp. 72–3). That last sentence reads:

> This means that, while henceforth speaking in an *adequate* fashion of everything that is given to him, post-historical Man must [*doit*] continue to *detach* "form" from "content," doing so no longer in order actively to trans-form the latter, but so that he may *oppose himself* as a pure "form" to himself and to others taken as "content" of any sort. (IRH, p. 162, emphasis in original)

What Kojève gives us to think, Derrida argues, is precisely not that just one ("Americanized") kind of life will be an "eternal present" for Man in the post-Historical period but that a future for post-Historical Man remains to be thought once Man has attained to and come to terms with the finally final post-Historical condition of snobbish "Japanization". And it does so, Derrida suggests, in just the same way as he himself had proposed in "what we are nicknaming the messianic without messianism" (SM, p. 73). Derrida glosses Kojève's final sentence as follows:

> in the same place, on the same limit, where history is finished, there where a certain determined concept of history comes to an end, precisely there the historicity of history begins, there finally it has the chance of heralding itself – of promising itself. There where man, a certain determined concept of man, is finished, there the pure humanity of man, of the *other man* and of man as *other* begins or has finally the chance of heralding itself – of promising itself. In an apparently inhuman or else a-human fashion. (SM, p. 74)

Taking Kojève's thought rather rapidly in the direction of his own manner of speaking, Derrida's gloss does very little to reduce the enigma of the last sentence. However, that Derrida could take it in his own direction at all brings out the striking parallel between the two positions. For whether one is thinking (with Kojève) about life after the end of history, or (with Derrida) about the end of the road for the onto-theological conception of "Man" that would anticipate any such end (even a bizarrely orientalist projection of a "Japanized" one), one is effectively speaking of the same condition. And the point is that neither Kojève nor Derrida conceives this as the end of the old perfectionist interest in emancipation or progress for Man. Rather, both insist on seeing a new chance for that interest, now freed from any *teleo-eschatology* of human self-realisation that has a specific "content", in a newly trans-formed way to be for Man, as its anticipated end. For Kojève this is because the specifically "Japanized" "content" attained by Man-at-the-finally-final-end, its "*snobbery*" (IRH, p. 161), is something that *in itself* finds itself endlessly called to be something superior: the space is opened in that condition for endless perfectionist ambitions to attain an as yet unattained other possibility of being that I or we can be.

Derrida suggests that Fukuyama "is not interested in [Kojève's] enigmatic conclusion" (SM, p. 74). This is not entirely fair. Fukuyama devotes a whole chapter of *The End of History and the Last Man* (Chapter 29) to a question of his own that he takes the whole "Postscript" to help us think through: namely, whether "democracy's long-run health and stability can be seen to rest on the quality and number of outlets for *megalothymia* that are available to its citizens" (EH, p. 315). As this question perhaps suggests, Fukuyama's interest in the "Postscript" reflects and is limited by his conviction that liberal democracy gives the last word on political history, and on the history of democracy. So he reads Kojève's future futures in a way that sees ongoing "outlets" for perfectionist ambitions as (self-limited) by liberal democratic societies to exclusively non-political arenas (EH, p. 320). Interestingly, however, in the course of that chapter, and in support of his view, Fukuyama also cites an article by John Adams Wettergreen which has, as its concluding concern, the very "Postscript"-ending sentence that Derrida supposes has never been read, and which Fukuyama seems at least to have not taken to heart. In that article, Wettergreen does read the final sentence, and does so, in fact, more or less as Derrida does, and, significantly, without Fukuyama's de-politicisation. Thus Wettergreen states that "Kojève's analysis… culminates in the suggestion that even at the end of history truly human life *may* prevail [this "may" corresponds to Derrida's "chance" and "promise" SG]" even though "no particular *social or political* arrangement necessarily corresponds to it [so it is a "messianism without messianism" SG]" (SFV, p. 126, emphasis mine). What matters here is not whether perfectionist ambitions promise that this or that specific social or political arrangement will prevail (which they may or may not, and if they did those very conditions would still – if a "truly human life" is to prevail – have to hold the future open to further such perfectionist ambitions in those domains); what matters is that a perfectionist promise of human self-development beyond all presently attained conditions survives even as Man remains "post-Historical". "Post-Historical" people "should/must [*doit*] continue" to, as Wettergreen puts it, "oppose themselves to themselves and to 'just anyone' else *for the sake of humanity*" (SFV, p. 128, emphasis mine).

On the other hand, the Kojève/Derrida confluence is short-lived. Derrida does not think that history was ever telic, and his reading of the in-our-time "exhaustion" of the sense that it is or was thus calls for "thinking another historicity" (SM, pp. 74–5). What Derrida is especially keen to avoid is a conception that sees human history in terms of the "successive linking of presents identical to themselves and contemporary with themselves" (SM, p. 70). History is not a matter of one such historical-present followed by another such historical-present *ad infinitum*. Rather, every "present" has to be thought as structurally "always already" haunted (freighted, inhabited) by both the ghosts of the past and by the apparitions of what has yet to appear "in the opening of the promise or expectation" (SM, p. 163). So "no time is contemporary with itself" (SM, p. 111). This irreducible spectrality of what goes on in (every) "our time" does not ruin every effort of studying events "in their historical context", but it does imply that such a context can never be rigorously circumscribed, delimited or saturated or even single (there are many histories running through our time, and at different speeds, some archaic, some hyper-modern), and it opposes every "historicism" which sees the future extruded from the past like toothpaste from a tube, one historical-present after another, each one forced out by the present that preceded it, linked in an intelligible line of "development". For Derrida, the future, at any time, appears on the scene in what remains in our present that heralds itself as still lying ahead of us. And then one can do what one can to make it so that what proclaims itself in our time as still to come for us *will have been* "prefaced" by what we do with the inheritance that we are; so that our lives will have been the first "apparition of the inapparent" (SM, p. 125).

In the first volume of this book, I said that the story of Europe that I am relating will be a ghost story. It really is. The ghosts do not arrive one day from outside to inhabit an un-haunted European world: "haunting would mark the very existence of Europe" (SM, p. 4).

V

We are not following Kojève's sense of an attained sense of a final end of history any more than we are Fukuyama's. Nevertheless, as I have suggested, what we are reading here as the exhaustion rather than the fulfilment of that sense leaves us (conceptually) in exactly the same enigmatic place with the same enigmatic future: "there where a certain determined concept of history comes to an end", and "there where man, a certain determined concept of man, is finished", the messianic and emancipatory interest in what remains to come for us and for any others is not over – but is now freed from every teleology that anticipates a determinate "content" as its finally perfected end.

Look at the sequence in this history of concepts of history as we have been examining it, this history of history which is above all a history of the process of democratisation. First, there are the "modern" conceptions of history that are fundamentally messianic eschatologies. As we have seen, Marxism belongs, at least in part, to that history. As Derrida puts it "Marxist ontology… carries with it and must carry with it, necessarily, despite so many modern or post-modern denials, a messianic eschatology" (SM, p. 59). Something is coming – a definite end is in view, projected and promised on the basis of an understanding of the whole history of the world: the universal union of the proletarians of all lands in a communist society to come. On the other hand, Derrida is right to stress the break in the history of universal history that Marx inaugurates. "Despite the fact that it necessarily participates in them, it cannot be simply classified among the ideologems or theologems whose critique or demystification it calls for" (SM, p. 59). In other words, while there is "this messianic eschatology common to both the religions it criticizes and to the Marxist critique" (SM, p. 59), there is also a decisive difference in Marx that distinguishes the Marxist conception of the history of the world from anything that had been witnessed in the history of the history of the world hitherto: it was entirely non-religious. Marxism is a messianism without religion. In our time, however, the situation has changed again. In what Derrida calls a radicalisation of Marx (SM, p. 86), "messianism without religion" is now increasingly conceived as a "messianism without messianism", a messianism without a final content or final perfection (SM, p. 59).

Perfectionism undergoes "democratization" in this condition, to draw again on Cavell's telling phrase (PDAT, p. 131): it is a perfectionism that "asks for each the right to seek a step toward an unattained possibility of the self" (PDAT, p. 131). But such a democratised condition is not a merely personal affair. Democracy is itself, in this way, democratised; its own promise itself conceived in terms of its open-ended and unpredictable perfectibility not the attainment of a final perfection. From now on, that "*other man*", that other who is the as yet unattained but attainable future for us, that other Man who would be "man as *other*" to both ourselves and any others today, is no longer thought from its final end (there is none), but from its opening in our own efforts to "seek a step" beyond our attained condition, whether individual, social or political.

So what gives itself to us today as that opening to the future? What for us, for "we, the Europeans", has the chance of heralding itself in the "there" that is the spectral virtuality of the "somewhere where we are" that is Europe today? The very "*archeo-teleological* program of all European discourse about Europe" that is exhausted in our time has made it so that what heralds itself for us is simply not up for grabs (OH, p. 27). Indeed, it imposes itself on us beyond the possibility of struggle or resistance, "in an apparently inhuman or else a-human fashion": it gives itself *ineluctably* – with the force of the "*doit*" – in a manner that appears quite unlike a merely human pro-posal. "There where a certain determined concept of history comes to an end", and "there where man, a certain determined concept of man, is finished", what interests us, "we, the Europeans", what we are not indifferent to, what we cannot duck, and what Derrida unlike Fukuyama ties internally to the European concept of democracy itself, is responsibility for the ongoing and interminable promise of human perfectibility itself, the promise of a fully human way to be – but now, and from now on, thought "*as* promise and not as onto-theological or *teleo-eschatological* program or design" (SM, p. 75). As the heirs of the exhausted world of Man and his teleology, the space is open once more in *our* heading for *other* headings to come, the headings of the promise to respond to "everything that is given" *for the sake of humanity.*

Nietzsche had already seen this chance ("the sea, *our* sea, lies open again"). Still concerned above all with the future of Man in his thinking of European Man, Nietzsche saw the chance of an escape from what is exhausted in Europe, and hence an escape that embraces the "conclusive transitoriness" that belongs to our now thoroughly decentered understanding of Man in the wake of the death of God. Indeed, he wants us cheerfully to welcome this new condition. From now on, there is no longer any future for conceiving Man as "the collaborator, let alone the centre, of becoming" (WTP, 12). As we saw in Chapter 5, Nietzsche's philosophical contribution to thinking the future of Man involves him turning away from a vision of philosophers as those who possess special knowledge of Man and his teleology: rather, for the "real philosophers" to come, "their 'knowing' is *creating*" (BGE, p. 123). It is, that is to say, a matter of taking "the most comprehensive responsibility" for creating – i.e. *being* – a new meaning of Man, an ambition that he frames, as we have seen, with the thought that "in Man, *creature* and *creator* are united" (BGE, p. 136).

Freed of the old modern conception of Man and his teleology, Berlin too invites us to consider ourselves not as formatted in our being by a teleological programme but as "unpredictably self-transforming". Neither Nietzsche nor Berlin deny our creatureliness, nor progress in scientific knowledge concerning ourselves as such. But neither do they circumscribe our being in a scientific construal of it. Thinking about what it is to be human should neither exclude (in an obscurantist anti-scientism) nor get overwhelmed (in a crude positivism or scientism) by positive scientific findings about human life. "Even the human genome is not Man", as Derrida nicely put it (HG, p. 209). Of course, Derrida too belongs to our little list of thinkers of Man beyond modernity, affirming (in Heidegger's wake in fact) that we are the being that has awakened to the question of its own being (HG, p. 123). He insists, in this regard, that while it is indeed "always better to know than not to know" whatever the sciences discover regarding human life, that very injunction or norm has "nothing to do with science itself" (HG, p. 213). We should not suppose that we should or in principle could look to science for the ground of such norms: here lies our creativeness.

On the other hand, if we are, today more than ever, liable reductively to over-estimate our creatureliness, we are equally liable to be misled by false pictures of our creativeness. To think, for example, that the kind of norm I have just mentioned is the upshot of "autonomous rational deliberation" is equally problematic. We like to think of our own decisions and choices as the conclusion or output of free and rational calculations. But even with all the knowledge in the world available to me (which anyway can never be everything) and all possible time given to deliberation (which anyway can never be forever), I am still left with, must still be left with, "an infinite leap before me" when a decision or choice is actually made (GPC, p. 372). Such choices, if indeed they are choices, cannot be reduced to anything predictable or programmable, "neither by science nor consciousness" (GPC, p. 372).

Outlining a conception which is, as John Gray has suggested, close to "post-modernism" (IB, p. 109), Berlin also affirms an idea of this kind of "radical choice" in the face of incommensurable (and hence non-calculable) alternatives that contrasts sharply with the old modern idea of autonomous rational control over one's life, or of self-fashioning that would be somehow free of ghosts, free of the historical "deposit of the choices made by others" or "the inherited choices... of others" (IB, p. 108). Berlin, who really valued the chance of leaving a measure of choice to the chooser, had no illusions about such autonomy, insisting that this kind of "choice-making" is "a power of agents whose identities are always... inheritances, deeply shaped by the language and form of life that is contingently theirs" (IB, p. 109):

> Many of the most momentous "choices" we make may turn out on examination – if [this] belief of Berlin's is at all well-founded – not to express "decisions" we have made, but to be summations or precipitates of...the forms of life to which we belong. (IB, p. 109)

The idea of self-fashioning through self-choice is an illusion, and "autonomous freedom" would be better regarded, perhaps somewhat paradoxically, as "*heteronomic* in its essence" (HG, p. 206). We give ourselves a picture of our autonomy that comfortingly masks us from the fact that our own choices most often follow predictable patterns of what Derrida calls, recalling Heidegger's thought of the everyday self as a "they-self" (BT, p. 167), "reproductive programming" rather than anything especially inventive or new (HG, p. 206). Nevertheless, to see choice-making, as Berlin does too, as necessarily faced with the non-calculable and the "undecidable" (IB, p. 106), means that a radical unpredictability invades our understanding of ourselves as self-transforming beings. And this opens us to a new anthropology too, one that Gray calls an "*anthropological pluralism*" (IB, p. 112): a conception of Man that is not one, and a history that is "never of one text" (IB, p. 109). Such a view is totally incompatible with any idea of a meta-narrative that would provide "the text of universal history" (IB, p. 109), or a sketch of a philosophical history of Man with a definite end. As Gray emphasises, "the idea of a universal human history" of that (*teleo-eschatological*) sort cannot survive this understanding of the human as a radically unpredictable production, with its propensity "to form for itself a plurality…to invent for itself a variety of forms of life" (IB, p. 110). Berlin may share Marx's view of man as self-transforming (IB, p. 127), but without his *teleo-eschatology* there is no end to this drama, no single actor in its cast, and it unfolds in its variety without "the authority of a meta-narrative" (IB, p. 109).

And yet, as we have seen, this does not mean it is all over for Europe and the old interest in the emancipation or progress of Man. And we do not have to wait for "Japanized" Man to come to affirm this: there where we are, *we are already called* to "continue to *detach* 'form' from 'content,'…so that [Man] may *oppose himself* as a pure 'form' to himself and to others taken as 'content' of any sort". Berlin's "pluralism as an ideal" is just such an opposing detachment, as is Derrida's and Nietzsche's "complete" democracy as democracy to come. All of these bearing witness to a call for a democratisation of perfectionism that is "called for by the democratic aspiration" itself (CHU, p. 1). All of these are also, therefore, "messianisms without messianism". That is, they project a way in which we may be that does not project a final way in which we may be: no end of politics, no end of democracy, no end of perfectionist ambitions – no end of a future for humanity. This position is radically opposed to a "sense…of a final or perfected state that each is to attain or pursue" (PDAT, p. 121). Instead, it affirms what Cavell calls its "democratization", and hence a politics that "asks for each the right to seek a step toward an unattained possibility of the self" (PDAT, p. 131). Securing such a right is not a one-time affair but inseparable from securing an ongoing openness to the future for the unpredictably self-transforming production of democracy itself, and its unattained possibilities, an ongoing openness now understood as internal to "*our* heading". So, again, where are we now? Where are we heading?

VI

When, in 1976, Wiggins discussed the twentieth century condition as more resistant than the eighteenth or nineteenth centuries knew how to be to mystical and metaphysical conceptions of Man and history, he had described our time as a time "after Darwin". And of the three blows that Freud describes, it is hard not to think of the Darwinian blow as especially significant. In 1861, Marx saw Darwin as striking a "death blow" to all teleology of nature (RC, p. 345). In 1906, Valéry was struck that it was not just natural history that Darwin upsets: "if Darwin was right, the whole of history is changed. I mean all thinking about history" (HP, p. 516). The upheaval over the idea of "*homo sapiens*" – the animal which, after all, if not simply "Man" is also the being that, in the becoming-European world, *called itself* (to be) "Man" – provoked by Darwin seems central to everything decentring in our world. Writing in 1974, Derrida affirmed the same thought:

> It was Darwin, not Freud, who had struck the greatest blow: a powerful and ample chain from Aristotle, at least, to our day...binds onto-theological metaphysics to humanism. The essential opposition of Man to animal – or rather, to animality, to a univocal, homogeneous, obscurantist concept of animality – always serves the same interest there... Of the three wounds to anthropic narcissism, the one Freud indicates with the name Darwin seems more intolerable than the one he has signed himself. It will have been resisted for a longer time. (Derrida, *Glas*, 27: column 1 insert)

In this text, Derrida highlights just one of the three blows that he would later see accumulating their force in the "Marxist *coup*". The blow to Man that "Freud indicates with the name Darwin" transforms our thinking about "the essential opposition of Man to animal", and is for that reason the most damaging of the three to everything that had been thought special about Man. No doubt resistance to the Darwinian blow is not over. However, as we do begin to come to terms with it (insofar as we have) we are perhaps also coming to see – as I will shortly show – that it is the blow-not-over that Derrida did not mention at all in 1974, the first blow, the Copernican blow, that more and more most marks our time as ours.

Philosophical history was always a concern with Man as Man, Man as such (if there is such a thing as Man as such, which we may now doubt). But this focus on Man has never concerned itself only with Man: an understanding of ("mere") animality always belongs (contrastively) with it too. And this is the significance of the Darwinian blow in our time. As the old European understanding of Man loses its grip on our thinking and feeling, so a new understanding of our mortal lives in relation to animals – those who we increasingly respond to as our fellows in mortality, our most other others, those for whom we are the other – is taking new shape too. I do not want to delay this book's ending with a study of the work that is going on today rethinking human and animal lives. However, something one might anticipate in view of that proliferating literature is that what is most human is no longer experienced, felt, attested or understood only in terms of our capacity for cosmopolitan sympathy with our "fellow men", but also in terms of a capacity to attest to a fellow-feeling beyond the human: the growing sense or awareness that a fellow-creature response to non-human animals should/must [*doit*] belong in the range of responses that best express "the pure humanity of man".

The call for what one might call "cosmopolitan friendship" beyond the human – something brought to light, for example, in Cora Diamond's astonishing work (see, for example, Diamond, 1991) – goes to the heart (and indeed from the heart) of the first steps in the movement of rethinking our relation to other animals. This movement seems extremely promising, even if there will likely be contributions that are less than welcome too. One might be particularly anxious, for example, about the emergence of a new purism, a purism about the sacredness of life as such (where "Thou shalt not kill" becomes a universal prohibition, applicable to all living things), a purism that Derrida (with considerable unease) predicted might mark the religion of the future (FK, p. 50). Nevertheless, we must surely be learning to overcome the "univocal, homogenous, obscurantist concept of animality" (GL, p. 27) that was based on the old European, onto-theological, humanist, logocentric – and we should add ethnocentric and androcentric – anthropology of Man, and learning too to see ourselves as the other of the other animal. Such developments, and the light they shed on the endlessly rich, complex, diverse and deeply interconnected lives of all living things, do not reduce the significance we attach to the idea of the human/animal difference but affirm it, and affirm too its historicity: at issue is a movement or mutation in which humans are called – ineluctably – to find their humanity (or find it "once again", see Kant, p. 225) in the extension of the fellow-creature response beyond the human. It would be the end of what Wiggins called the easy distinction between human welfare and the natural world.

If this easy distinction is felt, more and more, *un*easy, as I think it is, perhaps this is because it is not Freud or even Darwin whose blow is experienced most strongly in our time, but the blow struck by Copernicus. On our fragile, threatened and globalised planetary home, we more and more inhabit a Copernican Earth; we are more and more living in a time after Copernicus. Although he speaks of our time as a time after Darwin, Wiggins's text is alive to this other blow too: "we have more or less abandoned the idea that the importance of emancipation or progress (or a correct conception of spiritual advance) is that these are marks by which our minute speck in the universe can distinguish itself as the spiritual focus of the cosmos" (TIML, p. 91).

It is not so long ago that this Copernican understanding of our planetary-cosmological condition could be opposed with a completely non-Copernican counter-thesis about the Earth. As recently as the 1930s, for example, Husserl could still contrast the "*here*" of our lives as that might be disclosed by objective sciences, with an idea of the "*place*" or primordial ground of any such investigation. Calling that place "the Earth", Husserl insists, with solid reason, that the Earth is non-Copernican: "It is on the Earth, toward the Earth, starting from it, but still on it that motion occurs…It is in relation to the Earth that motion and rest first have sense…For us all, the Earth is the ground and not a body" (IOG, p. 84).

This extraordinary contrast between *the Earth* as the ground, the "place", the "thereabouts", for "every objective determination of space and spatial motion" (IOG, p. 85), and *the planet*, the global body, that is disclosed to objective thinking from that place, is completely vertiginous. On the other hand, the idea of such an Earth-ground does make sense. Look around you at some great or small vista, and you can see it: the surface of the Earth on which and in relation to which all movement takes its measure. The car drives across it, rivers run through it, the leaves fall onto it, the grass grows from it and blows in the wind, so does the plastic. But the ground itself neither moves nor stands still. It can shake, it can break open and explode lava from its depths, it can flood, and from it, one can chart the movement of the stars and watch the passing of the day into night, but the Earth itself is just there, as the ground of all motion and rest.

And yet planet Earth moves! The planet we are on is moving at thousands of miles per second – and so are you. What? If you were in a car, and the car suddenly stopped you would fly forward at the velocity of the car before it stopped. It is the same for the planet. But because we are always there (unless we go into space) it serves as the whereabouts of every measure of movement. It is like the famous standard metre in Paris that Wittgenstein discussed, which, when it was used, was the one thing about which one could not say it is either one metre long or not one metre long, since it was the point of reference for all metric measuring (PI, §50). So also what we call "the Earth" neither moves nor stands still, but is the fixed reference point for all motion and rest.

Now, my point about the Earth becoming increasingly Copernican is not about motion, or picturing the Earth as a ball in space, but the impossibility, *for us*, of holding fast to a distinction like Husserl's between our home-world of the Earth and the Copernican planet. The extensiveness of our politics as a geopolitics without limit – along with the global warming, air pollution, ocean pollution, ground contamination, water contamination, soil depletion, deforestation, habitat destruction, animal and plant extinction, in short, the relentless spoliation of nature – that our life on this planet is bringing about, is making it so that the inhabited *world* of our time (in so far as it is inhabitable) is *from the inside* global and planetary. Planet Earth is no longer simply an external and objective view of our lived-out whereabouts, but belongs to the home-ground of our existence and self-understanding.

The old modern European self-understanding – it is ending in our time. And into the space left vacant by that ending we have only the discourse of economic progress, prosperity, efficiency, performativity of the system, everything that Fukuyama summarises so blithely under the "the flowering of modern technological civilization as Europe industrialized, bringing in its train extraordinary material prosperity" (EH, p. 331), and what he calls "the blossoming" there of an economic neoliberalism: the "thoroughgoing *economization* of life" (EH, p. 190, emphasis in original). As we have seen, where economic efficiency and performativity rule as the only criteria for "modern progress", life in our time increasingly has the aspect of taking place on a planet which is no more than a mobile life-support system, and of lives that do nothing and go nowhere higher than sustaining a survival there. The Covid-19 crisis just as much as the climate emergency have demonstrated to everyone that sustaining a survival cannot be secured within a form of life that presumes such a life-support eco(n)-system can be insulated from the natural world. Indeed, immunitary insulating efforts only expose that system to catastrophic auto-immune vulnerability.

The external view – a view of our life as lived out in a planetary condition – is today increasingly part of the internal view. Nevertheless, *from the inside*, for participants, there is, along with (and in part because of) this external view brought inside, something new: our coming to regard ourselves as belonging to a newly un-bound Burkean immemorial community; a sense of cohabitation with others in which "doing the right thing for '*us*'" belongs more and more to forms of thinking that "us" which have no definite beginning – all the dead – and towards a future with no definite end – all of those yet to be born. On an increasingly Copernican Earth, there where the old European thought of the "pure humanity of man" had opened itself (typically violently but not always so) to the lives of every other, a newly decentred self-understanding is making its way, announcing a new cosmopolitan horizon – not only in relation to those humans who are not white, not European, and not men, but, in the name of humanity, beyond even the human.

VII

The guiding thread of this book is that a satisfactory engagement with Europe in our time must be alive not only to political and geopolitical developments but also to what in Europe's identity is philosophical and geophilosophical. It is not enough just to trace recent events or trends or crises in political or economic affairs in the world. We need to attend to the mutations of the world within which such events and changes take place, and hence need to attend to the great modern discourse of understanding the world and the significance of our lives – the Greco-Biblical, onto-theological conception of Man – which had framed the horizon of modern European lives.

We live in a time of mutation. We – who? We the inheritors of the understanding that belongs to the Greco-Biblical epoch we still (sort of) inhabit. This mutation belongs to a movement of decentring and deconstruction: the displacing, dismantling and un-bolting of a discourse in which Man holds a special position or distinction at the centre of nature and history, and European Man at the centre of the centre. In this mutation, Man and European Man is effectively decentred. We the inheritors of the understanding of the world and the significance of our lives that belongs to the epoch of *archeo-teleo-eschatological reason* – the epoch of logocentric, anthropocentric, androcentric and ethnocentric cosmopolitanism, the age of Europe's modernity and its centrality – we live in a time of epochal exhaustion in a whereabouts that is increasingly global and planetary. *There*, here, where a certain conception of ourselves as Man and his teleology is finished, *there*, here, where conviction in the old notation with Man at the centre and European Man as the centre of the centre has come to an end – the horizon is open once more for perfectionist developments for the unpredictably self-transforming beings that we are. And when the horizon is so open (it is no longer capable of domestication in the form of a "crisis") it is both a monstrous threat and a still promising chance.

"What are you going to do TODAY?", Valéry pointedly asked (HP, p. 228). Taking up the challenge sixty-four years later, Derrida wagered that "we *today*" want "a completely new 'today' of Europe" (OH, p. 12); a today in which one no longer finds it remotely adequate to respond to Europe today by indulging in either Eurocentric back-slapping and self-congratulation or anti-Eurocentric avowals of guilt and self-accusation (OH, p. 13). Beyond the programme of these "exhausted programmes", Derrida finds, nevertheless, that the traditional conceptuality of "all European discourse about Europe" (OH, p. 27) – that is to say, the discourse of Man and the end of Man that is the invariable theme of the discourse of Europe's modernity – "imposes" a responsibility "on us", an irrecusable responsibility beyond old ideas of autonomous choice on the matter, to "make ourselves the guardians of an idea of Europe" (OH, p. 29). Not, he emphasises, merely the guardians of a specific regional culture, not, as Louisa Passerini has suggested, a Europe that should from now on learn to live "within its own limits" and "to accept its own particularity", "for example" as "a cultural region" among others (MU, p. 107), "*but*", Derrida says,

> of a difference of Europe that consists precisely in not closing itself off in its own identity and in advancing itself in an exemplary way toward what it is not, toward the other heading or the heading of the other, indeed – and this is perhaps something else altogether – toward the other of the heading, which would be the beyond of this modern tradition". (OH, p. 29)

In this brief, compact and difficult passage Derrida draws together three themes that are central to the argument of *The Other Heading*, three themes that he wants to keep in view around the "grammar and syntax" of the expression that gives the book its title: "the other heading", "the heading of the other", and "the other of the heading" (OH, p. 17). It is the last (and most syntactically obscure) of these three that leads us, he suggests, to the "beyond" of Europe's modern self-understanding. Taking our bearings from Derrida's three themes, and the special significance that he gives to the last, I will (with)draw a final conclusion of this history of Europe's philosophical history.

VIII

Borrowing the idea of a heading from air and sea navigation, where a vessel "heads off" towards its destination (the idea then of "*our* heading"), Derrida wants to identify three distinctive variations on this theme to characterise what, in our inherited idea of Europe, he thinks announces itself today as still unexhausted. First, the (destinal) idea of "the *other* heading". This idea connects above all with the virtuous form of autoimmunity, democratic self-critique, that we have already explored: that "our heading" is "toward a destination that is its own but that it can also change course" (OH, p. 13). This is central to the specification of European cultural identity that Derrida wants to preserve from its own history: its openness to a change of course for itself – a break with itself – while precisely remaining faithful to itself in so doing. The second (destinal) idea is "the heading of the *other*", which is what the old modern European "specialism" – "specializing in the sense of the universal" (Valéry) – inevitably opens onto in its "missionary" spreading out: encountering other human ways to be, the headings of non-European cultures; encounters that have been historically more likely to have been marked by colonial violence, projection, and incomprehension rather than respectful interest and understanding. We did not have to wait (but also, sadly, we did have to wait) for the decolonisation independence movements of the twentieth century for Europeans to come to see that universal "reciprocal recognition" was a profoundly "just cause" (TC, pp. 161–2). Indeed, it was with an already clear sense of the fundamental injustice of European commercial colonisation and imperialism that Kant had raised the question of whether it is possible to organise a cosmopolitical response to a situation in which the big markers of human cultural identity and difference (religion and language) could be lived in a way that would at least minimise that historically typical unjust outcome. For Europe, advancing in an exemplary way towards the heading of the other remains as crucial as advancing in an exemplary way towards the other heading. The former concerns a relation of difference to the other, the latter a relation of difference to itself. But what of the third variation: Europe advancing itself in an exemplary way towards "the other of the heading". The what?

Whatever this third variation is getting at, it is also conceived as belonging in some way to Europe's existing self-understanding: it already runs deep in Europe's memory, and, like the other two variations, is "as old as the history of Europe" (OH, p. 17). But it also belongs, he suggests, to something that is also "newly new" for Europe (OH, p. 17): it belongs to a Europe that "seeks or promises itself *today*" (OH, p. 30), a new "exemplary way" forward for Europe in our time that would take it "beyond" its modern tradition (OH, p. 29).

So how should we understand the third variation, "the other of the heading"? There are two leading lines of interpretation in the secondary literature, two very different construals represented by the readings it has been given by Michael Naas and Rodolphe Gasché. Naas, on one side, focuses on the diversity of human cultures, and contrasts a point of view that would see each of them as samples or particular instances of (or subsumable under) a general concept "Man", and a point of view that eschews seeing each as a putative example of something general. The idea of "the other of the heading" is intended to provide, he suggests, the rubric for an acknowledgement of "the irreducible singularity of each example" (OH, p. xlvii). Each one is not a mere instance of a genus, an example of the same thing, rather each one is the only one, each one is one of a kind, and each can be gathered together with others only in that respect. Each one is an irreducibly singular example of a unique culture *of* Man; each one the "creation" *of* a "creature".

This emphasis on singularity goes to the heart of what we have called, following John Gray, anthropological pluralism. For Nass, speaking of the particulars of the plurality of cultures of Man in terms that describe each, for Europe, as "the other of the heading" is intended to foreground that it is *only* "the irreducible singularity or exemplarity [of each] that would allow for the 'unification' – though never the subsumption – of these particulars" (OH, lvi). Each culture is "the same" only as a singular culture *of* Man, each the unique creation *of* a creature. And there are only such cultures: we do not have an independently specifiable and universal genus "Man" with respect to which each would be a subsumable instance. For the being which has opened the question of its own being, that being "is not" apart from the creation of some singular and unique understanding of its own creaturely being. Each with its own heading, each attests to a unique conception of the being that we are: each, for Europe, is the other (one) of the heading. Aficionados would know that this stress on singularity is classic Derrida.

Rodolphe Gasché, on the other hand, construes the idea of "the other of the heading" as something internal to Europe's own characteristic way of identifying itself and its own heading by way of a binary and oppositional contrast with the other that it is not, internal to the binary logic at work in distinguishing its (own) cultural "self" from its (own) cultural "other". Gasché thus takes Derrida's third variation to have something in view that modern European thinking about its own identity necessarily presupposes but which is literally unthinkable in its own modern-tradition binary terms: a quasi-transcendental condition for thinking "the difference of identity and non-identity", that is not itself of the order that it makes possible (EIT, p. 126), something that is (if the binary terms in play are "our heading" over against "the heading of the other"), therefore, altogether the other of the [binary order of the] heading. For Gasché, then, the other of the heading refers to "the very thing from and thanks to which the binary opposition of [our] heading and the other heading, of self and other, of identity and non-identity, can distinguish their meaning" (EIT, p. 128).

These are dark conceptual waters, and one might be forgiven for thinking it too dark to see anything at all. But Derrida's own gloss on the idea of the other of the heading is not unhelpful in this regard, and, in fact, suggests that Naas and Gasché are, at bottom, both right, or at least both on to something essential. Derrida says that when we "recall ourselves" to "the other of the heading", we are recalling from within our own heritage the idea of "a relation of identity with the other that no longer obeys the form, the sign, or the logic of the heading, nor even of the anti-heading – of beheading, of decapitation" (OH, p. 15). At issue here is a point of view or focus which would orient us towards a relation of *identity to the other* that is, as Gasché might say, anterior to any binary distinction between our heading and their heading, a relation which cannot be thought within a system of such differentiation but nevertheless makes such a distinction possible (it depends on what it cannot conceptually incorporate). Aficionados would know that this stress on identities that do not exclude internal difference ("*différance*", "iterability") as conditions of (im)possibility for traditional binary oppositions is classic Derrida.

At issue for Gasché, then, is not the idea of a relation to another culture without any heading in view, as if there was a culture *of* Man that does not imply a heading *for* Man, as if a beheaded or decapitated culture was still a culture, but it is not a relation of difference from the other either. It concerns, Derrida says, "a relation of identity with the other", something that must therefore be thought both in some way prior to and yet not simply cut off from all thinking of cultural differences and the different headings they articulate: a relation of identity that is not simply opposed to difference, a relation which is presupposed by all binary self/other differentiation, and in terms of which it remains unthinkable.

It is at this point that we may see the virtue of Naas's equally classic reading. For what is brought into view with the emphasis on singularity is precisely the thought of *similarity in incomparability*. This may seem unduly obscure but, in fact, we have already come across this idea in the last chapter in relation to the idea of *an altogether other "me"*. Indeed, the focus Naas recommends on the idea of "the other [one] of the heading" is nothing other than the cultural counterpart of that kind of focus on a person: it concerns the relation to *an altogether other "we"*. Let's follow this up.

In the case we explored in the last chapter, the thought concerns the exemplary friend-like relation to "personal" singularity, the relation to the singularity of personal individuality: an interest in *the singularity of another person's life*. Derrida's book *The Other Heading* is concerned, of course, with cultural, not individual identities. But he is quick to note that the conception of singularity that he wants to discuss holds "whether this singularity be individual, social, national, state, federal, confederal, or not" (OH, p.72). In other words, this distinctive interest, "an attitude towards a soul" in the case of individuals, is not reserved only for the singularity that belongs to unique and irreplaceable individuals. In the context of cultural relations, where the altogether other at issue is an altogether other "we", here too, we find a case of singularity: *the singularity of another way to be human*, and each one not as a mere sample of (general) humanity, but each one a unique example of what it means to be human, each the creation *of* a creature. "No cultural identity presents itself as the opaque body of an untranslatable idiom, but always, on the contrary, as the irreplaceable *inscription* of the universal in the singular, the *unique testimony* to the human essence and to what is proper to man" (OH, p. 73).

Each and every cultural identity gives itself to be understood in relation to what it means to be human – and in each case the exemplarity of its own heading thus understood is unique. What is shared then, what makes them the same, the relation of identity with the other, is only this "unique testimony", each one the example of human exemplarity itself. Here there is a "unity of Man" that cannot be represented in terms of something common to all: each heading is a unique, irreplaceable and singular example of human exemplarity. "Anterior to the difference of identity and non-identity" (EIT, p. 126), the relation to the other [one] of the heading is not the other conceived without a heading or with a different heading than our own, but the other conceived in its "irreducible singularity" (OH, p. xlvii). The other of the [binary order of the] heading (Gasché's sense) *is*, that is to say, the other [one] of the heading (Naas's sense).

Europe's new "beyond modernity" exemplarity in this dimension would then lie in the possibility of recalling itself to what, in Europe's heritage, already opens it to the other of the [binary order of the] heading: the infinite demand to respect the other [one] of the heading; recalling itself here to a thought of all people's equality which affirms that every other "is owed the effort of understanding" (IBWD, p. 104). Every other cultural identity is an example of an exemplary heading, each one in their own right counting for us, in their singularity, as another culture of the heading of Man, another creation *of* a creature. And respecting the alterity of that singularity then calls on us to cultivate the capacity to *read* the "irreplaceable *inscription* of the universal in the singular" that is its own. It is not as an altogether foreign opacity – as if there were literally no "shared human behaviour" that provides the first point of entry into the alterity of what is not shared (PI, §206) – but another unique inscription and testimony of a self-understanding of what it means to be human, another conception of what it is to be the being we are, requiring of us "a capacity to see how things look to *them*" (IBWD, p. 138).

To be a new advancing guardian for a Europe which sees the cultivation of this capacity as part of *its* heading is never an exclusively or exhaustively theoretical affair, nor, once more, does it mean staring at our own convictions with ironic amazement, still less losing interest in them or disavowing them. On the contrary, it would be to affirm the exemplarity of *Europe's* heading to lie in its capacity to advance in this way towards the culture of the other in *its* exemplary singularity, one which is equally owed the effort of understanding.

Derrida's overall claim is that all three of his heading variations are in a certain way already centrally important to European cultural identity and its history in its singularity. That is to say, the "*inscription* of the universal in the singular" that belongs to "our heading" should be read in relation to all three variations: the idea of Europe is the idea of a culture in which each one of them, "the changing of the heading, the relation to the other heading or to the other of the heading", is to be understood as never excluded, "always possible" (OH, p. 17). In other words, "our heading", will have already been constitutively caught up in a responsibility for each of the three heading-variations Derrida identifies (OH, p. 17). Without forgetting their entanglements with Eurocentrism and colonialism, we have, with the first variation – the relation to the other heading – the most "Greek" moment: the abiding significance for us of the possibility of self-critique that never ends; and we have, with the second variation – the relation to the heading of the other – the most "Kantian" moment: the abiding significance for us of the cosmopolitan tradition. But it was the third variation – the relation to the other of the heading – which Derrida regarded as most important, most promising today, giving, he said, "the true title" of his reflections on Europe in his

Europe book. For with its invitation to focus on the incomparable singularity of every cultural identity as a culture *of* Man, it draws up a European memory of all people's equality, the most "Christian" moment, that Derrida thought had the chance of opening a future for Europe "beyond" the "*archeo-teleological* programme" of Europe's own "modern", "exemplarist" (and very Christian) discourse about Europe (OH, p.27). Here above all, we can anticipate the possibility of a politics of friendship – another cosmopolitics – that organises a response to, that takes responsibility for, the infinite (and hence impossible) demand that *everyone* is owed the effort of understanding, the most "Judaic" moment. An opening onto "the possibility of the impossible" (OH, p. 41); "the beyond of this modern tradition" which, in both its religious and its apparently and explicitly secular forms that tradition itself frees up (OH, p. 29).

"The beyond of this modern tradition". Over the course of two volumes, I have wanted to make a path through the history of Europe's philosophical history towards a compelling affirmation of this "beyond". Beyond Europe's modernity, its old *archeo-teleological* universal histories, its old humanitarian universalisms, its old Eurocentrism and anti-Eurocentrism, beyond its old anthropocentric, ethnocentric and androcentric models, a new narrative for the development of European culture becomes visible once more: not of Europe as the singular *avant garde* of a culture of universal humanity – but as the *avant garde* of a universalisable culture of singularities. In view, would be the development of the culture of a still-promising European ("Greek, Christian and beyond") memory that calls us to reconceive our own identity not from a thought of cultural self-sameness but in terms of a relation to otherness. It is in this, above all, that Derrida wants to bear witness to the possibility of a newly "epic gesture" for the development of European culture in our time, to go back to the theme that opened this volume: "to assign identity from alterity" (OH, p. 30); to see *our* heading as strictly inseparable from the endless possibility of the *other* heading, and an inexhaustible interest in the *other* of the heading.

We need to stand by our heading, even as we are prepared for the other heading which that might require. And this can mean "to take risks, to stick one's neck out" (OH, p. 49), it can mean "taking the lead in taking an initiative and sometimes even to go on the offensive" (OH, p. 49); and on the offensive, above all, for what gives *our* heading a future: for democracy, and, once more, for democracy not as something attained now or given-once-for-all (even in idea) but a conception of democracy as, in every here-and-now, remaining to come. It means to give strength and speed to the promise of democracy: the chance of guaranteeing for all men and women "as much independence as possible in their opinions, way of life and occupation" (HH, p. 344). It calls us to be as faithful as possible to the European memory of all people's equality, to give a future for an irrecusable and endlessly challenging imperative: "Let us be human.–" (CV, p. 36).

One should still recognise in this the idea of a universal right to the culture of what the Greeks called "philosophy". The Greek and Biblical *archē* of Europe articulated a distinctively European self-understanding which was fundamentally a conception of Man based on the logocentric anthropology of antiquity (the "*zōon logon echon*") and the theomorphic anthropology of Christianity (the *ens creatum* "made in God's image"). The "pure humanity of man", was understood as theomorphic rational animality, and the history of Man was the providential unfolding of Man's being towards the realisation of its proper end, with Europe at the head. I have not been trying to defend that Eurocentric conception nor provide a critique of it from an anti-Eurocentric point of view but, from the inside, have engaged in an interpretative undertaking – a "hermeneutic" movement in which one's own understanding folds back on itself and its history – in which the modern text of "European Man" reads its own unravelling. And I have done so not in order to forget or reject the heritage of "the Bible and the Greeks" and put it behind us, but to give it a future beyond its modern tradition. Addressing itself to, especially, "the *uniquely* European heritage of an idea of democracy" (OH, p. 78), and its opening onto a culture that would cleave to *our* heading in its constitutive responsibility for the other heading, the heading of the other, and the other of the heading, this old but still-promising, still-unexhausted Europe can still send itself on – onward, outward, into the dark. Sail on, sail on.

IX

Tomorrow, and tomorrow, and tomorrow. Can't we say anything about tomorrow? Well, you should say what you think best concerning the right thing to do today to improve all our tomorrows.

But let's think about what this means in terms of political and putatively democratic speech-making in our crowded and argumentative public squares. When Kant explored the dynamics of what he saw as the cosmopolitan heading of Man he stressed the importance of sympathy for human suffering beyond one's own national citizenry as central to everything. But he also highlighted a resistance to making the effort of understanding others who intrinsically merit respect closer to home, a resistance internal to what he called the "unsocial sociability" of everyone as their basic social condition; a condition of "*antagonism*" within society that he thought drives history (Kant, p. 44). The basic form of this antagonistic propensity is something I have touched on at various points in this book, particularly with regard to Kant's suspicions about so-called "rational cosmopolitans", and the "desire for...power" in general, where, whatever their avowed commitment to democracy, "everyone wants to be a ruler" (Kant, p. 44). Facing a social situation we regard as not being how it ought to be, we cannot but think that if only I (or "we") were in power things really would be different, and better – and that is why there are crowded and argumentative public squares in the first place. The characteristic social situation, then, is one of someone "wanting to direct everything in accordance with his own ideas" – and of others *not* agreeing with them (Kant, p. 44).

There is a fundamental logic to this social condition: one does not stand in the same relation to one's own attained understanding on any topic as one does to someone else's. Speaking one's mind on what should be done – political speech-making in the widest sense – is to speak from a position already understood in the sense that one says at any time what, by one's lights, most makes sense to you as the right thing to do. Of course, what makes most sense to any of us does not fall from a tree, nor is it unalterable. But that you can express what you think (perhaps after some struggle) without having to go through the kind of "effort of understanding" that is characteristic of listening to the views of others means that whatever you think (with all its "obscure causes and effects" (IBWD, p. 13)) cannot but stand for you as at least provisionally the thing to be thought about the thing to be done. And the social-political antagonism problem arises because, as an equally undeniable fact, other people just don't all think the same as you do. In the face of this condition, one might want to institute a despotism with no escape: my way (what we normally like to think of as "our way") or the highway. For the democrat, by contrast, what matters most is not that *I* at least get to have my say along the way, but that every other should (equally) have theirs. This is not, recall, a question of throwing your convictions away, or staring at them "with ironical amazement" (IBWD, p. 13). But it does imply accepting that the reason of the strongest is not for that reason the strongest reason: "one thing can be taken as an axiom, that *might does not imply right*, that power itself does not justify" (IBWD, p. 5) – and this is so whoever wields the biggest club, and whatever their avowed reasons. (Hence Kant affirms that what he calls "*democracy*, in the truest sense of the word", i.e. what is called "direct" as opposed to "representative" democracy, where the laws are made and executed by the same power, is necessarily a *despotism*" (Kant, p. 101).)

The strongest reason should, we want to say, belong to the strength of reason itself. But it is a total fantasy of the giving and taking of political reasons to suppose that there might be political speech-making that could be "rationally compelling" for all or even nearly all (a picture of speech that would speak to the "rational cosmopolitan" in each of us as it were, if only we were not labouring under delusions). Nevertheless, a certain universality can still be thought of as what political speech aims at: namely, as speech that wants to address itself not to everyone but to anonymity, to anyone.

This is the significance of what, in Chapter 3, I called the *timely* address. ("This is a timely address", Blair said of his 2005 speech to the European Parliament). It is an address that speaks to us today, speaking from and to the space of attained conditions and speaking towards an as yet unattained, but (putatively) attainable condition for us; and, if it is democratic, addressing listeners who are always simply and diffusely "the public at large" (IBWD, p. 57). There is no way, *a priori*, of judging whether we are being duped by the rhetoric of a "democratic" speaker who promises to "speak truth to power", or who promises "a better condition for all" (see Scatter 1, *passim*). Moreover, given the always historical and ultimately always somewhat "obscure causes" of anyone's believing, both speakers and listeners may have internalised as "good sense" a conception of attained conditions which serves only to reproduce the reason of the strongest (c.f. Williams's "*critical theory principle*", IBWD, p. 6; see also INP, chapter 4). Nevertheless, insofar as it intends to be a democratic address, it cannot present its own presently attained sense of what makes most sense as the thing to do here-and-now as the last word on anything. On the contrary, it should want to keep the space open for others, others with understandings other than its own, even as it presses its own presently preferred case. It is to want no end of political thinking.

Writing on Dostoevsky struggling to depict a form of human life with a "voice" capable of bringing social conflicts and tensions "to a point of stability or equilibrium", Rowan Williams notes that this is "a far less straightforward exercise than at first might appear" (DLFF, p. 112). The problem is not literary, psychological, ideological or even obviously political: rather it is simply due to the fact that "any form of human life is capable of drawing out diverse response" (DLFF, p. 112). "There is", he continues, "no manifest and unchallengeable last word in the process of human exchange" (DLFF, p. 113). We are in the swim of an "open-ended dialogue", and "formed by the exchange of words" we participate in (DLFF, p. 113). New words, new exchanges, can shape us to unpredictably new responses, new thoughts, and new forms of life can make their way. We should not want an unchallengeable last word or last sentence. As Rowan Williams memorably puts it, "silence" is "the Devil's aim" (DLFF, p. 113).

Affirming this open-endedness holds equally for our attained sense of what makes most sense to us as obviously political, and, indeed, what makes most sense to us as democratic. Hard to understand, difficult to decipher, accessible at first only to a few, texts which flex our attained sense of what makes sense belong to those arrivals who, in Chapter 3, I called *untimely*. Here we have texts made in our language that are inventively addressed not to "everyone", in the sense of a democratic ethic of "accessibility for all", but still to anyone; for anyone, but perhaps also to almost no one presently living: for readers who perhaps we as yet know none so that there may be such readers. These are the future-producers, the few, those who open the space of possibilities (the world of what most makes sense to us) beyond itself, *waxing the world* – the poets, writers, philosophers, and political leaders through whom, as Heidegger might say, the world most decisively worlds.

There are powerful reasons why timely politics remain indispensable. However, even the best political address – a discourse which is "apparently and explicitly pluralistic, democratic, and tolerant" – will, if it wants to be democratic, destroy the very thing it wants to save if it substitutes the democratic call to address anyone with the despotic claim to speak for everyone, "to speak in the name of intelligibility, good sense, common sense, or the democratic ethic", only to "discredit anything that complicates this model" (OH, p. 54), imposing "a grid of intelligibility" (OH, p. 39) that, despite its lovely democratic watchwords of tolerance, pluralism and diversity "suspects or represses" anything that "bends or even questions" it (OH, p. 55). A culture that celebrates inclusivity, daily intoning that every other deserves the effort of being understood, has no future at all beyond the levelling herd-animal life of the Last Man when it denounces as obscurantist everything that is not immediately "accessible to all". But all is not lost: the power of such grid-keeping is never unlimited. Where self-critique still survives, where "one part of its large body" does not remain "silent", *if even its littlest finger is lightly let loose*, "untimely developments that escape its grid of readability might one day take over without any resistance at all" (OH, pp. 103–4). This is the most radically messianic moment of the "messianism without messianism" that spurs democracy as democracy to come.

There are no guarantees here, and no programmes. We today remain in a condition of the exhaustion of "a globalization that is running out of breath, however irresistible and imperial it still may be" (FK, p. 30). And "we do not know and by definition cannot know" (FK, p. 30) whether that world disorder nevertheless "holds a future" (FK, p. 30), still less whether our time holds in store "untimely developments" that might "one day take over without any resistance at all". We do not and cannot know. Moreover, just as a timely address might dupe us or simply reproduce the reason of the strongest, claiming to be a writer of untimely texts certainly doesn't mean that you are one. (I am obviously not one. I am, perhaps, the kind of "fool" that is a "modern journeyman" or, at a pinch, a "postmodern journeyman" (MJ, p. x and p. 155).) Untimely writing is not a "method" or "practice" or "strategy", and it does not presuppose a rejection of one's own heritage, or a celebration of transgressive practices or identities either. What could be more familiar than all that? It is very hard (perhaps especially in universities today) to go further than the happy scattering of the specious glitter of unmeaning promises.

The age of dreaming that the future should or could be the realisation of some finally attained human perfection, the construction of a form of individual and social life which, here and now, we somehow manage to conceptualise in terms which are the absolutely correct ones, and which leaves nothing left to be thought or desired; a single form of human life that would express or realise best – once for all, and independently of any future experience – what we should understand by "the pure humanity of man", that age is over. But this is not a cause for regret at all. In the enlightenment granted our time by the onto-theological or *teleo-eschatological* philosophical heritage, we have begun to free ourselves from a conception of human history – precisely the one that conceives it in the form of an "onto-theological or *teleo-eschatological* program or design" – that simply "locks up" the historicity of history (SM, pp. 74–5). In this new but perplexing space, a new cause is announced: to welcome the friends of Europe's still-promising memory, and the chance for its future-producers – whether medically dead or not, ethnically white or not, geographically European or not, sexually male or not – who wax the world for a new enlightenment to come. Philosophical history, the heritage and inheritance of the *Idee zu einer allgemeinen Geschichte in weltbürgerlicher Absicht* – it is not over.

"And this one was Kant. And Kant begat Hegel, and Hegel begat Marx, and Marx begat..."

BIBLIOGRAPHY

Benedict Anderson, *Imagined Communities*, London: Verso (2006)

Deland Anderson, "The Death of God and Hegel's System of Philosophy", *Sophia* 35: 1 (1996)

Aristotle, *History of Animals*, Cambridge, Mass: Harvard University Press (1965)

Aristotle, *Politics*, London: Penguin (2000)

Samuel Beckett, "The Capital of the Ruins", in *The Complete Short Prose: 1929–1989*, New York: Grove Press (1995)

Geoffrey Bennington, "Demo", in *The Politics of Deconstruction*, ed. Martin McQuillan, London: Pluto Press (2007)

Geoffrey Bennington, *Scatter I*, New York: Fordham University Press (2016)

Jeremy Bentham, *An Introduction to the Principles of Morals and Legislation*, Mineola, New York: Dover Publications (2009)

Isaiah Berlin, "Two Concepts of Liberty", in *Four Essays on Liberty*, Oxford: OUP (1969)

Isaiah Berlin, "Message to the 21st Century", accepted speech on the occasion of receiving an honorary degree of Doctor of Laws at the University of Toronto. Unpaginated online text, archived at https://www.nybooks.com/articles/2014/10/23/message-21st-century/ (1994)

Robert Bernasconi, "Hegel at the Court of the Ashanti", in *Hegel After Derrida*, ed. Stuart Barnett, London: Routledge (1998)

Robert Bernasconi, "With What Must the Philosophy of World History Begin? On the Racial Basis of Hegel's Eurocentrism", *Nineteenth Century Contexts*, Vol. 22 (2000)

Robert Bernasconi, "The Philosophy of Race in the Nineteenth Century", in *The Routledge Companion to Nineteenth Century Philosophy*, ed. Dean Moyar, Abingdon: Routledge (2010)

Robert Blanch and Julian Wasserman, *From Pearl to Gawain*, Gainesville: University Press of Florida (1995)

Allan Bloom, "Editor's Introduction", Alexandre Kojève, *Introduction to the Reading of Hegel: Lectures on the "Phenomenology of Spirit"*, Ithaca: Cornell University Press (1980)

Allan Bloom, *The Closing of the American Mind*, London: Simon & Schuster (1988)

Pim den Boer, "Europe to 1914: The making of an idea", in *The History of the Idea of Europe*, eds. Kevin Wilson and Jan van der Dussen, London: Routledge (1995)

Andrew Buchwalter, *Dialectics, Politics, and the Contemporary Value of Hegel's Practical Philosophy*, Abingdon: Routledge (2015)

Judith Butler, "Uncritical Exuberance?", unpaginated online text, archived at https://angrywhitekid.blogs.com/weblog/2008/11/uncritical-exuberance-judith-butlers-take-on-obama.html

Stanley Cavell, *The Claim of Reason: Wittgenstein, Skepticism, Morality and Tragedy*, Oxford: Oxford University Press, 1979

Stanley Cavell, *Conditions Handsome and Unhandsome: The Constitution of Emersonian Perfectionism*, Chicago: Chicago University Press, 1990.

Stanley Cavell, Philosophy the Day After Tomorrow, Cambridge, Mass: Belknap Press of Harvard University Press (2005)

Gabriel Citron (ed.), "Wittgenstein's Philosophical Conversations with Rush Rhees (1939–50)", *Mind*, 124: 493 (January 2015)

I. Bernard Cohen, *Revolution in Science*, Cambridge, Mass: Harvard University Press (1987)

Mitchell Cohen, "Rooted Cosmopolitanism", *Dissent* 39 (Autumn 1992)

Rebecca Comay, "Hegel's Last Words", in *The Ends of History: Questioning the Stakes of Historical Reason*, eds. Amy Swiffen and Joshua Nichols, Abingdon: Routledge (2013)

Simon Critchley, "What's Left After Obama?" unpaginated online text, archived at http://16beavergroup.org/articles/2008/12/08/adbusters-simon-critchley-whats-left-after-obama/ (2008)

Simon Critchley, "The Problem with Levinas", unpaginated online interview with *Four by Three Magazine*, archived at http://www.fourbythreemagazine.com/issue/deception/simon-critchley-and-alexis-dianda-interview (2015)

Norman Davies, *Europe: A History*, London: Bodley Head (2014)

Jacques Derrida, *Of Grammatology*, Baltimore: Johns Hopkins University Press (1976)

Jacques Derrida, "Violence and Metaphysics", in *Writing and Difference*, London: Routledge (1978)

Jacques Derrida, *Glas*, Lincoln: University of Nebraska Press (1986)

Jacques Derrida, *The Ear of the Other*, ed. Christie McDonald, Lincoln: University of Nebraska Press (1988)

Jacques Derrida, *Of Spirit*, Chicago: Chicago University Press (1989)

Jacques Derrida, *Edmund Husserl's 'Origin of Geometry': An Introduction*, Lincoln: University of Nebraska Press (1989)

Jacques Derrida, *The Problem of Genesis in Husserl's Philosophy*, Chicago: Chicago University Press (1990)

Jacques Derrida, "The Ends of Man", in *Margins of Philosophy*, trans. Alan Bass, Birmingham: Harvester Wheatsheaf (1991)

Jacques Derrida, *The Other Heading: Reflections on Today's Europe*, Bloomington: Indiana University Press (1992)

Jacques Derrida, "Back from Moscow, in the USSR", *Daimon: Revista Internacional de Filosofía*, Issue 5, (1992)

Jacques Derrida, *Specters of Marx*, Abingdon: Routledge (1993)

Jacques Derrida, *Politics of Friendship*, London: Verso Books (1994)

Jacques Derrida, *Deconstruction in a Nutshell*, New York: Fordham University Press (1996)

Jacques Derrida, "Faith and Knowledge", in *Religion*, eds. Jacques Derrida and Gianni Vattimo, Stanford: Stanford University Press (1998)

Jacques Derrida, "Of the Humanities and the Philosophical Discipline: The Right to Philosophy from the Cosmopolitical Point of View (The Example of an International Institution)", *Studies in Practical Philosophy*, Volume 2, Issue 1, (2000). This text is also

available online, with free access, in *Surfaces* 4: 310 Folio 1: https://www.pum.umontreal.ca/revues/surfaces/vol4/derridaa.html
Jacques Derrida, *Of Hospitality: Anne Dufourmantelle Invites Jacques Derrida to Respond*, Stanford: Stanford University Press (2000)
Jacques Derrida, *On Cosmopolitanism and Forgiveness*, Abingdon: Routledge (2001)
Jacques Derrida, *Acts of Religion*, ed. Gil Anidjar, Abingdon: Routledge (2002)
Jacques Derrida, "The University Without Condition", in *Without Alibi*, ed. Peggy Kamuf, Stanford: Stanford University Press (2002)
Jacques Derrida, "What I would have said…", in *Negotiations: Interventions and Interviews*, 1971–2001, Stanford: Stanford University Press (2002)
Jacques Derrida, "Economies of the Crisis", in *Negotiations: Interventions and Interviews*, 1971–2001, Stanford: Stanford University Press (2002)
Jacques Derrida, "Globalization, Peace, and Cosmopolitanism", in *Negotiations: Interventions and Interviews*, 1971–2001, Stanford: Stanford University Press (2002)
Jacques Derrida, "The Aforementioned So-Called Human Genome", in *Negotiations: Interventions and Interviews*, 1971–2001, Stanford: Stanford University Press (2002)
Jacques Derrida, "Politics and Friendship", in *Negotiations: Interventions and Interviews*, 1971–2001, Stanford: Stanford University Press (2002)
Jacques Derrida, *Philosophy in a Time of Terror: Dialogues with Jürgen Habermas and Jacques Derrida*, ed. Giovanna Borradori, Chicago: Chicago University Press (2003)
Jacques Derrida, *Rogues: Two Essays on Reason*, Stanford: Stanford University Press (2005)
Jacques Derrida, *Learning to Live Finally*, Derrida's last interview, with Jean Birnbaum, New Jersey: Melville House Publishing (2007)
Jacques Derrida, *The Beast and the Sovereign*, Volume 1, Chicago: Chicago University Press (2009)
Cora Diamond, "Eating Meat and Eating People", in *The Realistic Spirit*, Cambridge, Mass: MIT Press (1991)
Myrto Dragona-Monachou, *Stoic Arguments for the Existence and Providence of the Gods*, Athens: National and Capodistrian University of Athens (1976).
T.S. Eliot, *Notes Towards the Definition of Culture*, London: Faber and Faber (1948)
Simone Emms, *The Modern Journeyman*, thesis submitted for a Master in Education, Auckland University of Technology (2005)
H.A.L. Fisher, *History of Europe*, Volume III, London: Eyre and Spottiswoode (1935)
Sigmund Freud, "Civilization and its Discontents", in *The Standard Edition of the Complete Psychological Works of Sigmund Freud*, Volume 21, Oxford: Macmillan (1964)
Peter Frick, *Divine Providence in Philo of Alexandria*, Tübingen: Mohr Siebeck (1999)
Francis Fukuyama, "The End of History?", *The National Interest*, No. 16 (Summer 1989)
Francis Fukuyama, *The End of History and the Last Man*, London: Hamish Hamilton (1992)
Rodolphe Gasché, *Europe, or the Infinite Task: A Study of a Philosophical Concept*, Stanford: Stanford University Press (2008)
Simon Glendinning, *In the Name of Phenomenology*, Abingdon: Routledge (2008)
Simon Glendinning, "Derrida and the Problem of Consciousness", in *Consciousness and the Great Philosophers*, eds. S. Leach and J. Tartaglia, Abingdon: Routledge (2017)
John Gray, *Isaiah Berlin: An Interpretation of His Thought*, Princeton: Princeton University Press (2013)
Denis Guénoun, *About Europe: Philosophical Hypotheses*, Stanford: Stanford University Press (2013)
Jürgen Habermas, *Between Naturalism and Religion*, Cambridge: Polity Press (2008)
Jürgen Habermas, *The Lure of Technocracy*, Cambridge: Polity Press (2015)

G.W.F. Hegel, *The Philosophy of History*, trans. J. Sibree. London: Bell (1894)
G.W.F. Hegel, *Faith and Knowledge*, New York: SUNY Press (1977)
G.W.F. Hegel, *Introduction to the Philosophy of History*, trans. Leo Rauch, Indianapolis: Hackett Publishing Co. (1988)
G.W.F. Hegel, *Philosophy of Right*, Kitchener: Batoche Books (2001)
Martin Heidegger, *What is Philosophy?*, Lanham, Maryland: Rowman and Littlefield Publishers (1956)
Martin Heidegger, *Being and Time*, Oxford: Blackwell (1962)
Martin Heidegger, "Memorial Address", in *Discourse on Thinking*, New York: Harper and Row (1966)
Martin Heidegger, "Nietzsche's Word: God is Dead", in *The Question of Technology and Other Essays*, New York: Garland Publishing (1977)
Martin Heidegger, "Letter on Humanism", in *Basic Writings*, ed. David Farrell Krell, London: Routledge (1993)
Martin Heidegger, *Introduction to Metaphysics*, New Haven: Yale University Press (2000)
Martin Heidegger, "Heidegger Speaks: Part 1", online video archived at https://www.youtube.com/watch?v=1ngHZr8sAj0
Adolf Hitler, *Mein Kampf*, trans. James Murphy. All references are to the pagination of the online copy of the text at www.greatwar.nl/books/meinkampf/meinkampf.pdf
Jonathan Hopkin and Caterina Paolucci, "The business firm model of party organisation: cases from Spain and Italy", *European Journal of Political Research* (1999)
Paulin J. Hountondji, *African Philosophy, Myth and Reality*, Bloomington: Indiana University Press (1983)
Stephen Houlgate, "World History as the Progress of Consciousness", *The Owl of Minerva* 22: 1 (1990)
Edmund Husserl, *The Crisis of European Sciences and Transcendental Phenomenology*, Evanston: Northwestern University Press (1970)
Simon Jenkins, *A Short History of Europe: from Pericles to Putin*, London: Penguin (2019)
Daniel Johnson, "Seven Minutes that Shook the World", Standpoint Magazine, unpaginated online text archived at http://www.standpointmag.co.uk/seven-minutes-that-shook-the-world-features-november-09-daniel-johnson-berlin-wall?page=0%2C0%2C0%2C0%2C0%2C0%2C0%2C0%2C0%2C0%2C3 (2009)
Anjali Joseph, "Us to Them: the pesto is now another country", *The Times of India* (2016). Unpaginated online text archived at https://timesofindia.indiatimes.com/home/sunday-times/all-that-matters/Us-to-them-The-pesto-is-now-another-country/articleshow/52919052.cms)
Immanuel Kant, *Critique of Pure Reason*, trans. Norman Kemp Smith, London: Macmillan (1973)
Immanuel Kant, *Kant's Political Writings*, Cambridge: Cambridge University Press (1991)
Immanuel Kant, *Opus Postumum*, Cambridge: Cambridge University Press (1995)
Alexandre Kojève, *Introduction to the Reading of Hegel: Lectures on the "Phenomenology of Spirit"*, Ithaca: Cornell University Press (1980)
Wolfram Keiser, 'Introduction', in *Christian Democracy and the Origins of European Union*, Cambridge: Cambridge University Press (2007)
Philipe Lacoue-Labarthe, *Heidegger, Art, and Politics*, Chichester: Wiley-Blackwell (1990)
Philipe Lacoue-Labarthe, *Heidegger and the Politics of Poetry*, Urbana and Chicago: University of Illinois Press (2007)
V.I. Lenin, *State and Revolution*, London: Penguin (1992)
Jean-François Lyotard, *The Postmodern Condition*, Manchester: Manchester University Press (1984)

Emmanuel Levinas, *Is it Righteous to Be?* Stanford: Stanford University Press (2001)

Emmanuel Levinas, *Alterity and Transcendence*, New York: Columbia University Press (2001)

Karl Marx, *Critique of Hegel's Philosophy of Right*, Oxford: Oxford University Press (1970). References give the pagination in the online transcription at https://www.marxists.org/archive/marx/works/download/Marx_Critique_of_Hegels_Philosophy_of_Right.pdf

Karl Marx and Friedrich Engels, *The Communist Manifesto*, Oxford: OUP (2008)

J.S. Mill, "On Nationality and Representative Government", in *Three Essays*, London: Penguin (1975)

J.S. Mill, *Utilitarianism and On Liberty*, Oxford: Blackwell (2003)

J.S. Mill, *On Liberty and the Subjection of Women*, London: Penguin Classics (2006)

Dermot Moran, "'Even the Papuan is a Man and not a Beast': Husserl on Universalism and the Relativity of Cultures", *Journal of the History of Philosophy* 49 (4):463–494 (2011)

Stephen Mulhall, *Philosophical Myths of the Fall*, Princeton: Princeton University Press (2009)

Stephen Mulhall, *The Self and its Shadows*, Oxford: OUP (2013)

Iris Murdoch, *The Book and the Brotherhood*, London: Penguin (1987)

Kalypso Nicolaïdis, "Braving the Waves? Europe's Constitutional Settlement at Twenty", *Journal of Common Market Studies*, Vol 1, no. 17 (2018)

Kalypso Nicolaïdis, "European Demoicracy and its Crisis", *Journal of Common Market Studies*, Vol. 51, no. 2 (2013)

Friedrich Nietzsche, *Human All Too Human, Part II*, trans. Paul V. Cohn, New York: MacMillan (1913)

Friedrich Nietzsche, "The Anti-Christ", in *The Twilight of the Idols and The Anti-Christ*, Harmondsworth: Penguin Books (1969)

Friedrich Nietzsche, *Beyond Good and Evil*, Harmondsworth: Penguin Books (1973)

Friedrich Nietzsche, *The Gay Science*, New York: Vintage (1974)

Friedrich Nietzsche, *The Genealogy of Morals*, London: Penguin Classics (2013)

Friedrich Nietzsche, *The Will to Power*, London: Penguin Classics (2017)

Friedrich Nietzsche, "Twilight of the Idols", in *The Twilight of the Idols and The Anti-Christ*, Harmondsworth: Penguin Books (1969)

Friedrich Nietzsche, *Untimely Mediations*, Cambridge: Cambridge University Press (1997)

Louisa Passerini, *Memory and Utopia: The Primacy of Inter-Subjectivity*, Abingdon: Routledge (2014)

Robert Perkins, "Hegel and the Secularisation of Religion", *International Journal for Philosophy of Religion* 1 (3):130–146 (1970)

Robert Pippin, *Modernism as a Philosophical Problem*, second edition, Oxford: Blackwell (1999)

Karl Popper, *The Open Society and its Enemies*, Fifth Edition, London: Routledge and Keegan Paul (1966). References give the pagination in the online scan at http://www.naturalthinker.net/trl/texts/Popper,Karl/Popper%20-%20The%20Open%20Society%20and%20its%20Enemies.htm

Rush Rhees, (Ed.), *Ludwig Wittgenstein, personal recollections*, Oxford: Blackwell (1981)

Richard Rorty, *Contingency, Irony, and Solidarity*, Cambridge: Cambridge University Press (1989)

Pierre Rosanvallon, *Society of Equals*, Cambridge, Mass: Harvard University Press (2013)

Jean-Paul Sartre, *Existentialism and Humanism*, London: Eyre Methuen (1980)

Jean-Paul Sartre, *The Family Idiot* (Vol. 4), Chicago: University of Chicago Press (1990)

Carl Schmitt, *Political Theology*, Chicago: University of Chicago Press (2006)

Hagen Schulze, *Germany: A New History*, Cambridge, Mass: Harvard University Press (1998)

Judith Shklar, "The Liberalism of Fear", in *Liberalism and the Moral Life*, ed. Nancy L. Rosenblum, Cambridge, Mass: Harvard University Press (1989)

Paul Valéry, "La Politque de L'Esprit", *Variété III*, Paris: Gallimard (1936)

Paul Valéry, *The Collected Works of Paul Valéry Vol 10: History and Politics*, New York: Pantheon Books (1962)

John Adams Wettergreen, Jr. "Is Snobbery a Formal Value? Considering Life at the End of Modernity", *The Western Political Quarterly*, Vol. 26, No. 1 (1973)

David Wiggins, "Truth, Invention, and The Meaning of Life", in *Needs, Values, Truth: Essays in the Philosophy of Value*, Oxford: OUP (1998)

Bernard Williams, *In the Beginning was the Deed: Realism and Moralism in Political Argument*, Princeton: Princeton University Press (2005)

Bernard Williams, *Shame and Necessity*, Berkeley and Los Angeles: University of California Press (2008)

Rowan Williams, "Rome Lecture: 'Secularism, Faith and Freedom'", unpaginated text archived at http://aoc2013.brix.fatbeehive.com/articles.php/1175/rome-lecture-secularism-faith-and-freedom (2006)

Rowan Williams, *Dostoevsky: Language, Faith and Fiction*, London: Continuum (2008)

Ludwig Wittgenstein, *Tractatus Logico-Philosophicus*, London: Routledge and Keegan Paul (1974)

Ludwig Wittgenstein, *The Blue and Brown Books*, Oxford: Blackwell (1958)

Ludwig Wittgenstein, *Lectures and Conversations on Aesthetics, Psychology and Religious Belief*, Oxford: Blackwell (1966)

Ludwig Wittgenstein, *Remarks on Frazer's Golden Bough*, Doncaster: The Brynmill Press (1979)

Ludwig Wittgenstein, *Culture and Value* (Revised Edition), Oxford: Blackwell (1998)

Ludwig Wittgenstein, *Philosophical Investigations*, Revised Fourth Edition, Chichester: Wiley-Blackwell (2009)

P.G. Wodehouse, *Right Ho, Jeeves*, London: Everyman (2000)

INDEX

CPSIA information can be obtained
at www.ICGtesting.com
Printed in the USA
LVHW080812130522
718633LV00012B/418